The Malaysian Economy

The Malaysian economy has enjoyed considerable and increasing success since its independence in 1957. The author explores various facets of the current centrally-planned development policy and the colonial inheritance from which it derives. It becomes evident that rural bias is significant in the area of primary commodities, including rubber and tin, and in their relation to the economy as a whole. This is in spite of a conspicuous shift in the manufacturing sector toward export-orientated high technology products.

Malaysia has suffered many of the problems associated with urbanization in recent years due to the high concentration of the manufacturing sector in the urban area. Throughout, the author places a sustained emphasis on the fundamental Malaysian economic policy of combating inequality. It is this planning, he argues, which, together with ethnic problems, poses a substantial threat to the immediate economic success of Malaysia.

The author

George Cho is Lecturer in the School of Applied Science, University of Canberra, Belconnen, Australia. He is a Malaysian citizen permanently resident in Australia and has conducted extensive field studies in Malaysia, publishing widely on the subject.

The Malaysian Economy

Spatial perspectives

George Cho

London and New York

First published 1990
by Routledge
11 New Fetter Lane, London EC4P 4EE

Simultaneously published in the USA and Canada
by Routledge
a division of Routledge, Chapman and Hall, Inc.
29 West 35th Street, New York, NY 10001

© 1990 George Cho

Printed in Great Britain by
Billing & Sons Ltd, Worcester

British Library Cataloguing in Publication Data

Cho, George, *1946–*
    The Malaysian economy : spatial perspectives.
    1. Malaysia. Economic conditions
    I. Title
    330.9595

    ISBN 0-415-02096-4

Library of Congress Cataloging in Publication Data

Cho, George, 1946–
        The Malaysian economy : spatial perspectives / by George Cho.
            p. cm.
        Includes bibliographical references.
        ISBN 0-415-02096-4
        1. Malaysia – Economic conditions. 2. Malaysia – Social
conditions.
        3. Malaysia – Rural conditions. I. Title.
        HC445.5.C52   1990
        330.9595′054–dc20   89-24185
                                                                    CIP

CONTENTS

FIGURES

TABLES

ACKNOWLEDGEMENTS

This book is an attempt to provide a spatial perspective of the Malaysian economy. In order to cover the wide range of important topics which need to be included within this limited volume some detail has been sacrificed in favour of a general discussion. There is no lack of specialized journal articles and monographs covering some of these topics in greater depth. I have also made use of a significant number of works by local authors, partly because such works are of limited circulation but mainly because the local, regional perspective is assuming considerable importance in an academic and practical way.

I owe a great debt to a number of persons who have helped me to produce a readable script and in shaping my ideas and thoughts. Professor Terry McGee of the University of British Columbia offered useful suggestions on the structure of the book. Special thanks are due to my friends especially Annette Sugden-Chatwin who looked for 'fugitive' references at the Australian National Library, Canberra, Jenny Wookey of the Australian Bureau of Statistics, Canberra, who found valuable sources of data, and to my brother-in-law Mr Goh Soah Hee for searching data sources in Malaysia. I am indebted to Steve Britton of Auckland University and Dean Forbes of the Australian National University, who read through an early draft thoroughly and extended detailed criticisms. Barbara Banks gave valuable editorial advice while Keith Mitchell provided assistance with the cartography. At the University of Canberra I have enjoyed the opportunity of working with many colleagues who have been most encouraging, especially Terry Birtles, Sherrill Bell, Joan Roberts, and Eric Best. Thanks are also due to Mrs Robyn Mason and Mrs Rose Forace, who helped with the tables. I am also grateful to Professor David Drakakis-Smith of Keele University, who was instrumental in giving me this opportunity to write this book, for his constant encouragement and support and to the editors at Croom Helm (later Routledge) for their forbearance of my many queries.

Finally, I would like to record an appreciation for my wife Marion who provided all the emotional support and shared in all the trials and tribulations at various stages of writing. Since no thanks could be sufficient, I hope that this small mention at least demonstrates the depth of my gratitude. Carolyn did her best with her music to help me keep things in perspective. This book is dedicated to my parents in Malaysia and to Marion and Carolyn.

George Cho
Kaleen
Australian Capital Territory

Permission to use the following copyright material is gratefully acknowledged: Federal Land Development Authority for the use of Figures 2.2 and 3.2 from the publication *21 Years of Land Development* (1977: 33, 72) by *Tunku* Shamsul Bahrin and P.D.A. Perera; *Malaysian Journal of Tropical Geography* for the use of Figures 3 and 4 in Voon Phin Keong's article in vol. 3 (1981: 61, 62); and Oxford University Press, Kuala Lumpur for the use of Figure 8.1 and Map 8.1 in Chap. 8 by Benjamin Higgins in *The Political Economy of Malaysia* (1982).

ABBREVIATIONS

ASEAN	Association of South East Asian Nations
ATPC	Association of Tin Producing Countries
BN	National Front
CGC	Credit Guarantee Corporation
CHOGM	Commonwealth Heads of Government Meeting
CIC	Capital Investment Committee
CPI	Consumer price index
DAP	Democratic Action Party
DARA	Pahang Tenggara Development Authority
DDP	Draft Development Plan
EPF	Employees Provident Fund
EPU	Economic Planning Unit
EPZ	Export Processing Zone
FAO	Food and Agriculture Organization
FAS	Fringe Alienation Scheme
FEER	*Far Eastern Economic Review*
FELCRA	Federal Land Consolidation and Rehabilitation Authority
FELDA	Federal Land Development Authority
FFYP	First Five Year Plan
FIDA	Federal Industrial Development Authority
FIMA	Food Industries of Malaysia
FMS	Federated Malay States
FTZ	Free Trade Zone
HICOM	Heavy Industries Corporation of Malaysia
IADP	Integrated Agricultural Development Projects
IBRD	International Bank for Reconstruction and Development
ICU	Implementation and Co-ordination Unit
IGC	Inter-governmental Committee
IMP	Industrial Master Plan
ISA	Internal Security Act

ITC	International Tin Council
JENGKA	Jengka Regional Development Authority
JKKKK	Village Development and Security Committee
KADA	Kemubu Agricultural Development Authority
KEDA	Kedah Regional Development Authority
KEJORA	Johor Tenggara Development Authority
KESEDAR	South Kelantan Development Authority
KETENGAH	Terengganu Tengah Regional Development Authority
KLSE	Kuala Lumpur Stock Exchange
KPD	Rural Development Corporation (Sabah)
LME	London Metal Exchange
LMW	Licensed Manufacturing Warehouse
MADA	Muda Agricultural Development Authority
MARA	Council of Trust for the Indigenous Peoples
MARDEC	Malaysian Rubber Development Corporation
MAS	Malaysian Airline System
MCA	Malaysian Chinese Association
MCP	Malayan Communist Party
MIC	Malaysian Indian Congress
MIDF	Malaysian Industrial Development Finance
MIPS	Malaysian Industrial Policies Study
MM	*Malay Mail*
MNC	Multinational Corporation
NAP	National Agricultural Policy
NEP	New Economic Policy
NFPEs	Non-Financial Public Enterprises
NSP	National Spatial Plan
NST	*New Straits Times*
NUP	National Urbanization Policy
OBA	Off Budget Agency
OEP	Old Economic Policy
OPP	Outline Perspective Plan
OSA	Official Secrets Act
PASOK	United Pasok Nunukragang National Organization
PBS	Parti Bersatu Sabah
PERDA	Penang Regional Development Authority
PERNAS	National Corporation
PETRONAS	National Oil Corporation
PM	United Pasok Momugun National Party
PNB	National Equity Corporation
PPP	People's Progressive Party
RDA	Regional Development Authority

RISDA	Rubber Industry Smallholders Development Authority
SALCRA	Sarawak Land Consolidation and Rehabilitation Authority
SADC	State Agricultural Development Corporation
SCA	Sabah Chinese Association
SCCP	Sabah Chinese Consolidated Party
SEDC	State Economic Development Corporation
SFYP	Second Five Year Plan
SIC	Sabah Indian Congress
SLDB	Sabah/Sarawak Land Development Board
SMR	Standard Malaysian Rubber
TAB	Tariff Advisory Board
UDA	Urban Development Authority
UFMS	Unfederated Malay States
UMNO	United Malay National Organization
UNKO	United National Kadazan Organization
USNO	United Sabah National Organization
ZOPFAN	Zone of Peace, Freedom and Neutrality

Monetary units

Unless otherwise indicated all currency referred to in this book is in Malaysian *ringgit* ($) (100 sen). The exchange rates per U.S. dollar (US $) for the period under study are:

1950:	$3.06	1975:	$2.59
1960:	$3.06	1980:	$2.22
1970:	$3.08	1985:	$2.43

(*Source*: International Monetary Fund (1987) *International Financial Statistics Yearbook*, Washington, D.C.: IMF, pp. 468-9.)

Nomenclature

The word *Bumiputera* can be translated literally as 'sons of the soil' and was brought into use to distinguish indigenous peoples from the non-indigenous Chinese and Indians.

Yang di-Pertuan Agong is the title of the Supreme Ruler or King of Malaysia; *Yang di Pertua Negeri*, *Negara* are titles of the Heads of State of Sabah and Sarawak respectively.

Tunku, Tengku, and *Raja* are hereditary titles denoting links with the royal families of the peninsular states.

Tun, Tan Sri are conferred titles, accorded with federal awards made by the *Yang di-Pertuan Agong. Datuk, Datuk Seri* are also conferred titles, accorded with awards made by the rulers in each state.

INTRODUCTION
THE MALAYSIAN ECONOMY: SPATIAL PERSPECTIVES

This book gives a spatial perspective on the Malaysian economy since *Merdeka* (independence) in 1957. It is concerned with the variables which constitute growth, progress, and national aspirations. The book describes the impact of economic development on the land and its people.

Malaysian economic performance in the last three decades has been one of the most successful in South East Asia. However, in the 1980s Malaysia was in the grip of one of the most serious socio-economic and political crises since its formation. There has been increasing polarization of community groups among the Malays, Chinese, and Indians. Tensions between the ruling party at national level and the opposition at local level have resulted in a coalition of political parties in order to find some middle ground.

The industrialization and diversification of the Malaysian economy took place in a highly competitive world market as inflation and economic recession were occurring among major western economies. The slowdown of world economies affected Malaysian export earnings, which fell short of targets set by economic planners.

The Malaysian polity appears to be extremely resilient, having weathered a number of stormy periods such as the communist insurgency (1948-60); May 13th, 1969 ethnic unrest; the constitutional crisis of 1983; and various other challenges to the established *Barisan Nasional* (BN) (National Front) regime. From each of these it has seemingly emerged with new vigour and determination to survive and to succeed.

What factors contributed to the relative success of its economic performance? Is such performance due primarily to a favourable international economic environment for Malaysian primary and manufactured goods or have domestic factors provided the main impetus? What is the importance of the 'openness' of the Malaysian economy? What are the country's immediate and long-term economic prospects in the light of the new international economic order and a domestic socio-political environment which poses a threat to all the work of post-independence achievements?

This book addresses these important geographical issues by examining the record of national development since the late 1950s. Successive chapters analyse the planning for development, rural regional development, growth and transformation of cities, industrial restructuring, economic policies, and political stability impinging on development strategies.

Chapter 1 focuses on the nature of the economy and the social environment. This chapter provides the background to the discussions that follow. In particular, the geographical context of the country's regional and global status is described. This includes a comparison of Malaysia's economy with those of other countries in the Association of South East Asian Nations (ASEAN). In the Malaysian case, genuine national development has been pursued, guided by an economic plan that attempts to promote social justice for all Malaysians. Such equity objectives of development planning are being pursued with vigour by Malaysians of every background and at all levels of society in order to ensure the ultimate success of the economic plans.

Chapter 2 traces development planning from independence up to 1990. It is a review of the aims, objectives, achievements, and shortcomings of the eight formal development plans. In particular, shifts in emphasis of the development policy are highlighted and their spatial impacts are given particular attention. The evolution of the colonial economy is discussed as this has laid the parameters for Malaysian development since 1957. There is also a discussion of the communal structures and policy attempts to eradicate social and economic inequalities.

An examination is made in Chapter 3 of the *raisons d'être* of development policies and the conscious bias towards rural regional development. The success of the Malaysian economy rests on the strength of commodities such as rubber, tin, palm oil, hardwood timber, and petroleum. While these primary industrial commodities have been the mainstay of the economy in the past, how they will continue in the future will depend on the tactics that the government employs in developing the rural sector. These governmental decisions, however, must be viewed against the backdrop of world demand for these primary commodities, world prices, and economic trends. Here the examination seeks to detect shifts in development strategies in the rural milieu and to determine whether they produce tensions and policy contradictions. On the one hand, 'peopling' of the interior has been a basis of land development, whether it be on a macro-, meso-, or micro-scale. On the other, the economic foundations of such schemes may be seen as a weapon of rural policy, to ensure the continued dominance of Malaysian production of rubber and palm oil in world commodity markets.

In Chapter 4, attention is focused on the transformation of cities. Many cities in the Malaysian urban hierarchy are at a crossroads, whereby growth and concomitant transformations have brought about problems of adjustment, of urban blight, and urban management. Urbanization, rural-urban drift, and urban unemployment are highlighted since these have to be geared to the needs of the national and international demands of the formal urban economy. 'Informal' sector activities, while an indispensable ingredient to the proper functioning of any city in the Third World, at times conflict with the formal sector of the urban economy. These conflicts are sometimes intractable and sometimes tolerated. In part it is this friction between the corporate and unincorporated sectors that explains why Malaysian cities are at a crossroads.

In Chapter 5 the focus is shifted towards Malaysian industrial transformation and to policies that have been geared to ensure the replacement of previous import-substitution industries with new export-oriented heavy and high technology industries. There is also a discussion of industrial strategies and the failure of technology transfer, especially in export processing zones. The inherent dualism in the industrial structure and the future prospects of the industrialization strategy are also examined.

Chapter 6 has three parts. The first section is an amalgam of issues that includes perceptions of Malaysia as a nation as well as a critical self-analysis of the national outlook as portrayed in news journals. There is also the issue of communalism and how the 'minor' ethnic groups will fare with the prospects of the primacy of the Malays and *Bumiputera* (sons of the soil). An examination of the Malays, the United Malay National Organization (UMNO) and Islam shows that they have played and will play an increasingly important role beyond the year 2000. The second section examines the constitutional crisis of 1983 and the differences that arise between the elected ruling elite and the rulers. A third section evaluates the constitutional position of Sabah and Sarawak, the special position these 'Bornean' states have been given, and what might be expected if a more complete integration of Malaysian states is attained.

These issues are considered important in unfolding the geography of Malaysia because the interaction of socio-economic groups is determined as much by their ethnicity as by their socio-economic status. A political system that is based on the rule of law has a better chance to provide the foundations for the spread of development over geographic space. Where geo-political entities are non-contiguous, as in the case of peninsular

Malaysia and 'East' Malaysia, it is imperative to identify the factors that bind as well as those that divide when discussing regional integration.

In a concluding section, a postscript poses the rhetorical question as to whether a new or national economic policy will be prominent for the period after 1990. Such a question prompts one that asks whether political and economic power is to be 'traded' between the different communities and whether there will likely be a transfer of wealth within ethnic groups.

1
MALAYSIA: THE SOCIO-ECONOMIC BACKGROUND

INTRODUCTION

The Federation of Malaysia (henceforth Malaysia) is composed of two major land masses. Peninsular Malaysia, occupying the southern portions of the Malay Peninsula, is comprised of the 11 states that before 1963 made up the Federation of Malaya, and Wilayah Persekutuan (Federal Territory, henceforth Kuala Lumpur). The other land mass is East Malaysia, which consists of two former British colonies in northern Borneo, Sabah and Sarawak.

Malaysia is a relatively small country by South East Asian standards. Peninsular Malaysia has an area of 131,582 square kilometres. It shares a border to the north with Thailand and to the south, across Johor Strait, with the Republic of Singapore. Sabah has an area of 73,709 square kilometres while Sarawak is larger, with an area of 124,445 square kilometres. Separating peninsular and East Malaysia are between 650 and 1,600 kilometres of the South China Sea and interstitial islands belonging to Indonesia. On the landward side, East Malaysia has a long mountain border with the Kalimantan provinces of Indonesia. On the coast is the Sultanate of Negara Brunei Darussalam, a former British protectorate (see Fig. 1.1). Taken together the total land area of Malaysia is only half the size of Burma, and about two-thirds that of Thailand, whereas Indonesia is six times larger and Australia twenty-three times larger.

In legal or geographic terms, Malaysia as a political entity was non-existent before 1963. After that date, however, the Federation of Malaysia consisted of all eleven states in peninsular Malaysia, Singapore, Sarawak, and Sabah.[1] Any survey of the economic geography of Malaysia will inevitably have to contend with the problem of maintaining a consistent definition of its geographic area. Some early data refer to

Figure 1.1. Malaysia: Administrative divisions, main towns, and cities.

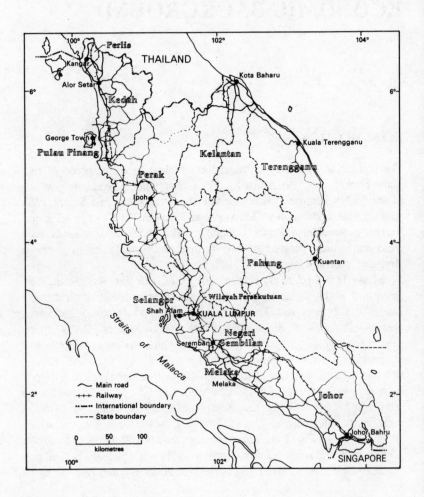

Figure 1.1. (cont.)

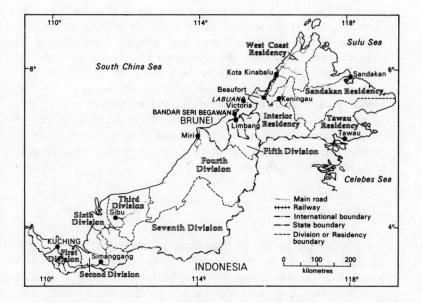

Malaya and Singapore, whereas more recent data refer to peninsular Malaysia to the exclusion of Sarawak and Sabah. Between 1963 and 1965 the Federation of Malaysia included Singapore, but in 1965 Singapore left Malaysia by mutual agreement. These definitional changes arising from changes to the territory also imply economic, social, and political adjustments to the organization of the national space economy. Therefore, to understand some of the dynamics of political and socio-economic change and development, this chapter begins with a brief historical sketch and then discusses some present-day socio-economic characteristics. We then focus on Malaysia in its regional and global context. These comparisons with neighbouring countries provide a broader picture of the relative strengths and weaknesses of the country *vis-à-vis* its neighbours. A discussion of the meaning of 'national development' follows to underline the basis of the particular perspective taken in this book in terms of development theory and the development experience of the country.

BRIEF HISTORY

Long before the coming of Europeans, Malay peoples had established settlements along the coasts and riverine estuaries of the Malay peninsula.[2] These were to become important trading posts and later the genesis of small kingdoms. Beginning in the 2nd century BC the Malay peninsula experienced over 1000 years of Indian or Indianized influence, and in the thirteenth century AD Arab and Indian Muslims brought Islamic and Arabic influence to the peninsula. The Portuguese were the first Europeans to arrive and a fleet under Alfonso de Alberqueque conquered Malacca (Melaka) in 1511. Then the Dutch, who had a foothold across the Straits of Malacca on the island of Java, laid siege to Melaka and succeeded in capturing it in 1641. However, it was the British who eventually prevailed over the Malay States. Their first beachhead was at Penang (Pulau Pinang) which was leased to the British East India Company by the Sultan of Kedah in 1786.

By 1867 Pulau Pinang had joined with Melaka and Singapore to form the Straits Settlements, a British Crown Colony. Some Malay states accepted British 'advisers' under the guise of British Residents and in 1895 these became the Federated Malay States (FMS) consisting of Perak, Selangor, Negri Sembilan, and Pahang. The remaining states, described as the Unfederated Malay States (UFMS), included Kelantan, Terengganu, Kedah, and Perlis, which had been extricated from the Siamese sphere of influence in 1909. Together with Johor, these were later brought into the British sphere. British political control over the whole of the peninsula radically transformed Malaya socially and economically and brought about stability which lasted until the Japanese invasion in the Second World War. Following the expulsion of the Japanese and the return of the British in late 1945, the attempts of the Colonial Office to organize Malaya into one state offended the Malays, who were determined not to revert to a mere colony.

In 1946 the United Malay National Organization (UMNO) was created under the leadership of *Dato* Onn bin Jaafar, and in 1948 a federation uniting all the states in the Malay peninsula, Pulau Pinang, and Melaka was formed. The Malayan Communist Party (MCP) immediately rose in armed revolt and attacked the British from sanctuaries in the jungle.

An 'Emergency' was proclaimed in 1948 and the British attempted to quell the revolt by military action as well as by removing its political causes. The latter was achieved by encouraging the attainment of *Merdeka* (independence) through the political co-operation of the two major races in the country. Under the new leader *Tunku* Abdul Rahman, the UMNO joined with the Malayan Chinese Association (MCA) led by Tan Cheng Lock to form the UMNO-MCA Alliance in 1952 to contest the 1955 national general elections. The Alliance, on a platform which was strongly anti-communist and anti-colonial, captured 51 out of the 52 seats. Britain responded to this mandate of the people by relinquishing its powers in Malaya. On August 31, 1957, Malaya secured *Merdeka*; however, the Emergency continued until 1960.

By this time Singapore, under Lee Kuan Yew, had secured full self-government in 1959. Singapore pressed for 'independence through merger' with Malaya, believing that its future could only be assured by uniting with the mainland. A merger was agreed to in order to forestall the growth of communist influence among Singapore's Chinese population. However, to offset the inclusion of a million Chinese of Singapore, Malaya suggested in 1961 that Brunei, Sabah, and Sarawak join in the merger. After considerable discussion and amidst increasing opposition from Indonesia and the Philippines, these states, with the exception of Brunei, established a new independent Federation of Malaysia on September 16, 1963.

Fears that the Malays would dominate the Federation led to the withdrawal of Singapore on August 9, 1965. Also during this period, Malaysia fought off armed 'Confrontation' mounted from Indonesia and resisted Filipino territorial claims over Sabah.

It was ironic that on August 8, 1967, the same group of actors - Indonesia, Malaysia, the Philippines, Singapore, and Thailand - came together to form the Association of South East Asian Nations (ASEAN). Though little progress was made in its first few years of existence, ASEAN was destined to become an important political, social, and economic grouping. As a regional organization, it is devoted to the promotion of regional co-operation in economic, social, cultural, and technical fields. Negara Brunei Darussalam joined ASEAN as a full member on January 7, 1984.

INTERNATIONAL AND REGIONAL CONTEXT

Within the ASEAN nations the contrasts between member countries in respect of physical area, population size, and stage of economic development are quite marked.[3] For instance, Table 1.1 shows that Indonesia is by far the largest country in terms of land area and population but its economic development lags behind that of other ASEAN countries. By contrast, the city-state of Singapore is smallest in geographical extent but its economic importance is relatively more significant. Malaysia appears to occupy a middle position within this regional context. The land area of Malaysia makes up only a tenth of the total and contains only about five per cent of the ASEAN population. For ASEAN as a whole, Brunei's population of 200,000 is by far the smallest, although it has ten times more land than Singapore.

In terms of the gross domestic product (GDP) Indonesia recorded the largest GDP in 1984, but the significance of this is diminished when the data are transformed into per capita income. Comparisons show that Brunei has a per capita income of US$21,600, while Singapore has US$6,922 per capita and Malaysia US$1,996 per capita. Partly because of relatively larger populations and smaller earnings, Indonesia, the Philippines, and Thailand have much lower per capita incomes.

The contrasts between Malaysia and other ASEAN countries show interesting patterns. Malaysia, for example, has less than one-tenth of the population of Indonesia but close to one-third of Indonesia's GDP. In similar terms, Malaysia's population is slightly more than one-fifth of the population of the Philippines and nearly one-third that of Thailand. But Malaysia's GDP is nearly nine-tenths that of the Philippines and three-quarters that of Thailand. In general, these suggest that Malaysia is a relatively more successful economy. Comparisons with ASEAN and other Third World countries shows that Malaysia has achieved outstanding economic success since its independence. This success is in stark contrast to countries in the region struggling to achieve similar growth patterns. There is little doubt that the contrasts are a result of the

Table 1.1. ASEAN countries: Physical and economic indicators

Country	Land area (sq. km.) (000s)	Index	Popn. 1985 (mil.)	Index	Popn. growth (%) 1977-84	GDP (US$ mil.)	Per capita income (US$)	Malaysia's Popn. as ratio of ASEAN	GDP
Brunei	5.8	0.2	0.2	0.07	2.4	3.9*	21,600	7,850	750.6
Indonesia	1,904.7	62.4	168.4	56.8	2.2	90.0*	566	9.3	32.4
Malaysia	329.7	10.8	15.7	5.3	2.2	29.2	1,996	.	.
Philippines	300.0	9.8	56.8	19.2	2.5	31.9	603	27.6	91.5
Singapore	0.6	0.02	2.6	0.9	1.1	17.7	6,922	603.8	164.9
Thailand	514.0	16.8	52.7	17.8	1.9	40.7	646	29.8	71.7
ASEAN	3,054.8	100	296.4	100	-	-	-	-	-

Sources: Far Eastern Economic Review, *Asia 1985 Yearbook;* International Monetary Fund, *International Financial Statistics Yearbook 1987.*

Note: * GNP not GDP.

differences in economic structure that engender differentials in growth rates as well as in historical trends of growth and decline.

While there is great diversity, the common thread binding all ASEAN countries seems to be the commitment to economic development and growth. To varying degrees all ASEAN countries subscribe to a style of democratic government. Internal political stability is thought to be assisted by sufficient regional equilibrium to the extent that expenditures earmarked for self-defence could be redirected towards the domestic economy. Thus, the 1971 ASEAN declaration of a Zone of Peace, Freedom and Neutrality (ZOPFAN) remains a centrepiece of the idea of regionalism. Malaysian foreign policy is closely identified with this declaration and it seems will continue to be so in the future.[4]

In an international context Malaysia has been a member of the British Commonwealth since its independence. While the relationship with Britain has been cool in the 1980s, commercial relations have begun to pick up in the latter half of the decade. There has been some strain in relations with Australia in the late 1980s, but by and large these have been episodic and quickly mended. Malaysia has also endeavoured some kind of a leadership role among developing countries within the Asia-Pacific rim. The theme of South-South economic co-operation and the cause of the Non-aligned Movement has been taken up by Malaysia at various international fora. Malaysia's stand on Afghanistan, Antarctica, apartheid, and Cambodia has been heard at the Non-aligned summit in Harare, Zimbabwe in September 1987 and later at the United Nations. Despite the policy of looking towards Japan and Korea as major trading partners and sources of investments and loans disquiet has been expressed in terms of the lack of benefits in favour of Malaysia. For example, concern has arisen over the lack of technology transfer and the increasing debt with Japan as a result of the rising value of the Japanese currency. The strictly formal relations with China have remained intact with the latter reiterating that it has no links with the outlawed Malayan Communist Party (MCP). No doubt once initial uncertainties have been ironed out the trade relations between the two countries will be further expanded.

SOCIO-ECONOMIC PATTERNS

Size and Growth of the Population

In 1980 the population of Malaysia was estimated to be 13.7 million people, of whom 11.4 million (83 per cent) were in peninsular Malaysia,

1.0 million (7 per cent) in Sabah, and 1.3 million (10 per cent) in Sarawak. As seen in Table 1.2, the population grew at a rate of 2.3 per cent per annum over the ten-year 1970-80. This rate is relatively high by South East Asian and world standards, for example the average growth rate of 2.0 per cent per annum among ASEAN countries and 1.5 per cent per annum for China. However, the rate of population growth in Malaysia is uneven between the three regions, with a rapid rate recorded for Sabah (3.8 per cent), and a slower but comparable rate for Sarawak (2.4 per cent) and peninsular Malaysia (2.2 per cent). Continued growth in the Malaysian population is attributable to lower infant mortality rates, high levels of fertility among women of child-bearing age, and a greater number of women entering this age-specific child-bearing cohort (15-39 years). In the foreseeable future, it is expected that this rapid rate of population growth will be maintained, given the fairly young age structure of the population and concomitant high fertility rates.

The high growth rate recorded for Sabah is partly attributable to natural increases as well as to the large inflow of immigrants from the Philippines and Indonesia during the intercensal period (1970-80). Evidence of this phenomenon may be obtained from a study of the 1980 census data on immigration concerning place of last residence, and the length of present residence.

There is wide variation in growth rates among states in peninsular Malaysia; even within these, there are differences between urban and rural areas. In general, Pahang, Selangor, and Kuala Lumpur recorded high growth rates while Melaka, Perak, and Kedah recorded low growth rates. Apart from natural increases between the two groups of states, it is observed that the first group of high growth states were destination areas of internal migrants and the second group of low growth states were the source areas for these internal migrants.

It would have most instructive if data were available to show demographic differences between the various ethnic groups in the locational settings of urban and rural areas. As data on the crude birth rates, crude death rates, and infant mortality rates are unavailable, it can only be postulated that there are no real differences between groups given the strong growth rate between regions as well as locational settings and the relatively even growth trends among the ethnic groups.

Thus it may be seen that the effects of net internal migration from rural to urban areas, high fertility, and low mortality rates have contributed to the growth in size of the population. It may be added that in some instances, administrative changes in boundaries between rural and urban areas or jurisdictional changes (for example, the separation of

Table 1.2. Malaysia: Area and population, 1970 and 1980

State	Area (sq.km.)	Population (000s)		Population density*	
		1970	1980	1970	1980
Johor	18,984	1,277	1,638	67.3	86.4
Kedah	9,425	955	1,116	101.3	118.4
Kelantan	14,931	685	894	45.9	59.9
Melaka	1,650	404	465	244.8	281.8
Negri Sembilan	6,642	481	574	72.4	86.4
Pahang	35,963	505	799	14.0	22.2
Perak	21,004	1,569	1,805	74.7	85.9
Perlis	795	121	148	152.2	186.2
Pulau Pinang	1,033	776	955	751.2	924.5
Sabah	73,709	654	1,011	8.9	13.7
Sarawak	124,445	976	1,308	7.8	10.5
Selangor	7,957	982	1,516	119.8	184.9
Terengganu	12,955	405	541	31.3	41.8
W.P. / K. L.+	243	684	977	2,814.8	4,020.6
East Malaysia	198,154	1,630	2,319	8.2	11.7
Peninsular Malaysia	131,582	8,844	11,428	67.2	86.9
Malaysia	329,736	10,474	13,747	31.8	41.7

Sources: Malaysia, Jabatan Perangkaan (1972); Khoo (1982a).

Notes: * Persons per square kilometre (ppsk).

+ *Wilayah Persekutuan* (Federal Territory) Kuala Lumpur was part of Selangor at the 1970 Census. The population given here is an estimate from enumeration block data for areas within the territory boundary.

Kuala Lumpur from the state of Selangor) have led to misleading figures for the growth of population.

Using 1980 census data a person-land ratio was computed for each of the states. The data show that in Malaysia the person-land ratio is 41.7 persons per square kilometre - a relatively low population density by Asian standards. As may be seen from Table 1.2 there is, at the state level, considerable variation in population density. This pattern closely reflects the distribution of economic activity. Rapid urban growth, coupled with high rates of rural-urban migration and high concentrations of people in urban areas, is becoming the norm in the more developed and modernized parts of the country, for instance, Kuala Lumpur, Pulau Pinang, and Selangor. These trends may need to be arrested if problems of overcrowding and unemployment are to be avoided in areas of high population concentration. While it may be unrealistic to expect an even distribution of economic activity and hence population distribution, an awareness of the problem can at least alleviate the negative effects of overpopulation through far-sighted socio-economic planning. The low density of population in Sabah, Sarawak, and Pahang suggests that these states will serve as the potential destination of many internal migrants attracted by the employment opportunities generated by regional development programmes and land development schemes.

Composition of the Population

The 1980 Census of Population and Housing used the term 'ethnic group' to define persons possessing a common language, religion, and/or customs. Hitherto, various terminology had been used in the censuses in defining 'race' or 'community group' (Hirschmann 1987).

However, for the first time information on ethnicity has been based on self-identification by the head of the household or through replies from members of the household. Procedural instructions to census-takers have prevented them from assigning an ethnic code to a respondent simply on the basis of physical appearance or other criteria by which the ethnicity of a person is subjectively interpreted by the census-taker. Of course, there will be some discussion between the householder and interviewer before recording such information. However, self-identification does introduce peculiar problems of interpreting such data, especially in the grey areas. For instance, some people may perceive decided advantages in being classified as belonging to a particular ethnic group. Such a self-description will inflate the numbers in that particular group. There may be others who will have difficulty in classifying themselves, especially where there are mixed marriages, for example Sino-Indians and Sino-Kadazans.

Nevertheless, the data on ethnic composition show that of the 11.4 million people in peninsular Malaysia, 6.3 million (55 per cent) were Malays, 3.9 million (34 per cent) were Chinese, and 1.2 million (10 per cent) were Indians. In Sabah, of a total population of 1.0 million people, 83 per cent identified themselves as belonging to the *Pribumi* group,[5] a general category that embraces 28 different ethnic groups. These include Kadazan, Murut, Bajau, Orang Sungei, Kedayan, Malay, and Sino-native among others. The Chinese made up 16 per cent and 'others' less than 1 per cent of the total population. The ethnic composition of the population in Sarawak of 1.3 million is more diffuse. The largest groups here include: Iban (30 per cent), Chinese (30 per cent), Malays (20 per cent), Bidayuh (8 per cent), Melanau (6 per cent), and the remainder is made up of smaller ethnic groups (7 per cent).

The annual growth rate of the Malays during the intercensal period was much higher than that of the other ethnic groups. The lower growth rates of the Chinese and Indians were due to their lower fertility level. Thus, as a result of the differences in intercensal growth rates in 1980, Malays made up 55 per cent of the population of peninsular Malaysia, as compared with 53 per cent in 1970. Conversely, the Chinese and Indians had reduced shares from 36 to 34 per cent and 10.7 to 10.2 per cent respectively.

The *Pribumi* group in Sabah grew at an annual rate of about 4.5 per cent between 1970 and 1980, higher than any other group in the state. Part of this high growth rate is attributable to the migrants from the Philippines and Indonesia who were also classified as *Pribumi* in the 1980 census.

The differentials in the intercensal growth rate among ethnic groups in Sarawak were not as wide as those in Sabah. As a result only small changes in the ethnic composition of the population have been recorded. For example, in 1970 Malays made up 18.6 per cent of the population in Sarawak; in 1980 they had grown to 19.7 per cent. However, the intercensal change for the other groups has been minimal, with Ibans (-0.8 per cent), Chinese (-0.6 per cent), and Bidayuh (-0.4 per cent) claiming a smaller proportion of the overall population while Melanau (+0.2 per cent), 'other indigenous' (+0.1 per cent), and 'others' (+0.4 per cent) gained slightly larger proportionate shares.

CHARACTERISTICS OF THE ECONOMY

In the mid-1980s the Malaysian economy was best characterized in terms of its high rate of economic growth and distinctive set of economic and political problems. Rather than describe at length the sectoral-industrial composition, market orientation of domestic and export production, level of technology, and productivity, the following focuses on four features. First, an analysis of the sectoral output provides a broad picture of the structure of the economy. Second, the spatial distribution of the GDP gives a background to the description of the pattern of economic activity as well as the regional contributions of various sectors of the economy. Third, labour force participation rates are given and finally, external trade data are discussed to demonstrate economic performance. Such a focus will characterize the distinctiveness of the Malaysian economy. However, the trends in growth need to be discussed initially in order to provide the background to that which follows.

In the period from independence to 1969, the gross national product (GNP) in peninsular Malaysia increased by 86 per cent. This substantial growth had been achieved in the context of a declining price trend for natural rubber and timber (see discussion on sectoral output below). The actual rate of growth of 5.3 per cent per annum during this period is considered one of the better ones in South East Asia and among developing countries generally. The comparatively successful economic performance has been attributed to its strong national government, a good physical and administrative infrastructure, a favourable ratio between land and resources to population, a broader based export sector, and a liberal and outward-looking economic policy framework which emphasized foreign trade and private enterprise (Snodgrass 1980: 7).

The decade of the 1970s witnessed the continuation of these liberal outward-looking economic policies albeit with a new emphasis that stressed the relative shares of the various ethnic groups in line with the New Economic Policy (NEP). During the 1970s, the average GNP growth rate of around 6 per cent had been won from an environment of sharp declines in rubber and timber prices. Moreover, deficits had begun to appear in trade statistics in 1975 which had grave implications for the attainment of growth objectives. The direct impact on many people would have been a fall in income and, as a consequence, a decline in demand for manufactured goods and services. Thus, in order to fulfil the political demands of the NEP and achieve racial economic balance, growth in the national economy was fundamental. One way that Malay wealth could be proportionately increased without potential divisiveness was to ensure that the overall 'national economic cake' continued to expand. Such endeavours have been successful, as the experience of the 1980s will show.

Between 1981 and 1985 the Malaysian annual GDP grew at a creditable rate of about 5.8 per cent in real terms despite a world economic recession. In addition, this growth was achieved even though there were structural problems in the domestic economy and major commodity prices continued to weaken. Growth in the economy was the result of greater domestic price stability, structural adjustment measures aimed at achieving higher productivity and efficiency, and a reduction in the rate of inflation to a single digit. As measured by the consumer price index (CPI), inflation rose by about 4.6 per cent per annum during the period 1981-85. At current prices, the GDP grew by 7.9 per cent per annum, thus enabling the per capita income to rise by 4.4 per cent per annum from $3,719 in 1980 to $4,609 in 1985.

The trend in the average rate of growth in the economy was uneven, decreasing from 7.9 per cent to 5.6 per cent between 1980 and 1982, rising steadily to 7.6 per cent in 1984, but falling sharply to 2.8 per cent in 1985. The fall in growth rate in the last period under consideration was due to a decline in manufacturing and mining output brought about by a weak world demand (Malaysia 1986: 39). But these growth rates are well within the targets set by the Second United Nations Development Decade (1970-80), which recommended a 6 per cent GNP growth or 3.5 per cent per capita income growth.

In general, growth in Malaysia is dependent on the performance of the world economy. This reflects the comparative 'openness' of the Malaysian economy and its reliance on the export of a relatively limited range of primary products and some manufactured goods. While this may be considered a wide range of export commodities by Third World standards, there are structural problems in the domestic economy which reduce the potential for growth. In addition, there is the tendency to import inflation from other economies, thus necessitating counter-measures to reduce such problems.

Sectoral Output

Analyses of sectoral contributions to the GDP for the period between 1980 and 1985 show that the major impetus and contributor to growth has been the primary and tertiary sectors (see Table 1.3). However, within these sectors there have been changes in their relative contributions. For instance, in the primary sector, mining and quarrying showed a negative

Table 1.3. Malaysia: Gross domestic product by industry of origin, 1980-
85 ($ million at 1978 prices)

Industry	GDP		Average annual growth rate (%)		
	1980	*1985*	*1981*	*1985*	*1981-85*
Primary	*14,676*	*18,052*	*2.0*	*2.2*	*4.2*
Agriculture, forestry,					
and fishing	10,189	12,046	4.9	3.6	3.2
Mining and quarrying	4,487	6,006	-4.4	-0.7	6.0
Secondary	*10,998*	*14,405*	*6.5*	*-1.9*	*5.5*
Manufacturing	8,932	11,357	4.6	-3.0	4.9
Construction	2,066	3,048	14.6	2.0	8.1
Tertiary	*17,836*	*26,138*	*11.6*	*7.0*	*7.9*
Electricity, gas, water	640	988	7.7	11.0	9.1
Transport and					
communications	2,542	3,805	12.0	9.8	8.4
Wholesale, retail	5,383	7,551	5.8	6.2	7.0
Finance, insurance, and					
services	3,687	5,212	7.2	6.5	7.2
Government services	4,563	7,270	23.8	6.6	9.8
Other services	1,021	1,312	4.3	5.0	5.1
Less bank charges	854	1,675	-	-	-
plus import duties	2,046	2,424	-	-	-
GDP at purchasers'					
value	44,702	59,344	6.9	2.8	5.8

Source: Malaysia, Jabatan Perangkaan (1985a).

Note: Figures for 1985 are estimates.

growth in 1985 but an overall growth rate of 6.0 per cent between 1981 and 1985 based on constant prices. This is compared with modest growth in agriculture, forestry, and fishing. In the secondary sector, growth in 1985 was not clear-cut, with manufacturing showing a negative growth while the output in construction showed a growth of 2.0 per cent over the previous year. However, the secondary sector as a whole showed a growth of 5.5 per cent between 1981 and 1985.

In general the tertiary sector has been buoyant, with steady growth recorded for all components. The largest growth over the period was recorded in government services (9.8 per cent) with electricity, gas, and water and transport and communications (9.1 per cent and 8.4 per cent respectively) following close behind.

The data suggest strongly the effects of structural changes that have taken place since 1980. For example, manufacturing became the largest contributor to the GDP in 1984, superseding agriculture, which previously had been the largest sector. However, the 1985 data show the resurgence of agriculture as a result of a significant decline in the output of electronics, iron and steel, non-metallic mineral, and petroleum products. Moreover, this trend also demonstrated the effects of the government's policy on diversification of the economy in all sectors - primary, secondary, and tertiary. Palm oil overtook rubber to become the largest single commodity in agricultural output; petroleum showed an expansion in production while the contribution from tin declined (see Table 1.4).

The primary sector accounted for about one-third of total output and contributed to about one-fifth of the growth of the economy during the period. The origin of this growth came from increases in output in the mining sector. Agriculture contributed to about 20.3 per cent in 1985 of total output.

This consistency in contribution has been sustained largely by palm oil production of about 4.1 million tonnes in 1985, produced from 1.5 million hectares of oil palm. The result reflects increases in planted area under oil palm, favourable export prices, and improved techniques which increased production and yields, for example, pollination methods, field husbandry, and fertilizer use. Rubber production in 1985 was 1.45 million tonnes, slightly smaller than at the beginning of 1980. A combination of lack of world demand and subsequent depressed prices and a decline in rubber-growing area has seen the share of this sector in agricultural output drop from 23.4 per cent in 1980 to 18.7 per cent in 1985. The area under rubber fell from just over two million hectares in 1980 to about 1.95 million hectares in 1985. In terms of sawlogs, output declined because of poor prices stemming from weak demand, the depletion of accessible

Table 1.4. Malaysia: Value of commodity exports, 1980 and 1985

Commodity	1980		1985		
	share of total $ (m.)	(%)	share of total $ (m.)	(%)	Average annual growth (%)
Crude petroleum	6,709.1	23.8	8,970.0	23.6	6.0
Palm oil	2,515.3	8.9	3,944.0	10.4	9.4
Rubber	4,618.0	16.4	2,864.0	7.5	-9.1
Sawlogs	2,616.2	9.3	2,667.0	7.0	0.4
Liquified natural gas	831.3*	-	2,319.0	6.1	30.7+
Tin	2,505.3	8.9	1,595.0	4.2	-8.6
Sawn timber	1,178.3	4.2	1,020.0	2.7	-2.8
Cocoa	161.9	0.6	394.0	1.0	19.5
Copper	177.3	0.6	141.0	0.4	-4.5
Pepper	107.7	0.4	139.0	0.4	5.2
Manufactures	6,269.8	22.3	12,229.0	32.1	14.3
Other commodity exports	1,312.7	4.7	1,812.0	4.8	6.7
Total gross commodity exports	28,171.6	100.0	38,094.0	100.0	6.2

Source: Malaysia, Jabatan Perangkaan (1985b).

Notes: * Figure is for 1983 and excluded from total gross commodity exports.
    + Figure is for 1983-85.

timber resources, and the implementation of a National Forestry Policy to monitor and manage the exploitation of forest resources.

Other agricultural commodities such as padi, pepper, and cocoa showed the influence of external factors. Padi, for example, exhibited a decline in production of about 2.8 per cent per annum, attributable to unfavourable weather conditions in 1983 and 1984 and further aggravated by the lack of farm labour in padi-growing areas which led to the abandonment of the padi land. The migration of young rural labour to urban areas exacerbated the situation. Weak export prices for pepper in 1981 and 1982 contributed to the decline in output of about 9.7 per cent over the period. In mining and quarrying the growth of crude petroleum and liquefied natural gas (LNG) production expanded the performance in this sector. Crude oil production increased by 10.1 per cent per annum while LNG, which came onstream in 1983, produced 4.5 million tonnes in 1985. However, tin output declined by almost 41 per cent, from 61,400 tonnes in 1980 to 36,300 tonnes in 1985, because of a depletion of readily accessible alluvial tin deposits, rising costs of mining and mineral production related to the mining of relatively inaccessible lode-bearing deposits, and production quotas imposed by the International Tin Council (ITC). This last factor was attributable to larger releases from the United States stockpile, the collapse of the buffer stock operations of ITC, and subsequent suspension of trading on the London Metal Exchange (LME) on October 24, 1985. The number of mines in operation fell from 852 in 1980 to 235 in 1985.

The secondary sector, consisting of manufacturing and construction activities, contributed about 24 per cent of total output of the economy in 1985. Growth in the manufacturing sector had slowed in 1985 mainly because of poor external demand. For example, the demand for electrical machinery was high at the beginning of the 1980s but dropped off towards the middle of the decade. The same can be said of the demand for textiles, although there was increased production in 1984.

However, the construction industry showed a healthy growth rate of about 8.1 per cent per annum between 1980 and 1985. Growth in this industry was closely tied to public sector expenditure, for example in physical infrastructural facilities, and to the stock of non-residential buildings and private sector construction such as office space and hotels. Thus a slowdown in growth may be attributed to weak demand for residential construction because of higher prices, a glut in the supply of office space, the scarcity of credit, higher costs in servicing mortgage loans, and the freeze on housing loans for government employees. This latter freeze reflected the cut-back in government expenditures since 1985 and other budgetary constraints imposed by a sluggish economy.

The tertiary sector grew at an average rate of 7.9 per cent per annum between 1980 and 1985 and all subsectors - transport, storage and communications, wholesale and retail trade, financial and real estate, and business services - expanded. Government services, for example, expanded rapidly by 238 per cent between 1980 and 1981 as a result of the exercise code-named *Isi Penuh* (fill up) designed to fill vacant positions in the government service so as to guarantee the ability to implement government programmes. However, growth in this subsector decelerated because of financial constraints from 1983 onwards so that by 1985 growth in the government subsector was only about 6.6 per cent. It might be useful to note here that it is possible that the high-productivity segment of the tertiary sector grew most rapidly. The low-productivity services segment, as represented by the informal sector, did not grow as quickly. However, quantitative data to support these intuitive observations are unavailable.

Spatial Distribution of the GDP

The sectoral contributions to the GDP examined above can be further illuminated by an examination of state contributions to the GDP. Invariably, the strength of each state's economy bears directly on its final contributions to the total GDP for the country.

On a state-wide basis (see Table 1.5), Selangor and Kuala Lumpur occupy the top two positions of national GDP contributions in 1985, with $9,043 million and $8,971 million respectively. The economic hub of the country, these two areas also encompass the rich urban-industrial complex of the Kelang valley which stretches coastwards to Port Kelang, the nation's major international and premier port. Perak is the third-ranked state, with a GDP of $6,179 million mainly as a result of its importance as a tin mining centre and as a centre for secondary manufacturing. Johor, with a GDP of $6,163 million, is the fourth-ranked state because of its central location in proximity to the rich natural and agricultural resources of the southern regions of the country. None of the remaining states has achieved a GDP in excess of $5,000 million. Sabah and Sarawak, with GDPs of $4,570 million and $4,760 million respectively, come closest. Mineral resources such as petroleum and, to a limited extent, copper and timber exports of these East Malaysian states have contributed to this relatively healthy performance. The smallest GDP is that of Perlis ($430 million), which reflects not only the small size of its territory but also the absence of important resources - either natural or human - that would help boost its GDP to significant levels.

Table 1.5. Malaysia: Gross domestic product and per capita gross
domestic product, by state, 1980 and 1985

State	GDP at purchasers' value 1985 ($ m. at 1978 prices)	Per capita GDP ($)		Ratio of per capita GDP to Malaysian average		Per capita growth (% p.a.)
		1980	1985	1980	1985	1981-85
Johor	6,163	2,916	3,324	0.91	0.88	2.7
Kedah	2,855	2,102	2,358	0.65	0.63	2.3
Kelantan	1,786	1,489	1,740	0.46	0.46	3.2
Melaka	1,362	2,297	2,765	0.71	0.74	3.8
Negri Sembilan	2,405	3,440	3,846	1.07	1.02	2.3
Pahang	3,490	3,182	3,495	0.99	0.93	1.9
Perak	6,179	2,853	3,194	0.89	0.85	2.3
Perlis	430	2,265	2,604	0.70	0.69	2.8
Pulau Pinang	4,325	3,649	4,120	1.13	1.10	2.5
Sabah	4,570	3,066	3,572	0.95	0.95	3.1
Sarawak	4,760	2,292	3,085	0.71	0.82	6.1
Selangor	9,043	4,610	4,963	1.43	1.32	1.5
Terengganu	3,005	3,705	4,719	1.15	1.26	5.0
WP/Kuala Lumpur	8,971	6,367	7,783	1.98	2.07	4.1
Malaysia	59,344	3,221	3,758	1.00	1.00	3.1

Source: Malaysia (1986: 170-3).

A paucity of data prevents any discussion of either ethnic or rural-urban differences in the distribution of per capita income. However, macro-scale per capita GDP data are available on a state-wide basis. These data are used in the following analysis to give 'orders of magnitude' and thus are indicative only.

The patterns of distribution of per capita GDP for 1980 and 1985 are similar. No signs of either a convergence or a divergence in per capita GDP are evident. This observation might suggest that the various states have retained their relative positions and reflect the strengths of different regional economies. As may be expected, Kuala Lumpur and Selangor take the top two positions, with $7,783 and $4,963 per capita in GDP in 1985 respectively. However, the third rank is taken up by Terengganu, followed by Pulau Pinang. The ranking of Terengganu above either Pulau Pinang or Perak is due to its large GDP earnings from petroleum and its relatively smaller population. This size component of population plays a significant part in the computation of per capita indices such that physically smaller states and smaller populations like Perlis, Melaka, and Negri Sembilan display 'healthier' per capita figures.

To show the significance of such per capita figures by comparison to a national standard, the per capita GDP is given as a ratio of the national average. The data suggest that Kuala Lumpur has a ratio which is twice as large as the national average. Only four states achieved a figure above the national average: Selangor, Terengganu, Pulau Pinang, and Negri Sembilan. The remaining nine states all show a ratio below that of the national average. This suggests a wide disparity between the high-earning states (at least in terms of per capita GDP) and the low-earning states, an issue which is given further attention in Chapter 2.

Remarkable growth rates have been posted for Sarawak, Terengganu and Kuala Lumpur with 6.1 per cent, 5.0 per cent, and 4.1 per cent per annum respectively for the period between 1981 and 1985. During the same period, surprisingly poor performances were recorded for Selangor, with a modest 1.5 per cent per annum, and Pahang, with 1.9 per cent per annum. A lack of demand for manufactured products together with a depressed commodity market have been blamed for such a performance. However, growth rates for the country as a whole range between 2.3 per cent to 3.8 per cent per annum. Indeed, the overall per capita growth rate for the country in the period under consideration is a modest 3.1 per cent per annum, a creditable achievement given that the world's economy was experiencing a recession.

Labour Force and Unemployment

The examination of the patterns of employment, unemployment, and underemployment in Malaysia points to differentials that are the result of geographical factors (that is, between different regions of the country or between rural and urban areas), demographic factors (age and sex), skills and quality of the labour force, and changes in the structure of the labour force. It may be observed that towards the latter half of the 1960s in Sabah, despite labour shortages, the inflow of both unskilled migrants and skilled artisans from elsewhere was curtailed for 'policy' reasons because these people were non-Malaysians. On the other hand, in peninsular Malaysia the number of job-seekers outnumbered available opportunities. Moreover, there was an oversupply of unskilled labour, invariably in urban areas. Thus regional imbalances in the supply and demand of labour were quite apparent. As a result a significant volume of economic activity was foregone as a result of the shortage of both unskilled and skilled workmen. The lack of qualified manpower could be costly, but this is difficult to measure. Inevitably, the expansion of investments and job opportunities may be retarded due to shortages of people with specialized know-how.

The beginning of the period of the *Second Malaysia Plan* posed new challenges from the viewpoint of job creation in the face of rapid growth in the size of the labour force. The task was not only to create enough jobs but also of the right kind. The young, aged between 15 and 25, made up about 30 per cent of the labour force and unemployment among them was particularly acute. For example, in 1962 about 64 per cent of the age group between 15 and 25 were unemployed and this rose to 75 per cent five years later. Thus it seemed that unemployment was largely a youth phenomenon.

By the end of the 1970s it was recognized that the lack of trained manpower was a principal constraint in accelerating socio-economic development. Between 1971 and 1975 the 15-29 age group registered a faster rate of growth, as compared with the overall labour force growth (4.8 per cent compared with 3.2 per cent respectively). However, there was a reduction in the unemployment rate from 7.4 per cent in 1970 to 7.0 per cent in 1975. During this period employment grew at the rate of about 3.3 per cent per annum and the impact was greater in urban than in rural areas.

The decade of the 1980s began with a continuation of the theme that the development of human resources was a critical input in the economic and social development of the country. The most important features to be noted during this period were, first, the rapid increase in the participation of females in the labour force, particularly in non-agricultural sectors. Second, there was a high incidence of unemployment among secondary school leavers, and finally, structural changes in the economy necessitated significant changes in sectoral employment growth with a shift away from agriculture to the secondary and tertiary sectors of the economy. Overall, therefore, it could be said that shortages of labour were relatively 'skill specific'. To appreciate these observations, participation rates of the labour force in 1980 are given below with a commentary on geographical distributions and demographic differentials.

Of the 7.4 million persons aged 15 and over in Malaysia in 1980, some 4.6 million were classified as being in the labour force (see Table 1.6). About 82 per cent of the labour force was found in peninsular Malaysia, 7 per cent in Sabah, and 10 per cent in Sarawak. This distribution correlates with the population distribution of these three major territories. While data in the table show little difference in percentage participation rates, an examination of detailed data on variations in labour force participation rates reveals that those states with significant net in-migration, such as Kuala Lumpur, Pahang, and Selangor have higher participation rates than the rest. This feature may be explained by the relatively larger number of persons at the prime working ages and especially of the male population in these three states as a result of in-migration. In contrast, those states which had a large outflow of migrants, such as Melaka and Perak, showed significantly lower rates.

However, there were marked differences in participation rates for males and females as well as for urban and rural areas. The participation rate for males was higher than for females in all age groups between 15 and 64 years. When the examination is switched to the pattern of urban-rural, age-specific participation rates, rural-based males and females demonstrated higher rates than those in urban areas. For rural males, this difference may be due to higher rates of participation of the young and old, while for rural females it was due to higher rates of participation by those in the older age bracket. The ease of entry and perhaps necessity to work in agricultural occupations in rural areas may explain the higher participation rates. Low productivity and low remuneration make it even more imperative to work for either wages or payment in kind. Further differences are evident when participation rates are disaggregated by region. As expected, the rates are higher for Sabah and Sarawak since the agricultural sector plays a prominent role in providing employment opportunities. These areas also have a markedly higher dependence ratio (see Table 1.6).

The rate of unemployment between 1980 and 1985 increased in Malaysia from 5.7 per cent to 7.6 per cent. A smaller increase was

Table 1.6. Malaysia: Total population, labour force, and unemployment
rates, 1980 and 1985

Region	Total popn. (000s)	Working age (000s)	Labour force (000s)	Particip- ation rate (%)	Unemploy- ment rate*		Dependence ratio+
					1980	1985	1980
Peninsular Malaysia	11,428	6,209	3,846	62.6	5.6	7.3	84.1
Sabah	1,011	523	342	66.9	8.3	9.3	93.3
Sarawak	1,308	676	448	66.6	5.1	8.7	93.5
Malaysia	13,747	7,408	4,636	63.3	5.7	7.6	85.6

Sources: Khoo (1982a) and Malaysia (1986: 170-1).

Notes: * Age group 15 to 64 years (as a percentage).
+ Ratio of population below 15 and over 65 years to the population aged between
15 and 64 years, expressed as per 100 persons.

recorded for peninsular Malaysia (from 5.6 to 7.3 per cent) and Sabah (from 8.3 to 9.3 per cent), while Sarawak recorded the biggest jump in unemployment rates, from 5.1 to 8.7 per cent. This pattern of change was partly attributable to a slowdown in the growth of the economy, especially the onset of the world recession at the end of 1979 and the beginning of 1980, which affected the Malaysian economy. As a consequence there was little or no expansion in work opportunities. Coupled with this is the large number of young persons joining the work force, thus inflating the rate of unemployment. Sabah recorded the highest unemployment rate in the country, at least in percentage terms, yet it recorded the smallest percentage growth over the previous five years. Thus, much caution needs to be exercised when analysing such data since these may lead to a misinterpretation of the trends in unemployment. It is noteworthy that for Malaysia as a whole, percentage unemployment rates are still single digit figures.

The dependence ratio given in the last column of Table 1.6 is the ratio of the number of children below 15 years and elderly persons over 65 years to the number of persons of working ages (15-64) years. This ratio gives an approximate measure of the relationship between those who depend on the working population for material well-being, maintenance, education, and advancement in life. The measure is an approximate one since it is merely an age-based classification and may be unrelated to whether those within the reference age groups are at school, employed, unemployed, or retired. Such ratios are also linked to fertility rates, such that high rates will correspondingly increase the dependence ratio; and related to mortality rates, such that longer life expectancy through better health care and nutrition will produce a higher dependence ratio. From Table 1.6 we see that the dependence burden in peninsular Malaysia was 84 dependants per 100 working persons, as compared with higher values for Sabah and Sarawak (93 dependants per 100 workers).

Terms of Trade and Balance of Payments

Any discussion of the terms of trade and balance of payments, favourable or otherwise, will need to be based on the set of interlocking factors which invariably control overall economic performance. In the Malaysian economy, for instance, the decline in the value of traditional primary commodity exports may be attributable to price declines rather than to any contractions in the volume of exports. Increases in the prices of imported capital equipment and intermediate industrial products will be reflected in the capital account. Similarly, world-wide shortages of food grains including rice will drive up the price of imported rice and these changes show up in the value of imports. For example, during 1974 price increases in rice accounted for 3.5 per cent of total imports (Malaysia 1976: 24). Similarly, if the *ringgit* is allowed to float with respect to other currencies, the result will be a reduction in the price of imports because of the resultant upward revaluation of the *ringgit* as against the currencies of Malaysia's major trading partners; this will perhaps dampen imported inflationary pressures. This theoretical background provides a structure for the following description.

The performance of the Malaysian economy during the 1960s and 1970s, while unspectacular, was nevertheless sufficient to maintain growth and other demands. In the first half of the 1960s, for instance, exports grew extremely slowly while the value of imports grew at a rate of 3.5 per cent per year. Such a pattern may be explained partly by the rapidly growing population but more accurately by the substantial increase in inflows of private long-term capital for investments in agriculture and industrial ventures. As a result of a rapid growth in recurrent expenditure, the deficit on the current account became more pronounced (Malaysia 1965: 30-35). During the latter half of the 1960s, however, domestic demand grew only slightly and exports performed better than expected. The GNP exceeded gross national expenditure with a growing surplus on the current account balance of payments and a net surplus of $1,064 million for the period 1965-70 (Malaysia 1971: 30-35).

The decade of the 1970s began with a minimal difference in the balance of trade between exports and imports of goods. Overall, for the five years between 1970 and 1975 there was a trade balance of about $3 billion in Malaysia's favour. This surplus enabled the country to accumulate external reserves totalling about $1.9 billion over the first half of the decade, thus enhancing the financial strength of the *ringgit* and providing sufficient resources to sustain six months of retained imports. In the second half of the 1970s the balance of payments was favourable despite marked fluctuations in the world economic situation and continued slackening in economic activity of the country's major trading partners. The trade balance of $21,954 million between 1976 and 1980 is about four times that of the previous five years ($4,088 million). The growth in trade surplus was the result of higher earnings from merchandise exports because of higher volumes and prices and increases in the value of crude petroleum and manufactured goods.

The capital account showed a substantial net inflow of long-term capital from foreign borrowing and a sustained inflow of corporate investments. The latter was no doubt attracted to the favourable opportunities for investment in the productive sectors of the economy, in particular in petroleum production. External reserves of Bank Negara (the central bank) were estimated at $10,304 million at the end of 1980, sufficient to finance 5.5 months of retained imports at the 1980 level.

In the early 1980s Malaysia's international trade was badly affected by a weak external demand and poor commodity prices. Between 1980 and 1985 the terms of trade declined by 1.4 per cent per annum as export prices fell by 1.0 per cent per annum and import prices rose by 0.5 per cent per annum. The fall in export prices was far from even; agricultural commodities declined by 4.4 per cent per annum while export prices of minerals fell by only 1.1 per cent per annum. Despite this, during the period 1981-85 the export of goods and non-factor services grew at a rate of 6.9 per cent per annum. Gross commodity exports increased by 6.2 per cent per annum from $28,172 million in 1980 to $38,094 million in 1985. Major contributors to this performance were the higher export volumes of crude petroleum and electronics, a consequence of higher external demand for raw materials and semi-finished products from industrialized countries.

On the other side of the trade exchange, imports of goods and non-factor services increased by 6.0 per cent per annum between 1980 and 1985. Although total output increased by 5.8 per cent per annum, when adjusted for the loss in terms of trade, GDP in real purchasing power increased at a lower rate of 5.1 per cent per annum. The increases in import prices may be attributed to marginal increases in the prices of exports of developed countries which accounted for a substantial proportion of total imports. Also, the price of investment goods such as the import price of capital goods showed a growth of only 1.3 per cent per annum while those of intermediate goods (for manufacturing and petroleum by-products) rose by 1.2 per cent per annum.

The combination of weaker export prices and a fall in the volume of total commodity exports resulted in a deterioration in the balance of payments. The current account recorded a deficit of $620 million, or 1.2 per cent of GNP, in 1980. By 1982 the deficit was $8,409, million or 14.1 per cent of GNP, but the economy had recovered from this position in 1985 with a deficit of $2,230 million, or 3.1 per cent of GNP.

The large deficit on the current account meant that Malaysia continued to be a net capital importer. Historically, capital inflows from both private and official sources have played an important role in augmenting the pool of resources for development. For the period 1965-70 the inflow of private long-term capital, including reinvestments by foreign companies, had been around $155 million a year while official capital receipts and market loans averaged $76 million a year. Data for 1971-76 and 1976-80 show that the inflow of official long-term capital ballooned to $2,327 million and $2,786 million respectively. During the period 1980-85 the cumulative net inflow of long-term capital amounted to $34,811 million, with $13,111 million representing corporate investment and the remainder either official market loans or official project loans. The net inflow of long-term capital helped offset the current account deficit, giving an overall balance of payments surplus of $1,759 million. External reserves of Bank Negara amounted to $12,457 million at the end of 1985, sufficient to finance 4.9 months of retained imports (Malaysia 1986: 45-59)

THE COLONIAL LEGACY

Much of the present economic and political structure of Malaysia today can be traced to the era of British colonial rule. As discussed in a previous section, the first foothold in the peninsula was in 1867 with the 'Straits Settlements', comprised of Singapore, Pulau Pinang, and Melaka. Direct British intervention in the Malay States, however, is officially marked by the Pangkor Agreement in 1874 when the British government signed an agreement with the Sultan of Perak. Under this agreement a British Resident was installed whose advice 'must be asked and acted upon on all questions other than those touching Malay religion and custom'. In reality this arrangement simply sanctioned colonial activity in the region because previously the British had intervened to quell the civil war that broke out in the tin fields of Perak and Selangor among Chinese immigrant miners. Such indirect rule was extended to other states and in 1895 the Federated Malay States was constituted, comprising Perak, Selangor, Negri Sembilan, and Pahang.

British interest in minerals, especially tin and gold, in the Malay States provided the incentive for accelerating British rule over all states in the peninsula. The stability accorded by such rule probably stimulated further Chinese immigration. From the 1900s British and Chinese miners began to exploit local resources, especially tin, and then branched out into other commercial ventures such as cash crops and spices. An event of critical significance was the introduction of the rubber tree from Brazil via Kew Gardens in England and the Botanical Gardens in Singapore. The highly successful introduction of this crop required more labour than the Malays could provide. As a result large numbers of Indian contract labourers were brought in from India to work the rubber plantations.

Thus the structure of the emergent modern economy of Malaya began to take shape. It appeared that the Malays who did not participate in the new plantation and mining sectors were left to their own devices in particular geographical locations. The Chinese and Indians who were prominent in tin and rubber were located in the more developed west coast states of the peninsula. The non-participation of the Malays in the modern economy has been blamed on overt British colonial policy, covert discrimination by European employers, the poor conditions in the early camps of the tin mines and 'labour queues' of rubber estates, and the alleged lack of economic motivation and preference for a traditional peasant life. On the other hand, an immigrant culture was said to have pervaded the ethos of the Chinese and Indian workers which provided them with a stronger motivation to achieve.[6]

The present-day multiracial character of the country is thus a direct result of British economic policy before the Second World War which encouraged mass non-Malay immigration. Such policies also established distinct patterns of economic disparity between the Malays and non-Malays, given their differences in culture, occupations, and income. A further important effect was the development of a highly over-specialized economy in rubber and tin that was subject to external fluctuations in world demand. Thus, notwithstanding the relatively successful levels of economic performance compared with other countries in the developing world, there are tensions in the Malaysian polity which can be traced to the multiracial nature of the society as well as to the structure of the economy.

It was clear that by *Merdeka* the Malays, Chinese, and Indians were positioned differently in terms of their relative strengths and weaknesses. In economic terms the Chinese occupied the 'high ground' with their relative wealth amassed from various economic activities and their competence in adapting to changes to the economy. Politically, the Malays had seized the initiative based on historical legitimacy and their established nationalism. Such differences between the main ethnic groups would have put them on a collision course but for the 'Bargain of 1957'. Whereas the non-Malays desired citizenship, the use of English in addition to the Malay language, a meritocracy, and a *laissez-faire* economy, the Malays demanded the recognition of their 'special position' and policies designed to accelerate their socio-economic progress. The compromise was that substantial concessions with respect to citizenship for non-Malays were made while the special position of the Malays was recognized for all time.

These agreements have been incorporated into various sections of the Constitution. Yet they proved inadequate to avoid the inter-ethnic conflict that erupted in 1969 - the chief complaints being the breaking of the 'Bargain of 1957' when the non-Malays seemed to want more political power, and the Malays' dissatisfaction with the slow progress towards economic equality.

The concentration of economic activity in isolated pockets, especially on the west coast of the peninsula, as well as the accumulation of wealth in urban localities resulted in unequal development. Invariably, rural areas and, unfortunately, one particular ethnic group - the *Bumiputera* - were adversely affected. It is believed that there was a lack of national integration, spatially and ethnically, leading inevitably to polarization based on geographic location and communal identification. Furthermore, inequality in the distribution of wealth among the ethnic groups and the high incidence of poverty among all groups brought forward the need for new government policies and radical social change to avoid further inter-ethnic problems, as discussed next.

GOVERNMENT ECONOMIC POLICY AND SOCIAL CHANGE

After the inter-ethnic riots of May 13, 1969, the government put in place a New Economic Policy to provide a structure whereby all Malaysians would be given equal opportunity to participate in the development process. The riots also brought to the fore gross disparities in income and wealth distribution among different groups in the population and the rural-urban differences in economic opportunities. Thus, the NEP was put in place to reduce and ultimately eradicate poverty among all Malaysians irrespective of ethnic origin, and concurrently to bring about social change to remove ethnic identification with economic function.

Since the 1970s, much progress has been made in this direction. All target groups[7] benefited from anti-poverty programmes. The overall incidence of poverty in peninsular Malaysia, that is, the total number of households whose incomes fell below the poverty line, declined from 39.6 per cent in 1976 to 18.4 per cent in 1984. This represented a reduction from 764,400 households to 483,300 (see Table 1.7). As can be observed this programme of poverty eradication had the most impact in the east coast states of Kelantan and Terengganu where the total number of households in poverty has been reduced by about one-third (31.4 per cent and 27.9 per cent respectively).

Elsewhere in the country the programme has been successful, with reductions in the number of households in poverty ranging from one-fifth to a quarter, the most significant of the people concerned living in Perlis, Sabah, Sarawak, Kedah, Pahang, and Negri Sembilan. The lowest overall change in the number of households in poverty was in Kuala Lumpur,

Table 1.7. Malaysia: Selected social indicators, 1976-85

State	Percentage of households in poverty		Doctors per 10,000 population		Persons living in quarters with				Infant mortality (per '000)	
					piped water		electricity			
	1976	1984	1980	1985	1980	1985	1980	1985	1980	1985
Johor	29.0	12.2	2.1	2.7	48.8	69.0	40.3	62.9	20.0	17.3
Kedah	61.0	36.6	1.4	1.9	57.2	70.4	33.0	60.9	28.1	24.3
Kelantan	67.1	39.2	0.9	1.6	28.4	32.8	38.8	62.8	18.4	16.4
Melaka	32.4	15.8	2.5	3.3	76.5	84.4	54.2	70.9	18.7	20.3
N. Sembilan	33.0	13.0	3.2	3.3	72.8	79.6	68.7	91.6	19.3	14.8
Pahang	38.9	15.7	1.9	2.2	58.8	72.8	34.0	49.5	15.9	13.7
Perak	43.0	20.3	1.9	2.7	68.2	82.4	25.3	58.0	19.3	21.3
Perlis	59.8	33.7	3.4	4.6	57.2	70.4	68.4	90.3	31.4	34.1
P. Pinang	32.4	13.4	2.2	3.7	87.0	91.0	70.8	81.0	23.5	23.2
Sabah	58.3	33.1	1.3	1.6	34.8	51.5	26.7	48.0	47.2	11.5
Sarawak	56.5	31.9	1.4	2.6	31.8	43.8	33.8	49.3	215.4	132.8
Selangor	22.9	8.6	2.2	2.9	80.8	88.1	44.8	81.0	27.5	27.0
Terengganu	60.3	28.9	1.2	1.7	46.4	59.1	49.8	70.6	14.7	12.2
W.P. / K.L.*	9.0	4.9	10.2	11.4	80.0	88.1	71.4	95.7	-	-
Peninsular Malaysia	39.6	18.4	-	-	-	-	-	-	-	-
Malaysia	-	-	2.6	3.2	58.8	69.9	49.9	71.3	25.8	20.4

Source: Malaysia (1986: 88, 170, 510).

Note: * Wilayah Persekutuan / Kuala Lumpur.

with a reduction of only 4.1 per cent. The second lowest reduction was in Selangor (14.3 per cent).

The decrease in the total number of households in poverty has been achieved through government policies in new land development, *in situ* projects which directly involve the rural poor and were designed to improve their incomes, and the absorption of the rural labour force into higher-income jobs in the industrial and service sectors.

The strategy for reducing poverty levels also included efforts at improving the quality of life through improved access to modern public services and social amenities. Malaysia's infant mortality rate per thousand live births declined from 25.8 in 1980 to 20.4 in 1985. Although Perlis, Perak, and Melaka recorded an increase in infant mortality over the 1982 data, the impact of improvements to medical and social services has been quite even. This is because of the well-organized health care delivery system and a bureaucratic infrastructure that is able to cope with greater demands on its services. A further indicator of improvement is that the ratio of medical practitioners to population, while still low by western standards, has improved markedly from about 2.6 doctors per 10,000 persons to about 3.2 per 10,000 persons. Except for Kelantan and Sarawak, more than half of all households had piped water in their homes by 1985. Nearly two-thirds of all households in all states except Pahang, Sabah, and Sarawak have electricity in their homes.

The second prong of the NEP involved the elimination of the identification of ethnicity with economic functions and geographical location. This strategy was to be achieved through the reduction of income imbalances among ethnic groups and regions by the generation of employment opportunities to bring about full employment, as well as through the restructuring of the employment pattern, the ownership of capital in the corporate sector, and the creation of a *Bumiputera* commercial and industrial community. Through redistribution of the ownership of economically productive assets in the country by 1990, *Bumiputera* will own or operate at least 30 per cent of the total commercial and industrial activities in all categories and scales of operation.

As these issues will be taken up later in the book, the above discussion has been very brief so as to lay the groundwork for later analysis. It cannot be doubted that government economic policy will bring about tremendous changes, not least of which are those of a social character. The geographical impact of such socio-economic changes and policies is assessed in Chapter 6.

NATIONAL DEVELOPMENT AND THE SPATIAL PERSPECTIVE

This brief section argues that a 'national' outlook needs to be adopted and emphasizes the spatial perspective. Higgins (1981: 15) gives one view of national development planning. He notes that in advanced capitalist countries prior to the Great Depression of the 1930s, anything remotely resembling national development planning was anathema, smacking of socialism and totally contradictory to the official nineteenth century dogma with its sublime faith in the free market as a guide and mechanism for resource allocation, economic growth, and income distribution. However, as can be observed from examples in both capitalist and socialist countries, this idea has been proved wrong. Neither Adam Smith's 'invisible hand' nor even the Marxian or Maoist 'dictatorship of the proletariat' has proved workable.

If that is the case, what then is meant by 'national development'? Misra (1981a: 10) sees development as part of the process of growth and a tool to win political freedom during the pre-independence period. After independence the development theme was used to perpetuate the 'group' and to strengthen the state. This became known as national development, but this again was hardly what was meant since Misra (1981a) later observed that the policies and strategies used to promote national development were often a reflection of what the developed countries wanted the developing countries to do anyway. It is thus not surprising that this in part was reflected in the rigidity of the economy, an inheritance from colonial days.

In the Malaysian context this concept of national development is all the more important because of the diversity of ethnic groups in its population, comprised of both indigenes and immigrants, and the geographical separation of east and west Malaysia, which may act as a barrier to economic development programmes. Moreover, the disparity in the relative levels of development between the east and west coasts of peninsular Malaysia or even between the peninsula and East Malaysia, suggests the need for a truly national approach to the subject of development. Such an approach deserves attention not only because it transcends a purely econometric approach but also because it includes a spatio-temporal and socio-cultural treatment of the economy. Development can be steered in space and time into high-growth sectors (aspatial) and selected growth points or locations (spatial) to obtain desired patterns in the form of cities and regions, and a planned environment (spatial).

The spatial implications of development have become increasingly important for many governments. For example, knowledge about the location of poverty groups in many countries was not comprehensive with the result that the geographical focus of anti-poverty campaigns has tended to be diffuse. Consequently, the emphasis of these programmes was on socio-economic groups that were poor rather than groups residing in particular locations. It is the geography of poverty as well as the positioning of the poor in the socio-economic system that should be addressed. It may be said that the geography of their plight may explain their poverty.[8]

Another way of looking at this problem is to note that the development paradigm of the 1950s and 1960s, with its preoccupation with the growth of the national income, capital accumulation, technological progress, and structural change in the economy, was primarily aspatial. However, the various approaches to development in the Second Development Decade - the 'unified approach', the 'basic needs approach', 'another development' and 'self-reliance'[9] - all imply that national development should be planned in terms of communities, target populations, grass roots, and smaller political and geographical units. The feeling was that somehow these were more responsive to the aspirations and needs of the people than a central government could be (Higgins 1981: 33).

The approach adopted in this book is therefore at variance with Perroux's theory of growth poles and his insistence that *effets d'entrainement* (spread effects) took place in widespread 'economic space', as opposed to 'banal' or geographic space (Blaug 1964). A stronger counter-argument can however be made. For example, Vagale (1981: 317) was more forthright in saying that

in the preparation and realization of development plans, one of the common weaknesses noticed is that they are 'spaceless in outlook'. The plans seem to have shown very little consideration to the location and distribution of economic activities and their impact on urban and regional growth. National development endeavours do not seem to have been brought into a sharp spatial focus.

The conclusion is that industry, transport, power, water supply, and housing all operate and interact within the framework of a set of spatial co-ordinates. Development is therefore a process of structural change and such change is brought about by planning, that is, goal-oriented state intervention in the national economy.

Even so, it cannot be guaranteed that planning over space can be all encompassing. There will still be a sizeable group of people who, for a variety of sociological and psychological reasons, are not being reached by development. These target groups who have not heard of development 'consist primarily of those who are "poor" in quality of human capital, the elderly, the infirm, the more tradition-bound and unprogressive' (Corner 1981: 136). To counter this, it has been suggested that a macro-spatial framework should be adopted (Lo, Salih, and Douglass 1981: 19). This approach sought to provide a holistic view of the national development process. According to this approach, rural areas are the basis of development so that when the distortions in rural-urban relations are corrected, the pattern of unevenness will be eradicated and rural towns and small regions will have a vital role to play in directing the process of planning from below.[10] Such an approach is very close to the idea of 'barefoot planners' as it involves the target population directly in the planning and execution of development projects and programmes. However, it is still the government that directs the change process with the ultimate objective of raising living standards and, cumulatively, the national well-being.

While there is much controversy over the precise definition of development and its objectives, no one will dispute the fact that a key feature of the concept is the improvement of the condition of life and the opportunities to develop the capacities of the poor in developing countries, with their participation in decision-making at all levels (Hettne and Wallensteen 1978: 1). Development is also much more than mere participation in decision-making. Sunkel (1981: 230) sees it as a process that brings about a transformation of society.

This change is characterized by an increase in average productivity per worker and income per person. A further feature is that there are changes in the structure of classes and groups in social organization, transformations in culture and value, and changes in the political and power structure. All these may lead to improvements in the average levels of living. However, development is not just growth: the assumption that unbridled economic growth will promote good life in the long run is fallacious. Some strategies may lead to the worsening of living standards for some sections of the population. Indeed, the spectre of the increasing gap between the 'haves' and 'have-nots' is very real. The following conclusion is thus apposite:

[t]his monolithic and materialistic approach to development must change. In fact, it is highly ethnocentric, retrogressive and pernicious: it is anti-developmental.

(Misra 1981b: 115)

In sum, the real meaning of development in the capitalist world is that it is a process through which the quality of life of the participants in both their material and cultural values is improved. The values referred to are those of the people involved, not the values of the western world, or any other world (Jackson 1977: 19).

CONCLUSION

The NEP represented a departure for Malaysian development policy in that it confronted squarely the problems of inequality and poverty among various groups in the country. Whether there are hidden agendas behind the ambiguities and vagueness in policy statements is unimportant because the immediate problem is one of achieving economic growth and fulfilling the objectives of a restructured society. Ethnic polarization as well as the structure of the economy will remain bottlenecks in the path to economic development. There is also little doubt that, on the one hand, internal political instability would undermine the plans and policies set out in planning documents. On the other hand, the world economic environment could play an important role in determining the relative wealth of Malaysia and thus her economic progress. Thus an examination of national economic planning is required in order to appreciate the tasks at hand.

2
PLANNING DEVELOPMENT (1950-1990)

Planning development and development planning may appear to be the same at first glance. But on deeper consideration it will quickly be realized that one can attach distinct interpretations to each of the phrases. Planning development at the most elemental level is the process of putting together some strategy to bring about 'development', however interpreted. On the other hand, development planning is more holistic in concept and in usage. Implicit in this notion is the attempt to plan development so as to attain some objective in the future. The similarity of the two phrases therefore belies their theoretical and operational differences.

To begin, one needs to consider what constitutes a development plan and identify a conceptual framework for the analysis of development efforts in Malaysia. In this approach, the spatial dimension is seen as providing a unifying perspective for the analysis of development planning in Malaysia. The impact of such planning impinges on geographic space at a local, regional, and national scale. Using this theme, an examination is undertaken of what is labelled 'old economic policy' (OEP) - that is, development plans up to 1969. This date, and more particularly May 13, when the so-called 'racial' riots affected many areas of peninsular Malaysia, is said to mark a watershed at which the old gave way to a new economic policy of the government. The examination is then switched to analysing various development plans of Malaysia, the latest of which concludes in 1990. In examining each development plan since their inception an attempt is made to isolate its objectives, to evaluate the success or failure of development expenditure allocations for the major sectors, and to detect major shifts in the direction of economic policy. To avoid the tedium of analysing each of the plans in a purely mechanistic manner, the depth of discussion of any one element will depend on its overall importance in the particular plan as a whole.

Past development plans may be regarded as historical records of the changing policy preoccupations of planners and the governments of the day. The causes of such shifts could be ascribed to fluctuations in economic conditions, to social upheavals, and to political change. The plans by themselves also follow some theoretical framework as a guiding principle to achieve policy objectives. Such frameworks provide the unifying theme to the choice of a development strategy. A discussion of these should, therefore, assist in an understanding of the development process. In this discussion the spatial perspective is prominent and emerges as an important component in the study and interpretation of development planning in Malaysia.

PLANS, PLANNING, AND DEVELOPMENT

When discussing development in its broadest context, there is the dual implication of growth on the one hand and improvement on the other. Growth encompasses not only economic growth such as per capita income and gross domestic product, but also socio-cultural growth in which the values and aspirations of any particular group of people are further enhanced, progressing from one level of wealth and well-being to a higher level. In terms of enhancement there can be improvements in the quality of life, coupled with the quantitative indicators of standards of living: housing, water, power, and telephone and car ownership.

Here it seems that planning may be perceived as essentially a technical or social engineering exercise. In fact, more is involved because planning is also inextricably linked with concepts of social change, of class interests, of prevailing ideologies, and the promotion of development by institutions with vested interests. Thus, planning may be seen as the art of transforming what is politically feasible rather than what is idealistically desirable. There is a need, therefore, to consider the 'political economy' of planning in a particular context.

Where it is accepted that the primary objective of a development plan is to increase total per capita output of goods and services, then it is also implied that the increased output should be fairly and equally shared, to the greatest extent possible, among all people in that economy. A plan would indeed be unfair and wholly invidious if only a privileged few derived benefits from it. According to the United Nations (1968: 16),

> planning signifies essentially the process of choosing or selecting among alternative courses of action, with a view to allocating scarce resources to reach specified objectives based on a diagnosis covering all of the relevant factors that can be identified.

But simply constructing a national plan does not *ipso facto* ensure economic development and social change. The formation of a plan's objectives by itself is not actual planning. The development plan is not an end but a means to some end. The plan simply provides a device or a framework within which to proceed. Planning is the process that includes, as a rational decision-making process,

> the judicious application of a sound system of choices among the alternative channels of capital investment and other development potentials, based on a consideration of economic, social, physical and other costs and benefits.

> (Vagale 1981: 314)

To this may be added Todaro's (1981: 430) observation that government attempts at long-range economic decision-making are made so that the country may 'achieve a predetermined set of development objectives'. It seems therefore that economic development planning may be used to guide economic growth and change in the direction of some image based on authentic national concepts of welfare, justice, and cultural values.

Thus the conceptual framework that is suggested provides the dimensions of economic development. Conceived as an integrated system, it consists of an activity dimension, a spatial dimension, and a temporal dimension. While the activity dimension may be thought of as the various sectors of the economy - agriculture, industry and manufacturing, transport, government services, and trade - the temporal dimension indicates the processes of change that take place within these sectors. The function of the spatial dimension relates to the geographical, territorial space of planning areas and their corresponding administrative units. In this way the conjunction of these three factors gives meaning to the activities that take place in time and space.

Why the Spatial Perspective?

In Chapter 1 it was argued that some of the colonial legacy could be construed as positive in material terms. None the less, while the colonial period provided a solid economic structure based on two export commodities, rubber and tin, it also engendered a spatial 'unevenness' in the opening up and development of the country. The pattern of uneven development has therefore left some areas lagging behind and probably acting as a 'brake' on more rapid growth. However, poor national integration also had socio-cultural and political dimensions.

Differences in cultural and indeed in political outlook could pose impediments where 'national' objectives are sought. Much has been said about the pluralistic nature of Malaysian society and how it might have constituted a potential strength. But as events have shown there continues to be a great degree of polarization among the ethnic groups based on religion, politics, and relative wealth.

The 'narrowness' of the economic base requires little further comment except to note that it is one factor that urgently needs to be overcome. It is this single factor that has led successive governments to plan consciously for the diminution of the country's economic dependence on a narrow range of primary products. Some of the economic problems of the 1980s have already been highlighted in the previous chapter. Among those that have to be borne in mind are problems of relative poverty and inequality in income distribution, unemployment and underemployment, variability in GDP as a consequence of fluctuating world demand for Malaysian products, poor terms of trade, and an unfavourable balance of trade. Such a background has suggested to economic planners that a distinctive approach to development planning was sorely needed. The following discussion postulates that a spatial perspective may offer some solution to the problem of unbalanced development. It is against this background that the topic of development planning in Malaysia is explored and its 'distinctiveness' highlighted.

If we accept that there is an ideology of rapid, directed social transformation, the argument for the need of a national development plan is rendered unnecessary. Perhaps what is more important is to consider the content, objectives, and direction of the change that is desired through planning. To geographers there may be some merit in suggesting also that in many development plans the spatial dimension is often neglected (Katchamat 1978). Decisions are often made on how much of a scarce resource should be allocated to a given purpose in a particular sector. However, consideration is seldom given as to where those investments should take place. The spatial variable is taken as assumed. Such decisions have increasingly come under criticism, especially where the result is an inequitable distribution of the benefits of economic development. Indeed, allocation *sans* space has its dangers. Thus where the

pattern of allocation of resources is made with little or no consideration of their locations ... [it will] create disparities in the benefits of economic growth distribution among regions of a country.

(Friedmann 1973: 133)

However, as one Malaysian economist has already noted, in the area of population and development planning there has been an extension into the spatial context of attempts to achieve an equitable ethnic balance in employment and income.

For the first time in Malaysia, development planners have directed attention and effort to integrating the spatial component with the socio-economic sectors of development planning.

(Chan 1981: 428)

An equitable ethnic balance in employment and income is probably the critical reason for recognizing the importance of the spatial dimension in the Malaysian context. The next chapter will show that the concepts of development planning also have parallels with regional planning and that the spatial perspective is an integral part of the planning process. For example, Faridad (1981: 94) has defined regional planning as

the application of growth models to development planning with explicit reference to the spatial dimension of the development process. Alternatively, it can be viewed as the preparation of a government action plan with due consideration to the location of economic activities and regional development.

Part of the reason for Malaysia's distinctive approach to development planning may be found in the uneven spatial patterns of growth. Where there is a structural transformation of the agricultural and non-agricultural sectors of economic production, such changes must be reflected in spatial terms. Furthermore, where the benefits of development accumulate in certain areas or regions of the country, then inevitably there will be widening inequalities in economic growth and income distribution. The contrary argument to this, of course, is that some economic activities of necessity concentrate in certain agglomerations, for example, industry. The disparity in terms of income, housing, water, and other facilities then becomes a contrast between urban and rural areas. Whatever it is, a consideration of the 'where' question becomes an important one.

There is a further reason for this spatial perspective. It is said that Malaysian development planners lean towards thinking of development in terms of space because much of their experience in development has consisted of opening up new land. The pioneering of such land was either for mining or modern plantation agriculture. Thus, in order to manage such resources, these planners have to couch their thinking in terms of land use planning. This emphasis on land use in urban and regional planning gives Malaysian development planning its special flavour (Higgins 1982: 148).

The geographical perspective in development planning is also seen as the key to ensuring distributive justice. The Malaysian economy relies primarily upon private enterprise to guarantee economic growth, as evidenced by the dominant role of the private sector in total investment and total consumption. This permits the government to attach high priority to social justice among ethnic and social groups in its own efforts to promote development. Thus, as Higgins (1982: 182) notes,

> [b]ecause of the overlay of disadvantaged groups with retarded regions, the attempt to move towards greater social justice has been translated into an attack on regional disparities.

Here it may be said that the Malaysian government operates a form of 'indicative' planning rather than 'comprehensive' (or statutory) planning such as those found in master plans that control land use in cities. The main instruments of such indicative planning include government revenue and spending in the area of public investment, taxation, trade, and monetary policy.

DEVELOPMENT PLANNING IN MALAYSIA

Background

The inter-ethnic riots[1] of May 13, 1969, mark a watershed in the history of Malaysia on many counts. Government attitudes and policies towards poverty and the restructuring of society and especially the participation of Malays in the economic growth and development of the country changed

Table 2.1. Malaya and Malaysia: Development plans and reviews, 1950-90

Year of publication	Plan	Acronym
Malaya and Malaysia		
1950	Draft Development Plan 1950-55, 'Yellow Book'	DDP
1953	Progress Report on the DDP	
1956	First Malaya Plan 1956-60 (First Five Year Plan, also known as A Plan of Development for Malaya)	FFYP
1961	Second Malaya Plan 1961-65 (Second Five Year Plan, also known as The RED Book)	SFYP
1963	Interim Review of Development in Malaya under the SFYP	IR-SFYP
1965	First Malaysia Plan 1966-70	1MP
1969	Mid-term Review of Economic Development in Malaysia under the First Malaysia Plan 1966-70	MTR-1MP
1971	Second Malaysia Plan 1971-75	2MP
1973	Mid-term Review of the Second Malaysia Plan 1971-75	MTR-2MP
1976	Third Malaysia Plan 1976-80	3MP
1979	Mid-term Review of the Third Malaysia Plan 1976-80	MTR-3MP
1981	Fourth Malaysia Plan 1981-85	4MP
1984	Mid-term Review of the Fourth Malaysia Plan 1981-85	MTR-4MP
1986	Fifth Malaysia Plan 1986-90	5MP
Sabah		
1948	Plan for Reconstruction and Development 1948-55	
1959	Sabah Development Plan 1959-64	
1965	Sabah State Development Plan 1965-70*	
Sarawak		
1947	Development and Welfare Plan 1947-56	
1951	Revised Plan 1951-57	
1954	Development Plan 1955-60	
1959	Sarawak Development Plan 1959-63*	
1963	Sarawak Development Plan 1964-68*	

Sources: All Malaya and Malaysia Plans were published in Kuala Lumpur by the Government Printer. Sabah Plans were published in Jesselton (Kota Kinabalu) and Sarawak Plans in Kuching.

Note: * Incorporated into the *First Malaysia Plan 1966-70*.

radically. After 1969 government policy was guided and governed by the NEP. All later planning makes reference to the NEP as well as to the *Outline Perspective Plan (Outline Plan)* suggested in the *Second Malaysia Plan 1971-1975,* which will bring about the achievement of the objectives of the NEP by 1990. Coincidentally, 1969 also marked approximately two decades of development in Malaysia which included a short period under colonial administration and a period of self-government. It is thus proposed that this early period of development be labelled the 'old economic policy'. The word 'old' is used with circumspection because there is some similarity with development policies devised after 1969. But it serves as a convenient label since it will allow a review of all development plans drawn up for Malaya and then west/peninsular Malaysia as well as for North Borneo/Sabah and Sarawak and terminating with the *First Malaysia Plan 1966-1970.* Under the NEP, on the other hand, all development plans are for Malaysia as a whole, beginning with the *Second* and concluding with the *Fifth Malaysia Plan 1986-1990.*

In order to help the reader keep track of the various development plans a tabulation of all plans as well as interim or mid-term reviews is given in Table 2.1. The year of publication is followed by the plan's designated title. Also included are acronyms sometimes used to refer to these plans.

Unless otherwise noted, all sources of data reported in this chapter concerning development plan allocations or expenditures come from the plans. Secondary synthetic (or derived) data such as percentages, growth rates, and statistical comparisons are computed from data published in the plans. This chapter analyses each plan in chronological order, beginning with those falling within the period of the OEP. At the end of this analysis a synthesis provides the platform for launching into an examination of plans within the NEP, followed by a summary and evaluation.

'OLD' ECONOMIC POLICY, 1947-70

The First Two Decades

Development plans in Malaysia have marked the changes in the direction and content of Malaysia's overall development policies. Such changes result from having to satisfy the needs of political reality and meeting new challenges that have arisen in the social, political, and economic spheres. While the start and end dates of the OEP span the pre-independence and newly independent states of Malaya, Sabah, and Sarawak, there is no suggestion of a continuity between the colonial and post-colonial plans. For this to be so would imply that the political agendas set up by those in power were the same in the two periods.

National planning in the post-independence era can be distinguished by the need to protect the rights and interests of the Malay and *Bumiputera* community in a highly competitive and predominantly non-Malay economic society. Thus, as noted by MacAndrews (1977b: 296), planning in Malaysia is as political as it is economic in focus. On the one hand, there was the objective of developing the country's rich resources and on the other, the satisfaction of the demands of competing ethnic groups, particularly the *Bumiputera* group as regards their contribution to and share in the economic development of the country. In this sense, therefore, any study of the history of development planning in Malaysia - as reflected in the various plans - will provide the 'warp and the weft'[2], as it were, of orientations, changes, and shifts in official government policy.

However, the political agendas may not always be self-evident since the data in the various plans may only give a superficial view of the true nature of the policy initiative. This is convincingly demonstrated by Rudner (1975) who highlighted the quandary of Malaysian rural development strategy. It had been claimed that Malaysian development policy tended to overemphasize the development of the agricultural sector. The most commonly given reason for this bias was the political influence of the rural population. Perhaps an elegant gerrymander,[3] the sparsely populated rural areas were given disproportionately large representation in Parliament. Moreover, as the rural population was primarily Malay, the result was uneven parliamentary representation reinforced by the special position accorded to the Malay community. But Rudner (1975) argues that these rural interests represented a conservative, land-owning Malay 'squirearchy' so that the rural development programmes that were pursued came about without social and institutional change. This then is the quandary of the strategy - the dilemma of pursuing economic development without socio-institutional adaptation. There is also the dilemma of producing change in situations where vested interests may be in control and are influential in deciding the nature of the development process itself (Rudner 1975: 87). It would be unwise to place too great an emphasis on an examination of the allocation of expenditure in development plans; the milieu within which the plan is drawn up must also be considered.

Draft Development Plan 1950-55

This first *Draft Development Plan (Draft Plan)* for the Federation of Malaya is also sometimes known as the 'Yellow Book'.[4] It was

> an attempt to define the objectives of social and economic policy for the periods 1950-1955: to balance them in relation to each other, and to plan them within range of the resources available to finance them.

> (Malaya 1950: 2)

The *Draft Plan* addressed the development of social services; national resources and utilities; trade and industry; and provided an indicative summary showing the possible sources from which the six-year development programme was to be financed.

A close reading of the economic, social, and political climate of the period will leave no doubt to the claim that the pressure for economic planning came from outside the Federation rather than from groups within it (Arudsothy 1975). The Colonial Office in London was anxious about the increasing problems of economic viability in its overseas dependencies in the wake of the Great Depression of the 1930s. The prevailing attitude was to abandon those colonies which had become a financial burden and to concentrate resources in colonies like Malaya because of the lesser amount of wartime damage and to capitalize on the high level of international demand for rubber and tin. There was a concomitant growing awareness among the colonial administrators and the local populace alike of the agitation for political independence in Malaya. To this end, the Colonial Development and Welfare Act of 1940 had been promulgated, but the Second World War prevented its implementation in Malaya until after 1946. The jurisdiction of this Act extended into the colonies of North Borneo and Sarawak. The main provisions of the Act provided 'development' funds for Malaya, North Borneo, and Sarawak.

The main cause of the anxiety was the overspecialized economy of these colonies so that their orientation operated to the detriment of each colony's domestic industries. This overspecialization made these economies potentially unstable, economically unviable, and incapable of long-term economic growth. The passing of the Act was an implicit indictment of past colonial economic policy and represented a major shift in colonial policy in favour of the interests of the colonies.

Arudsothy (1985) has given convincing reasons as to why local groups were uninterested in formulating any sort of plan for development. Other than tacitly admitting that all was not well, the miners and the planters, the power-brokers in the local Legislative Council, were willing neither to consider attempts to diversify the economy nor to give up their strong monopsonistic positions in the market place.

Of a proposed capital expenditure of $214 million, the Colonial Development and Welfare Fund contributed about $28 million (about 13.2 per cent). The raising of loans of $127 million (59.2 per cent) provided the bulk of the development expenditure. Federation funds, namely government revenue, yielded $59 million (27.6 per cent) for development purposes.[5]

Under the *Draft Plan* proposals for development expenditure, agriculture was allocated about $48 million (22 per cent), transport and communications $40 million (18 per cent), utilities $68 million (32 per cent), and social services $58 million (27 per cent) (see Table 2.2).

This pattern of capital expenditure reflected the fact that the *Draft Plan* was no more than a compilation of several development projects submitted by various heads of departments in the Malayan administration, which at that stage was still staffed by Europeans. That the *Draft Plan* represented a compromise between interdepartmental rivalries was evident from the apportionment of capital expenditure: no more than three or four main departments were given grants and expenditure was organized under a bewildering and seemingly haphazard series of headings that appeared to cut across established areas of responsibility. This meant that the more influential departments were allowed to dominate the plan and that the rationale for a reasoned formulation of even an incipient national development policy was stillborn. For example, social services obtained less than a third while the remainder went towards either the export sector or those sectors that facilitated and assisted the export sector, such as infrastructure. One interpretation was that such an apportionment should not be surprising since it reinforced the colony's role as a supplier of primary commodities to the United Kingdom. If this were true, then it was probably one of the unwritten assumptions of the plan. Industrialization, employment creation, and the subsistence sector were ignored by the plan, again perhaps reflecting the partiality of the colonial administrators in the country towards building infrastructure such as roads, railways, and drainage as a visible sign of development and progress (Arudsothy 1985).

Other weaknesses of the *Draft Plan* included its fiscal doctrines as well as the perception of the government's role in economic activity. Past

Table 2.2. Peninsular Malaysia: Public sector development expenditure under four development plans, 1955-70

Expenditure category	DDP 1950-55		FFYP 1956-60		SFYP 1961-65		IMP 1966-70	
	$m	% of total	$m	% of total	$m	% of total	$m	% of total
Agriculture	47	21	227	23	459	18	912	25
Rubber replanting	-	-	153	15	121	5	116	3
Drainage and irrigation	28	13	38	4	109	4	329	9
Land development	3	1	17	2	130	5	310	9
Other	16	7	19	2	99	4	157	4
Transport	6	3	230	23	589	22	357	9
Road	1	*	119	12	417	16	186	5
Rail	-	-	71	7	51	2	47	1
Ports	1	*	37	4	61	2	83	2
Aviation	4	2	3	*	60	2	41	1
Communication	36	16	52	5	113	4	158	4
Telecommunications	31	14	47	5	85	3	119	3
Broadcasting	2	1	3	*	23	1	35	1
Posts	3	1	2	*	5	*	4	*
Utilities	68	32	239	24	536	20	654	18
Electricity	-	-	142	14	353	13	518	14
Water supply	-	-	81	8	175	7	129	4
Sewerage	-	-	16	2	8	*	7	*
Commerce and industry	-	-	12	1	59	2	137	4
Social services	58	26	139	13	414	16	638	18
Education and training	35	16	61	6	237	9	287	8
Health and family planning	17	8	13	1	102	4	114	3
Housing	3	1	65	6	69	3	181	5
Social welfare and others	3	1	-	-	6	*	56	2
General administration	-	-	65	6	167	6	109	3
Sub-total: Non-security	-	-	964	96	2,337	88	2,965	82
Defence	-	-	35	3	245	9	532	15
Internal security	-	-	8	1	63	2	113	3
Total	215	100	1,007	100	2,645	100	3,610	100

Sources: Malaya (1953: 2; 1956a: 7; 1961: 7-8); Malaysia (1965: 28-9; 1971: 68-71).

Note: * Indicates less than 0.5 per cent.
Some totals do not add to 100 per cent owing to rounding errors.

colonial administrators had adopted antiquated fiscal doctrines so that

> [r]evenue producing works [were] financed out of loan funds, annually recurrent expenditure out of revenue, and, to the limit of the funds available, non-revenue-producing schemes by grants from the Colonial Development and Welfare Fund.

> (Malaya 1950: 5)

In practice, however, the distinction between 'revenue yielding' and 'non-revenue yielding' was at best arbitrary. Rather, as Arudsothy (1975: 100) believes, the *Draft Plan* could have been more effective if the government had adopted a more realistic fiscal structure based on explicit social goals and on the needs of a developing economy.

Apart from the bias of colonial budgets that favoured export and related sectors, 'development policy' was confined to general administration and to the provision of such infrastructural facilities and social amenities as would comply with the time-honoured 'agricultural bias' of the *kampungs* (Rudner 1977: 10). There was no place for the government in other activities in the economy. More particularly, the benign neglect of the Malays by a colonial regime resulted in the confinement of this group to the underdeveloped peasant sector. No attempt had been made to diversify the domestic economy so that this group as a whole could participate in progress and development.

First Five Year Plan 1956-60

Also known as the *First Malaya Plan (First Plan)*, this document was formulated just before the granting of independence to Malaya in 1957. Close scrutiny of the planned and actual public investment programme reveals that one need look no further than the proposals for agricultural development and the industrial sector to judge the plan's main thrust and emphasis.

While agriculture was accorded a nominal first priority in the plan's design there was strong emphasis on the more advanced urban sectors such as industry, machinery, and manufacturing. This emphasis was based on the belief that backward linkages would operate to convey development into the rural economy. In order to provide the mechanism for such linkages the plan gave prominence to the building of physical infrastructural facilities so that transport, communications, and utilities together consumed a little more than half of the planned expenditures over the five-year period. Moreover, there was also the planned development of economic infrastructures such as marketing mechanisms, provision of rural credit and loan facilities, and the setting up of farm co-operatives. Despite these, the rural producers themselves were expected to sustain their efforts in agricultural development, especially in the newly developing rubber industry. For instance, taking the padi subsector by itself, data from Rudner's (1975: 81) study showed that the explicit objective of agriculture was 'less the augmentation of padi planters' income than an increase in physical production'. The lack of an official pronouncement on this leads one to presume from such a policy that the objective was one of self-sufficiency rather than a concern with income.

However, other factors also impeded development and modernization in the subsistence sector. Institutional barriers arising from the established customary system of land tenure encompassing leases, rents, succession to land, and sheer conservatism among the landed gentry did not help innovation in this sector. Moreover, poor marketing and credit facilities prevented either investment or capital accumulation from enhancing the rural economy.

An analysis of planned and actual development expenditures for the *First Plan* shows that agriculture attained 86 per cent of its target, an achievement only slightly better than that of communications (82 per cent). Public works, plant, and equipment achieved 181 per cent of its target while transport and utilities showed 93 per cent and 111 per cent success rates respectively. The expenditure for commerce and industry of about $12 million represented only 77 per cent of the planned target. Compared with total development expenditure, commerce and industry accounted for only 1 per cent of the outlay.

Under the *First Plan* no policy on industrialization was announced; this appeared to be in line with recommendations of the World Bank (1955) report. That report stipulated that industrialization in Malaya was to be confined to passive measures such as site development, provision of infrastructure, and a favourable climate for private investment. Second, import restrictions of any kind were proscribed because in the Bank's view the standard of living of a majority of the population would deteriorate. Third, tax concessions were discouraged since they would create a tax differential in favour of new firms. Established firms might wish not to reinvest either in agriculture or agricultural processing industries or in mining exploration and extraction.

However, when the *Report of the Working Party on the Encourage-ment of Industrial Development in the Federation of Malaya* was published in 1957, the government's first steps towards an industrialization policy were taken. This came about in the Pioneer

Industries (Relief from Income Tax) Ordinance of 1958. The more important provisions under this ordinance included exemption from tax on company profits, duty-free imports of raw materials, and some tariff protection, depending on product. But the impact of this legislation was minimal in so far as employment in manufacturing was concerned (Rao 1980: 15). As will be discussed later, the spatial impact of this policy also resulted in a high concentration of firms in Pulau Pinang, Perak, Selangor, and Johor, with Kuala Lumpur and the then industrial satellite of Petaling Jaya dominating the industrial scene.

The hallmark of the *First Plan* was that it followed closely the *Draft Plan* and as such it continued to display the deficiencies that were apparent in the planned expenditures for the next five years. But the lack of coherence and consistency resurfaced.

Second Five Year Plan 1961-65

As in other newly emergent countries, Malaya began to acquire confidence in its task of economic and social development and as a result expanded greatly its range of targets. One way of appreciating this new confidence is to state briefly the broad objectives of the *Second Five Year Plan (Second Plan)*. The objectives of the plan were:

1. to provide facilities and opportunities for the rural population to improve its levels of economic and social well-being
2. to provide employment to the country's population of working age which (was) likely to increase by about 15 per cent during the plan period
3. to raise the per capita output of the economy and to protect per capita living standards against the adverse effects of a possible decline in rubber prices
4. to widen the variety of Malayan production, emphasizing the development of other suitable agricultural products in addition to rubber, and giving every reasonable encouragement to industrial expansion which in the long-term offered perhaps the greatest promise for sustained development and diversification of the Federation economy
5. finally, while stressing the importance of development which met production and employment requirements, to improve and expand the social services needed to provide educational opportunities for the rapidly growing school-age population, to extend the public health services over a wider coverage of the rural as well as urban population,

to assist in large measure in the provision of housing and to provide more adequately for rural and urban utilities.

(Malaya 1961: 16)

The emphasis of the plan was quite clear: continuing provision of infrastructural facilities (46 per cent of total planned expenditure) and the expansion of social services, especially health, education, welfare, and housing in both urban and rural areas. More significant, however, was the plan's decided push in three areas: first, the aim of providing employment to the population of working age; second, the raising of productivity of the economy while protecting per capita standards against an anticipated decline in rubber prices; and third, the drive towards a diversification of the economy.

The political factor accounted for the strong rural emphasis of this *Second Plan*. Of a total planned public expenditure of $2,652 million, nearly $468 million or 18 per cent was earmarked for agriculture. Half of this amount was for rubber replanting and land development, and nearly a quarter for co-operatives, farm credit, and modernization (see Table 2.2 above). All these expenditures benefited the rural sector, where the Malays and the majority of the electoral votes were to be found. A further indicator of the government's commitment to rural development was the incorporation of a National Rural Development Plan into the *Second Plan*. Thus it is not surprising that the allocation for this sector doubled that of the *First Plan*. As a first step in this direction the administration of rural development was reorganized to mobilize the effort into a national goal. This came about with the introduction of the 'RED Book' (Rural Economic Development) at a district level which recorded objectives and achievements of the local Development Committees. There was also an 'Operations Room' with charts, maps, overlays, and progress statistics of all development taking place in the district. The RED Book was as much an index of a district's performance as it was a target for rural development. This scheme was put in place in each of the 70 administrative districts in the country, with varying degrees of sophistication and success. The pinnacle of this organizational framework was the National Operations Room ('Ops Room') which controlled all development in the country.[6]

While rural roads were regarded as the key to *kampung* development, drainage and irrigation lagged behind. The failure of the irrigation programme under the *First Plan* resulted in renewed emphasis on this activity and it was seen as the principal vehicle for rural development. Cost-benefit criteria were applied to all investments in irrigation works and every person whose farm was affected by development projects came to be involved in decision-making through the RED Book. Planned targets were substantially achieved by mid-term. For example, the area under double-cropped padi increased fivefold to 23,068 hectares at the completion of the *Second Plan* period (see Malaysia 1965: 28-29).

In general, the *Second Plan* succeeded in meeting its objectives, with output and income growing more rapidly than planned and employment proceeding as projected. The initial steps towards diversification had thus been taken (Malaysia 1965: Ch.2).

First Malaysia Plan 1966-70

This plan marked the completion of nearly 20 years of development planning in Malaysia. A growing sophistication was evident in the layout of the plan and the setting of targets. For example, a comparison of the objectives of this plan with those of its predecessors will show not only the similarity but also improvements in the framing of objectives to more specific ends. This was a serious shortcoming in previous plans to the extent that vague statements of targets were infeasible.[7] The main objectives of the *First Malaysia Plan* were:

1. the integration of the peoples and states of Malaysia by promoting the welfare of all
2. a steady increase in the level of income and consumption per head
3. an improvement in the standard of living of the rural population and other low income groups by increasing their productivity
4. the provision of employment opportunities for the additional labour force and a reduction in the existing level of unemployment and underemployment
5. a diversification programme in agriculture and industry so as to reduce the dependence on rubber and tin
6. an educational programme for all Malaysians so that they might participate effectively in the process of economic and social development
7. a programme for effective family planning to reduce the demographic pressure
8. a land settlement scheme to provide the landless with economic-sized farms
9. an efficient and sufficient infrastructure.

(Malaysia 1965: 2)

The targets set were simple, readily quantifiable, and attainable within the context of the social, political, and economic climate. It is to be noted that this plan, while giving aggregate descriptions and analyses of Malaysia's development over the previous five years, by and large refers to peninsular Malaysia because Sabah and Sarawak were separate economic and political units during the first half of the plan period.

The basic commitments of the *First Malaysia Plan* to overall national planning were altered little; what had changed was the emphasis of the plan. In previous plans there was extensive rural development through the provision of complex infrastructural works, land development schemes, and the modernization of rural areas. Gradually this had shifted towards socio-economic and welfare concerns such as the improvement of standards of living, income, productivity, and employment opportunities.

Employment was targeted to increase by 15 per cent in the five-year period so as to absorb an expected labour force increase of about 14.1 per cent in peninsular Malaysia. The aim was that unemployment would decrease only slightly to around 5.5 to 6.0 per cent of the labour force. In Sabah and Sarawak it was expected that employment would just about keep pace with growth of the labour force at 15.3 per cent for the period 1966-70 (Malaysia 1965: 53). These measures have been criticized as unsatisfactory by Lim (1973: 147-8; 1975: 218). First, simply expanding employment at the same rate as the growth of the labour force does nothing to solve the problem of unemployment. Second, the level of unemployment was underestimated and the hidden rate of unemployment was largest among young Malays in urban areas. Finally, available evidence suggests that the target of 377,000 jobs was unlikely to be fulfilled. Furthermore, it was doubtful if much reliance could be placed on the estimated number of jobs required to be created during the period.[8] In the event, 350,000 jobs were created over the plan period. Unemployment rose from 180,000 or 6.5 per cent of the labour force at the end of the *First Malaysia Plan* to about 250,000 or 8 per cent in 1970 (Malaysia 1971: 95-111).

Changes in the world economic environment also forced the planners to look closely at development strategies. During the period 1966-70 it was estimated that total merchandise exports from Malaysia would increase by less than 1 per cent per year. This was due to the expected decline in the price of natural rubber and palm oil, coupled with a diminishing exports by volume of tin and iron ore, and few offsetting gains from increases in the volume of rubber, palm oil, timber, and pineapple exports. The argument of the planners at the Economic Planning Unit (EPU), of the Prime Minister's Department was that import substitution was an essential part of the growth strategy and the best prospects were to be found in the industrial sector (Malaysia 1965: 9, 27, 44). Total merchandise exports for the period of the *First Malaysia Plan* experienced an average annual growth rate of 4.8 per cent. The export performance of new activities was especially significant in contributing to this growth rate, as were the revised export incentives for export growth (Malaysia 1971: 54-5).

The growth of manufacturing was a major element in the long-run diversification of the economy, leading to a decrease in dependence on primary exports (Malaysia 1965: 15). To achieve this, capital and intermediate goods were imported as a short-run measure. Unfortunately, this created problems since limited reserves of foreign exchange had to be used. Three policy suggestions which have been adopted in various ways were made by Johns (1973: 168). First, he noted that there were a number of Malaysian manufacturing industries that had already captured a world market. Their main drawback was that they were small-scale enterprises. The Malaysian government could provide financial incentives to exporting industries to enlarge their operations. Second, it seemed unwise to concentrate solely on establishing small-scale manufacturing industries to tap the large unskilled labour market. What was required was the use of labour with appropriate skills in conjunction with capital; this appeared socially profitable at world prices. Finally, it was desirable to continue the policy of encouraging foreign direct investments in manufacturing, because the necessary ingredients of available land, plentiful labour, and a favourable investment climate in which tax and other concessions were freely available were believed to be able to foster the growth of industries.

Government attitudes towards the industrial sector may be gauged from official pronouncements. After the May 13, 1969, tragedy, *Tun* Abdul Razak, the Deputy Prime Minister and Director of the National Operations Council (the government during the Emergency period) announced a new industrial development strategy:

[t]he Government will take the initiative in industrialization and, if necessary, will participate in the establishment of industries either by itself or in joint venture with the private sector both local and foreign.

(*Tun* Abdul Razak 1969: 2)

This strategy was pursued quite vigorously with the setting up of Perbadanan Nasional (PERNAS) (the National Corporation) and various State Economic Development Corporations (SEDCs).

A final policy initiative that was to play an increasing role in the government's development effort was the launching of the JENGKA triangle. This giant land development scheme consisted of 60,705 hectares and was designed to resettle approximately 21,000 families (Malaysia 1965: 118). While this aspect of land development is the subject of an expanded analysis in Chapter 3 one comment needs to be made.

When the JENGKA scheme was launched Malaysian planners had yet to accumulate the necessary experience and expertise for such a huge undertaking. Moreover, institutional structures for matters such as land administration had not yet been worked out. For instance, land has always been a state matter. The mechanism for giving up huge areas of land to a statutory authority was not yet in place. This difficulty also meant that such giant schemes were confined within individual states. Another problem was the jurisdictional issue of the national government and its relationship with a regional authority and the extent to which the former had control over the latter. At this stage, regional development appeared to some as simply the opening up of more land. To others, national development was an increase in total investment in particular regions and activities so as to achieve structural change (Higgins 1982: 156-7).

To conclude this discussion of the *First Malaysia Plan*, it must be recognized that it was a macro-economic plan. Investment requirements were first determined for meeting targets for the growth of the national income. Then the investment budget was allocated among sectors. A notable feature was the long-range *Outline Plan* for 1990 and the projected structural changes in the economy that would be required. The plan reflected the 'clear understanding that structural change was a *sine qua non* of continued high growth of the Malaysian economy' (Higgins 1982: 156).

While the federal government was grappling with problems of large-scale land development in peninsular Malaysia, the planning for the development of Sarawak and Sabah had taken a different course, as we discuss next.

Sarawak Development Plans 1947-70

In a memorandum on development in Sarawak, MacFazdean (1947) is quoted as having said that

the chief obstacles in the way of formulating and carrying out a balanced and ordered programme of development for Sarawak are the lack of basic information, the lack of staff and the lack of money.

(Grijpstra 1976: 39)

Certainly, these shortages were evident at the end of the Second World War. To remedy the inadequacies and to rehabilitate the colony from the ravages of war, the *Development and Welfare Plan 1947-56* was drawn up. It was revised in 1951 to cover the period 1951-57. However, this plan was superseded by the *Development Plan 1955-60* which in turn was followed by the *Sarawak Development Plan 1959-63*. On the formation of Malaysia, the Sarawak *Development Plan 1964-68* was incorporated into the *First Malaysia Plan* (see Table 2.1 for a chronological tabulation of Malaysian development plans).

As with their counterparts in peninsular Malaysia, colonial administrators in Sarawak were prompted to prepare and implement the 1947 plan as a result of instructions from the Colonial Office. These moves were further stimulated by the possibility of obtaining funds from the Colonial Development and Welfare Fund (from which the colony received $5 million for development purposes) as well as from the Colombo Plan.[9] Funds were also forthcoming through loans as well as from annual revenue surpluses and accumulated reserves.

This pattern of development funding is much the same as that which took place in Malaya during the same period. Even the heads of expenditure under the plan were similar: rural development, communications, and education. In the early period of development activity in Sarawak, much effort was given to the improvement of wet padi. The reason for this emphasis in Sarawak was the concern for the prevention of soil erosion and detrimental effects as a result of the activities of the shifting cultivators on the hill slopes upstream.

The financial policy which was pursued remained conservative, with no deficits in spending being the rule and loans raised with great reluctance. The colonial government was always anxious not to overspend. Recurrent expenditure which tended to remain stable over a number of years made up one part, and a 'development' budget the other. This second part fluctuated, depending on the financial position of the government and revenue from exports. Moreover, only activities which had the character of a finite investment attracted funds from the development budget, presumably because of the effect such expenses might have on future outlays and/or revenues.

Much of the colonial fiscal conservatism was still evident in the next *Development Plan 1955-60*. An examination of its main objectives will reveal the chief concerns of the administrators of the day.

1. to increase, with the aim of self-sufficiency, the production of foodstuffs, the most important of which was rice
2. to ensure as early as possible against a recession of trade which might be caused by a collapse or serious deterioration in the market value of natural rubber. There must therefore be a reduction in imports of commodities which could be produced in Sarawak and simultaneously a development of alternative export crops
3. to improve communications as an important prerequisite of economic development
4. to associate private enterprise with industrial development and to provide an opportunity for local investment
5. to improve and expand social services within the capacity of the country to maintain the increased recurrent expenditure.

(Grijpstra 1976: 41)

The thrust of the plan is self-evident. There was to be an increase in the volume of rice production without any corresponding decrease in the labour devoted to other agricultural products or productive activities. But the emphasis in agricultural development had changed. Following the failure to resettle shifting cultivators to the lowlands and unsuccessful attempts at experimental wet padi, more attention was given to the rubber industry following the Korean War boom. The import and production of high-yielding rubber plants received high priority. A rubber planting scheme was introduced which provided planting materials, fertilizers, and cash grants. The other commercial crop that figured largely in this change of emphasis was pepper. The Second World War had devastated this industry, and with the lack of demand, it had nearly vanished. Under this plan efforts were made to re-establish the industry.

In terms of the other objectives of the plan, it will be observed that the underlying philosophy was that an improvement in communications was a prerequisite for economic development. Thus, while after the war there were no roads outside the main urban centres, during the plan period the main project was the construction of a trunk road linking Kuching with Simanggang and Sibu and eventually joining up the other two Divisions in Sarawak. Attention was also given to the construction of feeder roads. At best this plan may be described as providing the framework to help speed up the implementation of the development programmes.

The next plan, the *Sarawak Development Plan 1959-63* was allotted about $255 million for development purposes (see Table 2.3). Of this nearly half went towards infrastructural facilities: roads, communications and utilities. Social services and agriculture were each given about 18 per cent of the budget. It was left to each of the departments concerned, who had submitted bids, to spend the money as they had proposed. This was reminiscent of colonial days in terms of the preparation and implementation of projects. Funds for development were obtained from local government sources as well as from British grants-in-aid for development projects and from other Commonwealth countries (Jackson 1968).

This plan was adopted against a background of uneven economic progress in Sarawak. While timber production had grown by about 9 per cent annually between 1955 and 1960, there was less satisfactory progress in other subsectors. The problems created by shifting cultivators and their methods were still to be resolved, rubber output had stagnated because the smallholder sector of the industry had failed to replant with high-yielding materials and little or no progress towards self-sufficiency in rice production had been made.

In the non-agricultural sector, growth was stimulated by private and government investment expenditure. With the formation of Malaysia, Indonesia adopted a policy of confrontation that included armed military conflict. Increased military activity in the state as a counter-insurgency measure stimulated the construction industry. Some evidence of this can be gauged from the expansion of total road length, which grew from 965 to 1,550 kilometres during 1961-65. With the exception of a 160 kilometre gap between Sibu and Bintulu and another gap in the Fourth and Fifth Divisions, a trunk road paralleling the coast of Sarawak was completed (Malaysia 1965: 144).

The formation of Malaysia necessitated some adjustments to the phasing of the development plans. The *Sarawak Development Plan 1959-63* ended at the half-way point of the *Second Malaya Plan 1961-65* so that a plan for Sarawak had to be drawn up to fill the intervening period. Thus the final plan for Sarawak as a separate entity was the *Sarawak Development Plan 1964-68* which was later incorporated into the *First Malaysia Plan.* This was a more comprehensive plan than its predecessors and allowed assessment in terms of its macro-economic as well as its sectoral targets. The main aim of the plan was to improve standards of living by achieving high output levels and employment targets. A continuing objective was to widen the variety of Sarawakian production, emphasizing the development of other suitable agricultural products in addition to rubber and also giving encouragement to industrial expansion. With the inauguration of this plan there was high expectancy that Sarawak would develop at a faster rate than under colonial rule. This plan also saw the installation of a highly formalized and bureaucratic style

Table 2.3. North Borneo / Sabah and Sarawak: Public sector development expenditure under two development plans, 1959-70

Expenditure cateogry	North Borneo/Sabah				Sarawak			
	Development Plan 1959-64		First Malaysia Plan 1966-70		Sarawak Development Plan 1959-63		First Malaysia Plan 1966-70	
	$m	% of total	$m	% of total	$m	% of total	$m	% total
Agriculture	18	9	55	14	47	18	131	
Rubber replanting	-	-	5	1	-	-	61	
Drainage and irrigation	1	*	7	2	2	1	7	
Land development	3	1	28	7	3	1	13	
Other	14	7	15	4	42	16	50	
Transport	68	33	69	18	90	36	112	
Road	50	25	54	14	76	30	80	
Rail	2	1	1	*	-	-	-	
Ports	8	4	8	2	9	4	26	
Aviation	8	4	6	2	5	2	6	
Communications	8	4	26	7	8	3	24	
Telecommunications	5	2	19	5	-	-	19	
Broadcasting	3	1	6	2	7	3	5	
Posts	-	-	1	*	1	*	-	
Utilities	29	14	58	15	34	13	33	
Electricity	14	7	15	4	16	6	24	
Water supply	15	7	43	11	18	7	9	
Sewerage	-	-	-	-	-	-	-	
Commerce and industry	5	2	2	*	6	2	3	
Social services	43	21	62	17	45	17	87	
Education and training	18	9	27	7	23	9	46	
Health and family planning	7	3	18	5	8	3	21	
Housing	10	5	7	2	8	3	8	
Social welfare and other	8	4	10	3	6	2	12	
General administration	33	16	27	7	20	8	12	
Sub-total: Non-security	204	100	299	78	250	97	402	
Defence	-	-	54	14	-	-	45	
Internal security	-	-	22	6	4	2	19	
Total	204	100	375	100	254	100	466	

Source: Malaysia (1965: 69-70).

Notes: * Indicates less than 0.5 per cent.

Some totals do not add to 100 per cent owing to rounding errors.

of development with the introduction of Development Committees, Operations Rooms, and RED Books (Esman 1972: 105). Also introduced in an effort to engender an excitement about development, especially with independence and the formation of Malaysia, and to make development more visible, were the so-called 'minor rural projects' (MRP). Under this MRP category villages were provided with basic amenities - roads, bridges, and piped water supply - on the recommendation of District Development Committees. The political ramifications are self-evident as these soon added up on the electoral balance sheet. But from an economic viewpoint, there were projects which did not bring the expected profitable returns.

Whatever the policy, the guiding principle was that

the government's investment [was] not an end in itself and it [was] the total results of the economy which matter[ed] to the people gaining their living from it.

(Sarawak 1963: 18)

Sabah Development Plans 1948-70

As with neighbouring Sarawak and peninsular Malaysia, the *Plan for Reconstruction and Development 1948-55* (North Borneo 1948) was prepared under nearly similar circumstances in that money for development was forthcoming from the Colonial Welfare and Development Fund. A sum of £6 million was provided for the rehabilitation and reconstruction of the economy and for development purposes. Not surprisingly, infrastructural facilities were given the bulk of development funds.

The next plan was the *Sabah Development Plan 1959-64* with an expenditure budget of $204 million; two-fifths came from the Colonial Welfare and Development Fund, a fifth from loans raised by the Sabah government, and the remaining two-fifths from surplus funds of the ordinary state budget (see Table 2.3). Transport, communications, and utilities took up about 33 per cent of the total budget. Social services, which included education, health, housing, and social welfare, took about 21 per cent. Agriculture was allocated only a very small proportion of the development budget, a meagre $18 million (about 9 per cent). To all intents and purposes this plan was simply a programme of public investment expenditure rather than a comprehensive development plan with explicit economic targets. Heavy investment was proposed in the transport and communications sector because the scattered population and difficult terrain made road construction quite expensive when compared with either peninsular Malaysia or Sarawak (Jackson 1968: 165). None the less, the length of metalled roads grew from about 1,232 to 2,240 kilometres between 1960 and 1965 and electricity generating capacity increased from 7,849 to 18,700 kiloWatts in the same period (Malaysia 1965: 39).

A high growth rate of about 7 per cent per annum was achieved during the period of the plan, the main impetus coming from the very rapid expansion of round timber production for export. Output of rice grew slowly, averaging 2.8 per cent per annum over the plan period, and rubber production stagnated as compared with its level in 1960. The main limitation on continued economic growth was the extreme imbalance of the export economy, the lack of an integrated infrastructure, and a shortage of labour. The youthful age structure of the population, the lack of skills and experience among the labour force, and inflation as a result of the timber 'boom' were other major impediments to the development process.

The *Sabah State Development Plan 1965-70*, which was incorporated into the *First Malaysia Plan 1966-70*, by contrast with the pre-independence plan (1959-64), was much more comprehensive and ambitious. It also set the tone and style of development for subsequent plans. Probably because of the new fraternity of states in Malaysia and partly because of a need to achieve consistency with the *First Malaysia Plan* and subsequent plans, its presentation and scope were of a high standard.

Long-term goals for the state were both economic and social in origin: the promotion of economic growth, rapid development of the state's human resources, an expansion of social and economic facilities, and a reduction of socio-economic inequalities. Matched against these were specific objectives which could be operationalized within the plan period: land development, education, trunk and feeder roads, communication systems, medical services, and a skilled labour force supply (see Gudgeon 1981; Lim 1986: 167-8).

Synthesis and Evaluation

During the period up to the *First Malaysia Plan 1966-70*, all plans, whether for peninsular Malaysia, Sabah, or Sarawak were merely a collection of public development projects rather than an integrated programme encompassing many individual projects. This meant that the establishment of a development programme and project priorities was not possible.

Yet an examination of strategies adopted and the implementation of these plans, including the *First Malaysia Plan*, reveals that the techniques used were not ideologically doctrinaire; neither were the plans overly ambitious or impractical. Rather they sought to be realistic in that while there were no alterations to the socio-political *status quo*, the different plans had set modest, achievable targets within the plan period. All through the period under consideration plans were prepared on the basis of the various sectors of the economy. Some regard was given to the equity of the benefits of economic growth distribution and allocation of resources, but this, by and large, was overwhelmed by concern with rural development, the provision of infrastructural facilities and generally asserting the new-found *merdeka* which the territories had obtained from the colonial government. Thus, it may be said that the plans prior to independence were aimed at developing the colonies for 'the greater welfare of the UK' (Lim 1975: 3).

After independence there were important changes in the stated priorities. The emphasis of the post-independence plans was on a high rate of economic growth, the reduction of economic instability due to the extreme dependence on a few primary products, and attempts to discard the 'apron-strings' which tied these former colonies to the needs of a predominantly British market. The need for greater stability was nowhere better demonstrated than in the Korean War 'boom' during which rubber prices rose to unprecedented heights.[10]

Also underlying these macro-economic objectives were social equity aims, in which every citizen was expected to share equally in the development process and to reap its rewards. A further socio-economic objective was that of providing jobs for everyone. However, a close examination of development plans after the *First Malaysia Plan* will show that such objectives were largely ignored in the first flush of the development process, mainly because the broader issue of enlarging the economic cake took precedence over all other considerations.

It may be concluded that the plans had adopted a 'satisficing' rather than a maximizing objective function. The completion of each project represented only a step forward and an attempt at a local rather than global solution to the problem.

Some available data show that on the whole federal grants per capita were higher for the less developed states with a large rural population than for more developed states. However, despite the large amounts that were poured into the Malay rural sector, the results have been meagre (see Lai 1975: 404). No comparable data of the kind used by Lai exist for

Sabah and Sarawak, but it may be suggested that the picture was similar despite the massive outlays on infrastructural facilities. The development in the Bornean states is largely a matter of frontier resource development in which the extraction of timber resources led to the opening of new land for agriculture (less in rubber and palm oil than in peninsular Malaysia but more in other types of commercial agriculture) and the expansion of industries closely related to the primary sector. Overall, the plans for development in Sabah and Sarawak were less detailed and extensive than those emanating from peninsular Malaysia. This soon changed with the formulation of the NEP. The problem of differentials in details of planning no longer existed because the preoccupation with distributive justice took centre stage.

'NEW' ECONOMIC POLICY, c. 1971-90

The Last Two Decades

The NEP spans a period during which greater concern was accorded to two interrelated policy themes:

> to reduce and eventually eradicate poverty, by raising income levels and increasing employment opportunities for all Malaysians, irrespective of race; [and] ... accelerating the process of restructuring Malaysian society to correct economic imbalance, so as to reduce and eventually eliminate the identification of race with economic function.

(Malaysia 1971: 1)

In one sense it was a political response to the events of May 1969; in another sense these policy goals arose directly out of the economic, social, and political problems created by the colonial economic system. As noted previously, up to and including the *First Malaysia Plan 1966-70*, economic policy was directed towards the attainment of a faster rate of economic growth, a reduction in dependence on the export of rubber and tin, a higher level of employment, and a more equitable distribution of income and wealth. The May 13 incident was but a reflection of the fact that some of these policy goals had not been achieved (Lim 1973: 298; Malaysia 1971: Chs. 1 and 3). For example, in 1970 about 49 per cent of all households in peninsular Malaysia received an income below the poverty line; of these, 88 per cent were found in rural areas. Farmers made up 48 per cent and 30 per cent were farm or estate labourers. The geographical distribution of the poor households showed that 42 per cent lived in the northern, largely Malay states of Kelantan, Perlis, Terengganu and Kedah (Anand 1983).

Yet it cannot be denied that there had been a significant increase in the pace of development since the early 1950s. The average annual rate of growth of real GDP was only 3.5 per cent between 1950 and 1960; it increased to 4.5 per cent in the next decade. This growth had been achieved through a programme of sustained diversification. For example, manufacturing activity at the time of independence consisted only of processing agricultural products for local use and this sector's contribution was less than 8 per cent of the GDP. However, by 1970, with newer industries such as chemical products, non-metallic mineral products, and printing, the share had risen to 13 per cent of the GDP.

In the agricultural sector the rubber industry's vitality may be gauged from its switch to high-yielding planting materials. The adoption of improved processing technology to produce 'block' rubbers and technically specified Standard Malaysian Rubber (SMR) illustrated the industry's dynamism. The production of palm oil also increased during the period. In 1950, only 53,000 tonnes of palm oil were produced - less than 10 per cent of total world production. By 1970, 400,000 tonnes were produced (about 27 per cent), making the country the world's leading producer of this vegetable oil. Rice production also increased with the improvement in drainage and irrigation, thus giving a greater degree of water control to the padi fields. In addition, double- and triple-cropping became feasible in certain areas in line with the 'Green Revolution'. However, production costs became much heavier due to the increased use of chemical fertilizers and higher labour inputs.

Together these developments in Malaysia have brought about some degree of economic stability through the diversification of export incomes. But these alone were insufficient to ensure long-term economic growth because the country had to contend with destabilizing factors of different kinds. Whereas the *Second Malaysia Plan 1971-75* was concerned with the elimination of poverty among Malays and the restructuring of society, the *Third Malaysia Plan 1976-80* could be viewed as the fine-tuning mechanism by which the poverty of all Malaysians could be attacked. By the *Fourth Malaysia Plan 1981-85*, attention was being switched to the theme of employment and, by implication, industrialization policies. The *Fifth Malaysia Plan 1986-90* was premissed on the completion of the objectives of the NEP with a drive towards privatization, regional development, and even perhaps a 'new' National Economic Policy.

Second Malaysia Plan 1971-75

The restructuring programme of the *Second Malaysia Plan* set out two quantitative targets. First, employment by sector should reflect the ethnic composition of the population: Malays and *Bumiputera* 54 per cent, Chinese 35 per cent, Indians 10 per cent and 'others' 1 per cent. Second, by 1990 Malays and *Bumiputera* groups should own and manage at least 30 per cent of the corporate sector, an increase from its 2.4 per cent share in 1970.[11]

The increase of the Malay and *Bumiputera* share would be through their active participation in an expanding national cake rather than through the 'disruptive redistribution' of existing wealth. Although not stated explicitly, it was assumed that employment was to be secured through new employment opportunities rather than by a displacement of existing workers. Redistribution of the capital was to be accomplished through public enterprises taking up share capital 'in trust' for Malays and Bumiputeras until such time as they were in a position to purchase them (Thillainathan 1975b: 313; Hainsworth 1979: 14).

Thus for the first time in the development plans there was an explicit ideological foundation. There was also a very broad perspective of development in that no longer was development equated with growth. It will be seen that there were policies, projects, and programmes designed to modernize rural life; active encouragement and government participation to bring about rapid and balanced growth of urban activities; education and training programmes provided at all levels; and efforts to create a Malay commercial and industrial community at all levels and in all categories.

The central assumption of the *Second Malaysia Plan* was that national unity would flow from greater equity and balance among Malaysia's social and ethnic groups. While it was true that an equitable distribution of income and wealth was a necessary but not sufficient condition of national unity (Malaysia 1971: 4), Lim (1973: 295) has shown that empirical research from other developing countries suggests that there may be no direct link between the two and that more research may be required in this direction.

The public expenditure programme for this plan was seven times larger than the actual expenditure for the *First Malaysia Plan* (see Table 2.4). There was to be a greater volume of public investment, from 38 per cent of total investments during the 1960s to about 45 per cent in 1971-75. Public consumption expenditure also rose from 23 per cent of total

Table 2.4. Malaysia: Public sector development expenditure under four
development plans, 1971-90

Expenditure category	Second Malaysia Plan 1971-75		Third Malaysia Plan 1976-80		Fourth Malaysia Plan 1981-85		Fifth Malaysia Plan 1986-90+	
	$m	% of total	$m	% of total	$m	% of total	$m	% of total
Agriculture	*2,129*	*22*	*6,487*	*21*	*8,924*	*12*	*12,330*	*18*
Rubber replanting	158	1	263	1	397	1	1910	3
Drainage and irrigation	271	2	779	3	1425	2	337	*
Land development	1,139	11	3,433	11	3,040	4	4,419	6
Other	561	8	2,012	6	4,062	5	5,664	8
Transport	*1,781*	*18*	*4,462*	*14*	*12,966*	*17*	*10,789*	*16*
Road	1,033	11	2,763	9	9,960	13	7,672	11
Rail	104	1	350	1	651	1	1,049	2
Ports	442	4	859	3	1,481	2	401	-
Aviation	202	2	490	1	874	1	1,667	-
Communications	*604*	*6*	*1,363*	*4*	*5,033*	*7*	*9,706*	*14*
Telecommunications	499	5	1,211	4	4,932	7	9572	11
Broadcasting	87	1	110	*	94	*	120	*
Posts	18	*	42	*	7	*	14	*
Utilities	*952*	*9*	*2,120*	*7*	*8,645*	*11*	*9,895*	*14*
Electricity	634	6	1,407	5	6,589	9	6,385	9
Water supply	297	3	542	2	1,828	2	3,126	4
Sewerage	21	*	171	*	228	*	384	1
Commerce and trade	*1,654*	*17*	*4,348*	*14*	*20,212*	*27*	*9,752*	*14*
Social services	*1,327*	*13*	*5,214*	*17*	*9,981*	*13*	*9,035*	*13*
Education and training	676	7	2,153	7	4,688	6	5,583	8
Health and family planning	174	2	529	2	737	1	715	1
Housing	235	2	1,706	5	3,935	5	1,980	3
Social welfare	242	2	826	3	621	1	757	1
General administration	*349*	*3*	*862*	*3*	*811*	*1*	*2,788*	*4*
Sub-total: Non-security	*8,796*	*89*	*24,856*	*80*	*66,572*	*90*	*64,295*	*93*
Defence	*765*	*7*	*4,969*	*16*	*5,836*	*8*	*2,804*	*4*
Internal security	*259*	*3*	*1,340*	*4*	*1,658*	*2*	*1,901*	*3*
Total	*9,820*	*100*	*31,165*	*100*	*74,066*	*100*	*69,000*	*100*

Sources: Malaysia (1976: 240-1; 1981: 118-25; 1986: 246-7).

Notes: * Indicates less than 0.5 per cent.
   + Estimates only.
   Some totals do not add to 100 per cent owing to rounding errors.

consumption in 1966-70 to about 25 per cent during 1971-75. In terms of sectoral pattern of expenditure, while in the period 1956-65 more than half of the development resources were given to infrastructural facilities, the allocation from 1971 onwards was to decrease to about a third. Similarly, expenditure on agriculture and rural development was to fall to about 25 per cent while commerce and industry, which previously had been receiving between 3-5 per cent of development funds, received 13 per cent of total development expenditure.

In sum, the whole of the *Second Malaysia Plan* and indeed development plans after 1970 have been consumed with the NEP and aspects connected with either poverty or the restructuring of society. Such an all-abiding focus has attracted its share of critics. The question remains as to whether these goals were achievable within 20 years of the *Outline Plan*. On the one hand, the quota goals (that is, employment reflecting the ethnic composition of the population and 30 per cent equity in Malay or *Bumiputera* hands by 1990) have been considered to be too ambitious. The measures taken to achieve these goals have impeded growth, a precondition for the fulfilment of the NEP. The majority of Malay or *Bumiputera* individuals have been unable to take up the shares reserved for them so that the equity is held by 'trust agencies' such as MARA (Council of Trust for the Indigenous Peoples) and PERNAS (Lim 1986: 160). The target of 9.4 per cent of all shareholdings to be in Malay hands by 1975 was not achieved. Of the estimated 7 per cent held by Malays at that date, 5.5 per cent were held by trust agencies (Malaysia 1976: 33-87).

On the other hand, the emphasis on ownership rather than control meant greater demands for government funds to achieve national policy objectives within the time set. There was also the danger of capital flight out of the country since nearly two-thirds of the corporate wealth was in foreign hands. Thus the NEP represented a major change in development philosophy. Previously, a *laissez-faire* attitude prevailed; with the NEP there was to be stricter governmental control of the economy. A critical issue seems to be that greater state intervention in the economy was necessary to overcome the deficiencies of the previous *laissez-faire* policy. These included the apparent neglect of the distributive impact of capitalist-type development and the externally oriented pattern of development, both of these leading towards instability in the economy and unevenness in development in spatial and structural terms.

However, a problem of economic efficiency has arisen when state enterprises are expected to run businesses. Senior managers are part of the bureaucratic machinery and therefore may not make good business managers. Moreover, the concentration of economic power in the hands of a few will put 'considerable pressure on public probity in handling and disbursing these enormous claims upon the national wealth' (Hainsworth 1979: 16). Scandals are already beginning to come to light in connection with the transfer of equity holdings.[12] While the same sorts of criticisms may be made about the concentration of power in private hands - as may have occurred under the OEP - a significant feature of the increased role of the state in the economy is that it may engender fear and uncertainty among investors to the extent that it may have detrimental effects on private investment in the economy.[13]

From a spatial perspective, the *Second Malaysia Plan* recognized that development should be integrated in space and in time. For example the *Mid-term Review of the Second Malaysia Plan* noted the correlation between ethnic and regional disparities in income. A correction was thus necessary 'so as to reduce and eventually eliminate the identification of race with economic function and *geographical location*' [emphasis added] (Malaysia 1973: 7). But the biggest problem facing the government from an equity viewpoint (and putting to one side efficiency considerations completely) was that

> its attempts to improve regional distribution of income and to reduce regional disparities in economic development may be perverse in terms of racial distribution of income

(Lai 1975: 407)

Third Malaysia Plan 1976-80

The *Mid-term Review of the Second Malaysia Plan* set the tone for the *Third Malaysia Plan 1976-80*. The plan was delayed for about six months following *Tun* Abdul Razak's death in January 1976 in London. *Dato* Hussein Onn became the country's third prime minister, and during the six-month delay in the publication of the plan he may well have influenced its direction and tenor.

The NEP still provided the foundations of the national doctrine for the *Third Malaysia Plan* but the programmes proposed were less preoccupied with the targets posted in the *Second Malaysia Plan*. Two themes were evident. In the first, the transformation sought was

> an economic order in which the well-being of Malaysians of all races, from all walks of life and in all regions of the country will be enhanced.

(Malaysia 1976: iv)[14]

Thus while the NEP exclusively addressed the problem of Malay poverty, in the context of the *Third Malaysia Plan* 'rural poverty' took on an expanded meaning. It now also referred to the poor living in New Villages and to estate workers. New Villages were created during the Emergency (1948-60) and are inhabited mostly by Chinese. Estate workers are mainly Indians who live and work on the rubber and oil palm estates (Malaysia 1976: 159-77).

When the theme of rural poverty was matched with the restructuring of Malaysian society the plan appeared to be one by which non-Malays would move into the rural sector with the Malays moving into the urban sector (Mehmet 1982b: 982). It is thought that such a plan could successfully be carried out so long as the cross-movement of groups took place where there was an expansion of both the urban and rural sectors. This method of expanding Malay-held capital was also to operate in areas of large foreign ownership of capital. Again there was to be no expropriation but a larger share for the Malays from an enlarged national cake.

For example, in a number of general and specific statements the plan was careful to emphasize that share capital holdings of non-Malays and foreign persons should not decline. Non-Malay holdings were expected to grow at around 15 per cent per annum, foreign-owned capital at 10 per cent per annum, and Malay-owned equity at a phenomenal 30 per cent per annum to 1990. The pattern of capital ownership was expected to change from the ratio of 3:34:63 for Malays, non-Malays, and foreigners respectively to 30:40:30 by 1990 (Malaysia 1976: 88-9).

A theme evident since the *Second Malaysia Plan* was the aim of achieving a 30 per cent share of the economy for Malays by 1990. This has been found to be impracticable within the time available. Moreover, the plan still failed to help substantially the majority of poor rural-based Malays (MacAndrews 1977b: 299). One reason for this failure was the geographical nature of the problem. Whereas the corporate sector is necessarily urban-based, the majority of the poor lived in rural areas. Even within this latter group there are inter- and intra-regional differences as well as differences that are socially based. The need therefore was for a disbursement of funds in a manner that would lead to the development of society and the economy in the less developed areas of the country.

Development expenditure for the *Third Malaysia Plan* was almost twice that of the previous plan (see Table 2.4 above). The private sector was expected to fund a greater proportion of this expenditure than the public sector in contrast to previous plans. Total government expenditure was estimated to be $18.5 million; the private sector was to provide $26.5 million in local and foreign investments (Malaysia 1976: Ch. 12). Careful reading of the plan will reveal that it was much more sympathetic to private investment and private savings. Such a switch had been brought about by a realization that the public sector on its own would find development expenditure increasingly burdensome. In previous plans the private sector had remained distant where new development initiatives were concerned. There was also 'a new sense of urgency ... to ensure the timely delivery of the fruits of development to the people, particularly the poor' (Malaysia 1976: vii). To this end a major policy shift in budgetary allocations was put in train so that as many people as possible would be reached.

First, there was less emphasis on land development, which until now had been the major weapon in combating Malay poverty. Instead, more attention was paid to the root causes of poverty such as landlessness, low productivity in human and capital resources, and unemployment. The response included raising the productivity of existing farms, increasing the area under high-yielding material for rubber smallholders, drainage and irrigation to enhance rice production, and fisheries and livestock-raising. A large proportion of overall development expenditure was committed to the agricultural sector because primary commodities such as rubber, oil palm, and timber were still major foreign exchange earners. Agriculture and rural development expenditure increased from 21.7 per cent to 25.5 per cent (Malaysia 1976: 96-8). This allocation of $4.7 billion made agriculture and rural development the largest recipient. None of this, however, was to go to more advanced sectors of the agricultural economy such as large-scale rubber and oil palm estates, agricultural processing plants, and agricultural marketing corporations; presumably this was left to private enterprise.

What was significant was that the enormous public investment in agriculture reflected the realization among government planners that solving the defects in agricultural infrastructure might go a long way in eradicating poverty. The problem of uneconomic-size farms, poor farming methods and hence productivity and even 'leakages', such as in marketing, credit, and loan facilities, which probably soaked up most of the increases in output, all needed parallel attention. Thus, programmes were aimed at higher productivity, expanding employment, and creating a dynamic economic and social environment in rural areas.

Second, state enterprises such as MARA, PERNAS, and the Urban Development Authority (UDA) were still supported in development expenditure as an institutional means of securing greater Malay participation in the economy. However, their roles were now perceived to be much less significant as compared with the initial stages of the NEP.

The *Mid-term Review of the Third Malaysia Plan* noted that domestic financing of private investment fell 10.5 per cent from the target of $11.4 billion to $10.2 billion, while public sector investment rose from a target of $6.3 billion to $10.6 billion (67 per cent). Foreign capital inflow amounted to $27.5 billion, or about $1 billion more than anticipated. In the measurement of the incidence of poverty the review recommended a downward revision of the poverty-line income from $180 per month per household in 1970 to $160 per month per household in 1980. The review concluded that on the basis of performance in the 1970s, the NEP targets for restructuring employment might not be attainable by 1990 as planned even though considerable progress was being made in that direction.

To conclude, the *Third Malaysia Plan* provided

a fascinating case study of the massive intervention and use of government policy and machinery to meet, contain, and shape political developments in the country sinxe the very scope and breadth of the plan is based, for all its economic strengths, on political factors.

(MacAndrews 1977b: 308)

Fourth Malaysia Plan 1981-85

This plan heralded the second decade of the *Outline Plan* and further elaborated and refined policy measures instituted in the *Second* and *Third Malaysia Plans*.It was also a period within which some of the targets of the NEP were due to be realized. However, at the beginning of this period the world economic environment was marked by inflation, slow growth, increasing protectionism, and a rise in the cost of petroleum. Yet the Malaysian economy performed strongly. The economic policies of the past decade had led to increases in per capita income of 12 per cent per annum in current prices. The harnessing of public and private sector investments had resulted in the growth of the GDP of 7.8 per cent per annum during the period 1971-80. While the share of the agricultural sector in total GDP declined, modern sector activities such as manufacturing uring and construction increased rapidly to the extent that unemployment declined from 7.8 per cent in 1970 to 5.3 per cent in 1980. The incidence of poverty (as measured by the number of households below the poverty-line income) declined from 49.3 per cent in 1970 to 29.2 per cent in 1980. In rural areas the incidence of poverty was higher but was reduced from 58.7 per cent in 1970 to 37.7 per cent in 1980, ultimately to a target of 25 per cent in 1990. Five elements were identified by the *Fourth Malaysia Plan* as being responsible for such a development performance.

First, more resources were devoted to development, from 8 per cent of GDP during 1971-75 to 10 per cent during 1976-80. Second, the economy used its own resources to finance its development efforts, the ratio of taxes to GDP having risen from 18 per cent to 21 per cent during the 1970-75 and 1976-80 periods respectively. Third, the industrial development strategy shifted from import substitution to export promotion. Fourth, regional development was given increased importance in order to bring about a more balanced distribution of economic activities and integrate the states of Malaysia. Finally, policies and programmes were implemented to control inflation and to minimize its impact on the poor. The consumer price index (CPI) rose by 7.3 per cent per annum during 1971-75 but by the 1976-80 period had been pegged back to 4.6 per cent per annum (Malaysia 1981: Ch. 1).

In terms of the objectives of the *Fourth Malaysia Plan* the agricultural sector continued to be a source of export earnings and raw materials for the manufacturing sector. An expansion in agricultural production was expected as a consequence of increasing productivity. The rubber industry, for example, stood to benefit from projected increases in energy costs which made the production of synthetic rubbers overseas more expensive and hence less competitive. Palm oil prices, however, were expected to decline with prospective increases in world supply of oils and fats. A National Forestry Policy was adopted in 1978 to monitor the conservation, management, and development of forest resources on a systematic basis. This step had been taken to ensure the long-term and continued supply of hardwood timbers to the world market. The policy of self-sufficiency in rice production was maintained through increases in area and yield.

The manufacturing sector was projected to grow at a rapid rate of 10.9 per cent per annum, principally from export expansion and import substitution. This sector played a vital part in the expansion of employment among the ethnic groups and regions. Processing of agricultural products and textiles was designed to tap the natural comparative advantages of the labour market. In 1980 manufactured exports accounted for 27.5 per cent of total exports; this figure was expected to increase to 41 per cent by 1990. The incentive and tariff system was to be reviewed to foster growth in manufacturing.

The mining sector was projected to increase by 4.4 per cent per annum during the 1980s with a slowing down of contributions from tin mining but with rapid increases from petroleum and natural gas. Value added in the construction sector was projected to increase at 9.5 per cent per annum during 1981-90, slower than the 9.6 per cent rate per annum achieved during 1971-80. The service sector as a whole was estimated to grow at 8.5 per cent per annum in line with the diversification of the economy and the modernization of services provided by the public and private sectors (Malaysia 1981: 162-6).

Against the background of these objectives must be set the reality of the socio-economic environment during the life of the plan. Here a focus on the employment strategies will highlight some of the shortcomings. First, employment growth projections were based on the view that the economic boom of the 1980s would generate jobs at an annual rate of 4.3 per cent. During the plan period a total of 860,600 new jobs were expected to be created, mostly in manufacturing, wholesale and retail trade, and the service sector - hotels, restaurants, and government services. However, the economy created only 651,600 new jobs, indicating that the view of the planners had been over-optimistic. Second, the Malaysian economy was still dualistic in structure, depending heavily on the commodity export trade and thereby vulnerable to swings in the world economy. Thus a slow-down in global economic growth adversely affected demand for Malaysian primary commodities with the result that the unemployment rate of 5.7 per cent could not be sustained. In 1985 the unemployment rate was 7.6 per cent (Malaysia 1986: 139-40).

It has been suggested that the government's restructuring policies performed dismally (Mehmet 1982b). For example, the Malay share of employment in the non-agricultural sector increased from 38 per cent in 1970 to 43.7 per cent in 1980 whereas the Chinese share fell from 51.3 per cent to 45.9 per cent in the same period. But the Malay share in agriculture was a little less in 1980 than in 1970, while the Chinese share remained constant and the Indian community became more concentrated in agriculture and less so in the secondary and tertiary sectors. On these data, Mehmet asserts, 'the policies have so far not been very effective except in creating a secondary labour market' (1982b: 83). Such a market may be described in the context of dual labour market theory. This theory postulates that there can be two separate markets for job allocations, one for high-quality jobs and a secondary market for casual, low-quality jobs. The emergence of such a secondary market may be a transitory phenomenon. Mehmet (1971) adds that labour market segmentation is not new in Malaysia. What is new is that it was actively promoted, albeit unwittingly, by industrialization and the restructuring of policies in the name of modernization and racial balance.

Furthermore, Mehmet predicted that unless very radical policies were adopted in the 1980s these employment restructuring targets were unlikely to be any more successful than they were in the 1970s. The solution was either to relax the NEP restructuring targets for 1990 or to insist on them rigidly regardless of a changing economic climate and risk disharmony. There was already nervousness among private investors in the face of adverse fiscal and economic policy conditions. This might also have a negative impact on private investments, especially those in the hands of the non-Malays. Paradoxically, this plan projected a greater reliance on private investment (72.2 per cent) than the previous plan (63.2 per cent). In the final analysis, the projections of the *Fourth Malaysia Plan* have been over-optimistic.

Fifth Malaysia Plan 1986-90

The *Fifth Malaysia Plan* represents the fourth and last segment of the twenty-year *Outline Plan* for attaining national unity. This plan views the last five-year period as the most crucial and challenging in the light of the NEP and the state of the economy. Lagging international demand and weak commodity prices have affected export earnings as much as increasing protectionism in overseas markets and debt servicing problems. As a result a strategy of moderate growth with stability is to be pursued. Thus public expenditure on development has been cut from $74 billion in the last plan to $69 billion for the current plan (see Table 2.4). The major cuts were in defence and security spending. Agriculture and rural development continued to be emphasized, with a push towards increased food production and a commitment to small-scale industries and small-scale business in urban areas.

The government will continue to provide an investment climate to stimulate certain domestic activities: road construction, low-cost housing, and rising standards of living in rural areas. The private sector, however, is expected to provide the dynamism in the economy with the progressive withdrawal of the government from the economic sector. In this the government expects that the private sector will switch from its preoccupation with finance, property development, and real estate to manufacturing for export. Malaysia Incorporated, a term adopted to refer to the integration of the roles and functions of the government, the private sector, employers and employees, and producers and consumers, has been adopted as the theme to help develop a united, just, stable, and progressive society.

The strategies for growth during the *Fifth Malaysia Plan* include

1. an increased role for the private sector, to import dynamism into the economy. Rules and regulations that constrain growth are to be phased

out. With the privatization policy the private sector will be expected to participate more broadly in the economic life of the country

2. efficient management of the economy, especially of the public agencies. A broad policy of encouraging efficiency, higher rates of industrial investment, and the development of new subsectors will be instituted

3. domestic resource mobilization. Domestic savings and borrowings are the two main sources of growth. In the 1980s public and private sector savings have been declining with a concomitant increase in foreign capital. Better saving habits are encouraged, *inter alia*, increasing the reward and security of savings and purchasing habits such as the consumption of local as opposed to imported products

4. revitalization of the agricultural sector. The National Agricultural Policy (NAP) of 1984 aimed at revitalizing agriculture through efficient utilization of resources and hence contributing to the economic growth of the country

5. stimulating industrial development. The Industrial Master Plan (IMP) will provide measures to stimulate foreign and domestic economic activities, including liberalization of equity guidelines for foreign investors, the establishment of new investment funds to finance new production capacity in the manufacturing, agriculture, and tourism sectors, the reduction of power, telephone, and telex rates to businesses, and provision of incentives to businesses using local raw materials in manufacturing export goods

6. fuller development of human resources. Increasing productivity of local labour is seen as an important strategy

7. greater emphasis on research and development. The role of science and technology as an important tool for development is emphasized

8. improving spatial planning. Planning at the regional rather than state level is given increased attention

9. developing urban centres. Urbanization will be used as an important means to bring about both industrialization and social change. Growth centres in Regional Development Areas (RDAs) are to be actively promoted.

(Malaysia 1986: 21-8)

In line with the objectives of the NEP, the overall incidence of poverty among all target groups in peninsular Malaysia fell from 49.3 per cent in 1970 to 18.4 per cent in 1984, with a target of 16.7 per cent in 1990. It is to be noted, however, that the data are from government sources which have claimed that the incidence of poverty has been reduced and will continue to be reduced in 1990. A poverty line has been mentioned in previous plans but there is no indication of how it is determined; whether there are differentials for rural as compared with urban dwellers; and how stable this datum has been over the last 15 years or so. There is also the question of relative poverty and the gap between rich and poor. Thus, much more statistical data are required in order to argue convincingly that the battle against poverty has been won (Malaysia 1986: 7).

The *Fifth Malaysia Plan* expects much growth to come from the private sector. A projected overall economic growth rate of 5 per cent is set as a target. However, the performance of the private sector has so far been dismal. Under the *Fourth Malaysia Plan* the private sector only achieved a 1.8 per cent growth as compared with the target of 10.7 per cent. Thus if 5 per cent growth is to be achieved under the *Fifth Malaysia Plan*, based on the past achievement of 1.8 per cent under the previous plan, it would require a 360 per cent increase in the performance of the private sector. It is suggested that this projected growth rate of 5 per cent is unduly optimistic (Malaysia 1986: Ch. 6).

The thrust of the IMP is towards an export-oriented industrialization that is both resource- and non-resource-based. This dependence on overseas markets also means that the economy will again be susceptible to fluctuations in the international economy and hence will be severely affected by any recession in the world economy. The manufacturing sector is seeking growth through the encouragement of foreign investment so that during the plan period foreign equity will rise from 25.5 per cent in 1985 to 30 per cent in 1990.

The significant reduction in public sector participation in the domestic economy has been prompted by increasing foreign debt and huge budget deficits. The withdrawal of the government will be brought about through its privatization policies. Under health services, expenditure has been cut from $776 million in the last plan to $698 million in the present one. This is in anticipation of leasing public hospitals partially or wholly to the private sector and permitting private doctors to practise in public hospitals. The danger here is that these services may be more costly although there could be some improvement in the delivery of medical services.

The allocation for housing has been cut from $3.9 billion under the *Fourth Malaysia Plan* to $1.98 billion in the *Fifth Malaysia Plan*. Of the projected 701,500 new dwellings required, the public sector will build only 21 per cent. These targets may need to be revised. For example, in the previous plan the private sector was able to build only 204,200 units as against a target of 524,700 units (a 39 per cent achievement rate). Moreover, the housing units to be built under the *Fifth Malaysia Plan* may be too expensive. Only 9.4 per cent (19,170 units) built during the *Fourth Malaysia Plan* were low-cost units.

A re-examination of some of these policies will be required if the targets set under the plan are to be achieved. The projected growth rate for the economy of 5 per cent is probably over-optimistic. The private sector may not be able to perform as expected either in terms of the rate of investment or in providing employment opportunities in new ventures other than the previous concentration on finance, property, and real estate sectors.

THE FUTURE

Since the formulation of the NEP, development planning in Malaysia has been preoccupied with the twin goals of poverty alleviation and the restructuring of society. In greater or lesser degree each of the development plans has given prominence to achievements in meeting the NEP targets. The *Outline Plan* which spelt out these specific targets is scheduled to terminate in 1990. The crucial decision for policymakers then is whether to 'go for broke' and do everything necessary to achieve the NEP's objectives or to accept that it might be difficult to achieve these and seek to extend the NEP beyond 1990. Ministerial pronouncements on this issue have been ambivalent and strong emotional overtones have arisen on all sides (James 1986: 208-22).

The Chinese and Indian households, especially the poor, are likely to become increasingly resentful of benefits being channelled towards their Malay neighbours and of the discrimination they feel when seeking personal advancement. The opening of new land for Malays, the subsidization of resource-based industries and employment reserved for Malays, and the provision of public amenities with Malays in mind may all provoke some sense of frustration for the perceived injustice of the whole system. On the other hand, were these programmes to be carried out in some covert manner, then the indictment would be even more severe.

Within this policy of putting Malays first there is also the problem of identifying those industries and sectors which are best suited to promoting Malay entrepreneurship. Once found, there is the added burden of ensuring that they will be successful and become viable, competitive, and progressive enterprises. Where such efforts succeed, they can be expected to generate continuing productivity increases as well as rising incomes. But to achieve this requires some form of stewardship to ensure that the policy is implemented effectively.

Elsewhere it has already been noted that the concept of trusteeship as a means of fostering a socio-economic restructuring of society has failed (Mehmet 1986). It seems likely that the 'opportunist interests' and not necessarily those of the poor will be rewarded with the biggest share of the proceeds (Chia and MacAndrews 1982: 10-11).

In the drive towards development the government has become only too aware of the need to achieve some form of distributive justice. It is also acutely conscious that these distributional problems transcend sectors, occupations, ethnic groups, and geographical regions. In the *Second Malaysia Plan*, especially, one finds that a direct assault was launched to tackle problems of disparities at a regional level. Thus it may be said that while early plans have been aspatial in conception, by the *Fifth Malaysia Plan* a spatial perspective had suffused economic policies and programmes.

3
THE RURAL CONTENT OF REGIONAL PLANNING

It can be argued that Malaysia is one of the few Third World countries in which there is no urban bias in development (Lipton 1977). Indeed, public development expenditure post-independence suggests a leaning towards rural development (Tan 1981: 218). This rural emphasis may be observed indirectly through the preponderance of rural-rural migrations as a result of government land settlement schemes and the predominance of urban-rural flows (Young 1977).[1] Taylor (1981: 276), however, has rejected the theory of a false dichotomy between urban and rural development since the interaction between the two subsystems was part of a larger systematic whole.

Nevertheless, whatever the merits of the views of Lipton and Taylor, the essential task here is to identify and evaluate the ongoing programmes, projects, and trends in Malaysian rural development. While this follows from the previous chapter's discussion of economic planning the concern here is with the pressing socio-economic issues confronting rural areas. What are the changes that result from rural development and what is happening to rural areas? How have these changes affected rural dwellers and what prospects are there of continued development and future growth, given current thrusts in public policy and initiatives? These questions invariably describe a tripartite relationship between planners, that is, those assigned the task of bringing about changes; the objectives and goals of public policy as a manifestation of the views of politicians, and the vested interests, namely the rural population who are affected by these activities, rural institutions and the controllers of the rural economy. The focus is therefore on the interactions and interrelationships between these three actors that are translated either spatially or in terms of potentials for future economic growth.

After clarifying the distinction between rural and regional development in part one, particular attention in part two is given to strategies of rural development and in part three to land development and settlement. These are attempts to describe the nature of the agrarian transformation from low- to high-capital-intensity enterprises. Such a focus also permits an examination of the related issues of poverty and economic redistribution among the have-nots in the rural areas in part four and the problem of uneven development which, together with poverty and redistribution, have an impact on contributions to economic growth in the future. Part five discusses the different facets of government response to the challenge of rural development by examining giant development schemes as an example of how the problems are being tackled. Case studies of public enterprise in the rural sector demonstrate the ideals and the reality of development. Part six shows that the eastern states of Sabah and Sarawak are a subset of the development equation. Because the needs, potentialities, and peoples are very different an entirely unorthodox approach is required but has not yet been implemented. The final section in this chapter looks at the human dimension as part of this process of economic development, since the participants of rural development have hitherto been given scant attention.

DEVELOPMENT: RURAL AND REGIONAL

Early in 1970 a United Nations Committee on Development Planning emphasized that

> what development implies for developing countries [was] not simply an increase in productive capacity but also major transformations in their social and economic structures

(United Nations 1970: 6)

The essence of development includes the expansion of participation in economic activities, the increase in levels of income for the poorest groups and a reduction in spatial and economic disparities so that a larger majority have an enriched quality of life (Rondinelli and Ruddle 1978: v). More specifically, rural development is seen as a means of leading a traditional society towards the path of modernization; development consists of managed economic and social change. Who manages change and how change is brought about depends on the framework and mechanisms of development. However, in the final analysis it may be argued that development is an inherently political process because the planners who initiate change have to plan within a given political and social power network. In addition, it could also be suggested that although

> [m]an [was] both an agent and the object of the development process ... not infrequently, man [was] merely considered in statistical terms rather than as a pivot in the development formula.

> (Voon 1981: 63)

The context of rural development was therefore to create:

1. a surplus of food and raw materials for an urban (industrial) labour force
2. an export surplus to generate foreign exchange
3. a labour surplus to give rise to an industrial labour force
4. an investment surplus for urban, industrial, and welfare investment.

This was to be done by transforming subsistence agriculture into capitalist agriculture, extending the area under production, and dramatically raising productivity. Extending the area under production involves more farmers while increasing the productivity of farms may improve the economic and social life of the rural poor.

The rural poor include small-scale farmers, tenants, and the landless. In addition, rural development programmes have to include provision for promoting non-agricultural activities in rural areas so that the linkages between the agricultural sectors on the one hand and the urban industrialized sectors on the other may be further strengthened (World Bank 1975). Thus, on any view, rural development programmes will have to solve closely interlocking socio-economic, cultural, and technical problems.

In the Malaysian context, rural development performed two essential tasks. First, it may be seen as part of primary export promotion, of concentrating on export commodities such as rubber, oil palm, cocoa, and pepper. Second, it takes the form of a strategy of poverty eradication among the rural population by increasing opportunities for higher income earning capacity. These tasks are interrelated. To enhance primary export promotion, agricultural strategies entail land development so that landless farmers may have land and therefore a means of production to extricate themselves from poverty. The strategies also include large-scale infrastructural development such as irrigation projects for rice-growing areas so that the availability of water when and where required can be ensured, thus increasing farm productivity. Another strategy has been improved access to general agricultural institutions such as marketing, credit, fertilizers, and farm subsidies. The policies therefore aimed at improving agricultural production and creating rural employment opportunities. Pricing policies that favoured village farmers and land settlement schemes that provided modern amenities were added incentives that anchored people in the rural areas. The success of these programmes, however, will depend to a large extent on the reach and access to them by people in the rural areas.

However, there are a bewildering number of ministries, authorities, and other agencies that are concerned with various aspects of rural development in Malaysia. In land development alone there seems to be a multitude of agencies, including a number with little or no competence in this field. It is the task of the next section to unravel these complexities and to provide some organizational framework in order to visualize the various parts of the rural development strategy and how they fit into the overall system.

A World Bank-UN Development Planning Adviser on Regional Planning, Ove Simonsen, has divided regional development in Malaysia into three phases (cited in Higgins 1982: 160). These are:

1. tacit recognition of regional planning, a period that roughly parallels the *First Malaysia Plan*
2. *ad hoc* regional planning - the *Second Malaysia Plan*
3. explicit regional policy - the *Third* to *Fifth Malaysia Plan*s.

Each period spells out clearly the types and intensity of development projects and programmes. As discussed in Chapter 2 these phases reflect not only the changing emphasis but also changed circumstances on the political, economic, and social fronts. In general, regional development planning in Malaysia was a top-down affair, highly structured and organized by authorities of the central government. However, because of interests in land and development planning on the part of the states themselves, the stage has not been reached in Malaysia at which 'regional development plans are one of the "building blocks" to national policy and plans' (Higgins 1982: 160). A cursory examination of the *Fifth Malaysia Plan* will show the significance of regional development planning. It may be said to be the outstanding feature of development in Malaysia up to the 1990s and beyond. This has come about because of the dissatisfaction of both practitioners and academics with the purely sectoral approach in previous planning that has neglected either locations or regions. The *Fifth Malaysia Plan* is designed to remedy that deficiency.

Robin Pryor's comment that the sectoral emphasis of the *Second Malaysia Plan* precluded a more desirable regional space economy approach to national development seems to have been heard in the Economic Planning Unit (EPU) of the prime minister's department. Pryor also noted that an economic locational strategy will necessarily have to be based on the evolution of a complete set of regions, rather than the *ad hoc* and often aspatial planning that was typical of the 1971-75 period (Pryor 1975b: 15-16). Thus, although regional planning was given token priority with a strong political orientation that seemingly was designed to satisfy the rural voters, regional planning suffered from a vagueness in so far as geographical orientation was concerned since no regions were overtly identified.

The *Third Malaysia Plan* formulated a regional policy aimed at integrating urban, regional, and national development. Its main strategy was to bring about social and economic cohesion among the states and a more balanced urban system, to limit growth in the Kelang Valley, and to promote the east coast, which was perceived to be lagging behind (Malaysia 1976: 199). According to Higgins (1982: 158) the EPU planners were rather impatient with the highly aggregative Domar-like models that featured so prominently in the 1960s and were convinced of the need to disaggregate. In fairness, sectoral disaggregation had been tried in the 1960s, but it had been unsuccessful because the various sectors were unable to function independently.

Within this context, there was a felt need for some conceptual framework to bind together not only the sectors of the economy but also the various areas in which the economic activities took place. The 'growth pole' concept provided this structure and was described by Higgins (1982) as highly seductive, within easy reach, and untouched (see also Stöhr 1981; Stöhr and Taylor 1981).

This concept of the growth pole is derived from the ideas of Perroux and his 'theory of the dominant economic unit' (Blaug 1964: 551-63). When adapted to regional development, the theory held that growth pole industries or activities would give rise to the 'diffusion of spread effects' and the 'trickling down' of benefits to peripheral areas, given appropriate linkages to the rural areas. Such spread effects were expected to take place in both geographical and economic space. The temptation to adopt this concept seemed irresistible to Malaysian planners.

However, the Malaysian use of growth poles in regional development was an adulteration of the original Perrouxian ideas. Instead of the characteristic propulsive industries and activities in the growth centres, Malaysia adopted cash cropping to create employment opportunities to help rural dwellers achieve high standards of living and assist the country's economic growth. However, cash cropping by itself does not fit into the scheme of things considered by theorists to be part of a growth pole strategy. Malaysia's strategy was agriculturally based.[2] Rural areas, given the appropriate infrastructure and technology, were considered the poles from which the diffusion of benefits was to take place. These areas were to be the key links in the chain to the higher-order regional urban centres. In retrospect, evidence suggests that the application of the growth pole concept to national development planning in Malaysia was much more cautious and sophisticated than in most other countries that have attempted it. For example, a thorough study of the anatomy and functioning of the Malaysian urban system was undertaken before the growth centre structure was defined and policies to produce the growth centres designed (Higgins 1982: 159).

Yet despite this cautious use of the growth pole concept, the *Third Malaysia Plan* failed to achieve its objective of reducing regional disparities. It seemed that there was inadequate integration between the separate regional authorities who appeared to be in competition with one another. As discussed later, the apparent inflexibility of the various regional development authorities in adjusting their master plan to unforeseen circumstances contributed to shortfalls in achievements. Moreover, at the federal level there was no body in total charge that could direct, arbitrate, and provide conciliation between rival claims to scarce national resources. It was only in 1976 that a Ministry of Land and Regional Development was established. However, it may be naive to expect that planning along these lines may provide the solution to a reduction in regional disparities. More likely, no amount of planning will produce these reductions in the absence of changes to social structures, power relations, and institutions.

In the *Fourth Malaysia Plan* the objective of regional development was to narrow the disparities in the standard of living between regions by accelerating the rate of growth of the less developed regions relative to the more developed. For the first time, planners had become more conscious of the 'region' as opposed to 'state-wide' development. The *Fourth Malaysia Plan* defined the region as:

a relatively contiguous land mass which is in a more or less uniform state of development, has similar resources and economic activities and is dominated by a single metropolitan area. A region, therefore, may encompass an entire state or a group of states.

(Malaysia 1981: 99)

This plan identified six regions: Northern, comprising the states of Perlis, Kedah, Pulau Pinang, and Perak; Central, including Selangor, Kuala Lumpur, Negri Sembilan, and Melaka; Eastern, made up of Kelantan, Terengganu, and Pahang; and the single state regions of Johor (Southern), Sabah, and Sarawak. In the case of single state regions, Sabah and Sarawak were considered distinct regions in view of their large physical size, location, and unique socio-economic characteristics. With regard to Johor, even though it had some characteristics in common with other peninsular Malaysian states, its pace of development and pattern of resource flow were influenced by its proximity to Singapore (Malaysia 1986: 166). It may be observed that there was a gradual shift from thinking along state lines towards regarding the region as a spatial entity containing one or more states. Since the region provided territorial contiguity, political state boundaries inevitably became blurred in this process.

The other need for regional planning, of course, stemmed from the necessity to integrate more efficiently urban and regional development for the whole country. As a consequence, regional development planning was adopted as the means of providing this integration to achieve the two related targets of economic policy: equitable distribution of income and economic growth. The socio-economic objectives of regional development emphasized the need to give rural workers higher incomes, employment in agricultural and non-agricultural occupations, and to make available social amenities found in urban areas. New town centres would provide the dormitory for the workforce in agro-industries as well as the surrounding plantations. The overall aim was to eliminate regional imbalances through the application of the techniques of regional science.

STRATEGIES FOR REGIONAL DEVELOPMENT

Regional development in Malaysia has been aimed at reducing regional disparities and to this end both agricultural and industrial strategies have been followed. Three aspects of Malaysian regional policy should be noted. First, the move to de-emphasize states in favour of regions for planning purposes has direct implications for industrial location and the selection of growth centres for priority development. The previous practice of establishing industrial estates at various locations spread resources too thinly while new townships in land settlement schemes experienced problems in attracting settlers.

Second, there was a need to strike a balance between 'people-prosperity' and 'place-prosperity' strategies. A people-prosperity strategy would move people to where the jobs were by accelerating growth in lead areas through either comparative advantages or economies of scale. The place-prosperity strategy envisaged the generation of employment for people living at particular locations and catered for people migrating into these areas. To these ends the *Fifth Malaysia Plan* attempted to reinvigorate and modernize the agricultural sector through rural urbanization programmes.

Finally, using the region as a planning unit, selected centres were to be developed to capture urban-bound migrants originating from the region. Such developments would include revitalizing rural activities so as to raise the income of the labour force (Malaysia 1986: 199-201). The underlying rationale for each of these orientations was to bring about a balance in the relative absorptive capacities of the regions. The policy affects all regions. For example, it was designed to limit the industrial expansion and population growth of the Kelang Valley. The Northern region was to be developed but Pulau Pinang was not to be disturbed by government policy because it was already relatively well-developed. Johor Bahru's deep-water port and international airport would serve as entry and exit points for goods and services. For the east coast, Kuantan was identified as the growth pole for the region, while Sabah and Sarawak were to be developed at a pace according to their respective needs.

Four types of regional development programmes have been employed in Malaysia (Mat 1983: 95):

1. *in situ* agricultural development programmes assist in the development of depressed and highly populated areas. Such programmes take the form of infrastructural improvements, extension services, credit, and subsidies for replanting crops such as rubber and coconuts. The Muda and Kemubu projects are good examples of irrigation projects for rice growing[3]
2. large-scale resettlement and new land settlement schemes, also known as resource frontier settlement and colonization. One characteristic of recent schemes involves collective land tenure and a community-based production system in which earnings are shared equally among participants

3. industrial dispersal strategy[4] involves fiscal incentives as well as the development of infrastructure such as power and roads to attract private investment to less developed regions
4. rural urbanization programmes and the creation of new growth centres in backward regions. It is expected that agglomeration economies would accrue through the growth of supporting industries and 'downstream' activities in urbanized areas. Typical of this is Kuantan, the growth centre that is to serve the Pahang Tenggara area as well as the states of Kelantan and Terengganu. Under the rural urbanization concept there will be a regrouping of villages of at least 500 families to form a new rural growth centre.

The administrative framework of regional development in Malaysia is shown in Figure 3.1. Development planning is administered at two levels. First, there are central agencies that come under the control and direction of the prime minister's department such as the EPU, the Implementation and Co-ordination Unit (ICU), and the Federal Treasury which finances all development expenditures. These agencies act as the clearing house for all national councils and committees and also determine implementing strategies. Second, ministries, statutory authorities, and other departments oversee implementation and make recommendations to central agencies to suggest improvements when developing appropriate policy. Also included are the individual state government planning units. At this level are found the various regional development authorities and city regions that complete the planning hierarchy. Regional development planning is basically top-down in structure.

A brief outline of the RDAs' activities will serve to illustrate their function in the overall planning structure shown in Figure 3.1. The Georgetown-Butterworth conurbation comes under the State Economic Planning Unit of Pulau Pinang[5] while Kuala Lumpur is under the Ministry of Federal Territory. The main tasks are to manage the urban environment and urban growth. Of particular interest, however, are the various regional authorities and agricultural development schemes.

The Muda Irrigation Project (MADA) located on the Kedah-Perlis plains in the northwest of the peninsula provides off-season water to about 98,000 hectares of padi land. This is by far the largest irrigation project in the country. A second, medium-sized irrigation project is the Kemubu Scheme (KADA) in Kelantan which incorporates 19,000 hectares of padi land and provides the opportunity to grow a second rice crop for some 23,000 families. Other small and minor projects based on mixed inter-cropping include those of Johor Barat, Barat Laut Selangor, and Asajaya in Sarawak. These are either part of integrated agricultural development

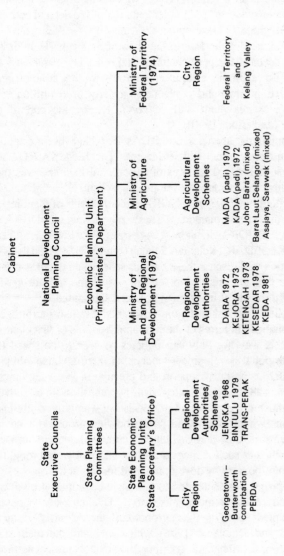

Figure 3.1 **Malaysia: Administrative framework for regional development**

Source: Higgins (1982: 167).

projects (IADP) or simply drainage and irrigation schemes. The Trans-Perak scheme is an irrigation project which also involves a concentrated, packaged, and synchronized implementation of IADPs and activities. The Bintulu Regional Development Authority serves the potential development area of the Fourth Division of Sarawak. Here an industrial site of 83 hectares for petrochemical and other heavy industry has been set aside. For example, a liquified natural gas plant at an estimated cost of US$1,016 million and a planned capacity of 6 million tonnes per annum and a urea plant will be completed by the end of the *Fifth Malaysia Plan* period (1990).

The remaining agencies are RDAs that have been established for agricultural development and settlement. The JENGKA RDA in Pahang involves about 126,000 hectares of agricultural land and was the first of the so-called 'giant land-development schemes'. Other RDAs are modelled along the lines of JENGKA either in terms of planning and/or in terms of the crops planted. These others include DARA (Pahang Tenggara), KEJORA (Johor Tenggara), KETENGAH (Terengganu Tengah), KESEDAR (Kelantan Selatan), and KEDA (Kedah) RDAs. As a later section will discuss these various schemes in detail it need only be noted here that the areas involved are very large, all are agriculturally based, and the scale of investment has been substantial.

The political appeal of the top-down model remains strong, especially when rationalized in terms of the economic benefits of 'trickle down' over time. In this way not only can policies be seen to be based on sound, objective regional development theory, but there are also added political bonuses such as political support and prestige in these settlements (Ness 1967; Tham 1983). The 'trickle down' hypothesis as an effective strategy has been much criticized (Corner, 1983) but was universally encouraged in situations where established power-holding groups did not intend to alter power structures and institutional arrangements. This usage casts doubt on whether such strategies at a social level have brought about an eradication of poverty by developing land for settlers.

These projects are intended to stimulate economic growth in lagging regions and reduce regional disparity. Diametrically opposed to the model adopted above is the 'agropolitan' theory initially suggested by Friedmann and Douglass (1975) which includes the idea of selective regional closure (Stöhr and Todtling 1977). The theory is based on the building of strength from within, using local skills and resources with no input from the outside (Friedmann and Weaver 1979: 200). The notion is one of 'basic needs', of 'self reliance', and 'development from below'. The belief is that capitalist development magnifies inequalities and will not eliminate poverty.

However, the idea of 'agropoles', conceived of as cities in the fields, has not been taken up as part of the development philosophy in Malaysia. The macro-spatial economy is tied so firmly to the international trading system that it would be impractical to abandon one method of regional development for another, despite the warning that inequalities will be magnified and poverty will persist where development is directed from above (Friedmann and Weaver 1979). Local needs and markets in Malaysia are too small to compete with the international economy if the idea of 'selected spatial closures' were to be adopted. There would be limited economic growth generated domestically since there could be no imports of wealth either from outside the region or from overseas. It would be a very radical step and would take a brave planner to suggest that Malaysia adopt the agropolitan approach to ameliorate the problems of regional disparity.

Taylor (1981) has suggested the development centre concept as a sort of grassroots bottom-up strategy.[6] The method should be viewed as a normative prescription for planning purposes. The development centre performs such functions as the diffusion of innovations, the provision of services for the hinterland, especially those related to basic needs such as health, education, housing, water, and electricity. Such a centre also co-ordinates government and local development planning, and becomes a point from which local ideas and initiatives can be discussed, refined, and further developed (Taylor 1981: 284). In the Malaysian context this idea would have a small following since most development is 'outer-directed', that is, from outside the area and from above. Spontaneous, inner-directed projects, while successfully employed in private agricultural enterprises, have not taken hold in land-based public enterprises.[7]

To demonstrate the record of regional development in the past few decades, attention is switched to the strategy of new land settlements based on the Federal Land Development Authority (FELDA) model. An analysis of this model follows.

LAND DEVELOPMENT AND RURAL SETTLEMENT

Tunku Shamsul Bahrin (1981: 132-3) has classified the objectives[8] of government-directed land-settlement programmes under four broad heads:

1. redistributive, to relieve population pressure in congested areas
2. economic, to raise national or individual incomes or to increase agricultural employment or production

3. social, so that governments can more readily supply services to compactly settled populations or strategically populate frontier zones that are at risk of invasion from external forces
4. political, to avoid the confiscation of established farm land entailed by land reform or to serve some particular segment of the population.

Such programmes therefore have socio-economic as well as geopolitical dimensions. The maximization of marketable output, redistribution of income, and supply of a means of production are examples of the former while the settlement of pioneer zones, occupation of territory, and nurturing of a future political power base are examples of the latter. While large-scale transfers of population require heavy public investment and a highly organized administrative structure (Myrdal 1968: 2140) the Malaysian government has nevertheless embraced land development as an integral tool for economic development. The agency used was FELDA, together with a number of other federal and state bodies.

The land development programmes are administered by the Ministry of Land and Regional Development. In 1971 a Land Development Co-ordination Committee was set up to streamline land development efforts in the country. However, this was unsuccessful because land settlement was then unintegrated and wasteful as there was duplication and competition among agencies for the same limited resources. A Ministry of Land Development was then created in 1973 and charged with overseeing the organization and administration of various resettlement projects. Three years later it was enlarged to incorporate regional development. Thus national land and regional planning machinery was put in place within 15 years to replace an *ad hoc* system with one that was highly structured.

The administrative structure for land development is given in Figure 3.2. The primary division is determined by whether the particular development is with or without a subsidy from the government. The next major branching occurs between federal and state-controlled schemes, which in a majority of cases includes some form of settlement on newly cleared land. The functions of each of the bodies are self-evident from their names. FELDA as an organization has been selected for critical examination not only because it has been instrumental in bringing large areas of virgin jungle under settlement but also because it is by far the most experienced agency in land development in Malaysia. FELDA has also devised technical and policy guidelines for scheme development and in this respect has built up an enviable record. The other federal and state agencies in Malaysia have based their strategies on the FELDA model.

Figure 3.2. **Malaysia: Land development strategies**

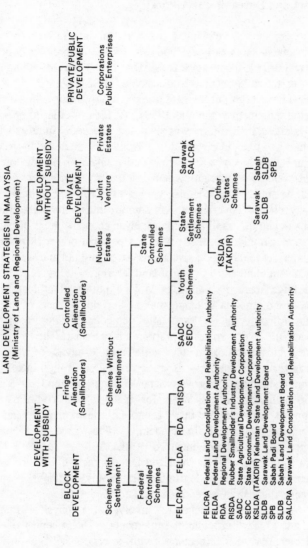

LAND DEVELOPMENT STRATEGIES IN MALAYSIA
(Ministry of Land and Regional Development)

DEVELOPMENT WITH SUBSIDY

BLOCK DEVELOPMENT
- Schemes With Settlement
- Federal Controlled Schemes
  - FELCRA
  - FELDA
  - RDA
  - RISDA

Fringe Alienation (Smallholders)
- Schemes Without Settlement

DEVELOPMENT WITHOUT SUBSIDY

Controlled Alienation (Smallholders)
- State Controlled Schemes
  - SADC SEDC
  - Youth Schemes
  - State Settlement Schemes
    - KSLDA (TAKDIR)
    - Other States' Schemes
      - Sarawak SLDB
      - Sabah SLDB SPB
    - Sarawak SALCRA

PRIVATE DEVELOPMENT
- Nucleus Estates
- Joint Venture
- Private Estates

PRIVATE/PUBLIC DEVELOPMENT
- Corporations Public Enterprises

FELCRA   Federal Land Consolidation and Rehabilitation Authority
FELDA   Federal Land Development Authority
RDA   Regional Development Authority
RISDA   Rubber Smallholder's Industry Development Authority
SADC   State Agricultural Development Corporation
SEDC   State Economic Development Corporation
KSLDA (TAKDIR) Kelantan State Land Development Authority
SLDB   Sarawak Land Development Board
SPB   Sabah Padi Board
SLDB   Sabah Land Development Board
SALCRA   Sarawak Land Consolidation and Rehabilitation Authority

Source: Syed Hussain Wafa (1972: 31).

Federal Land Development Authority

In Malaysia, land development has been an integral part of national development since as early as 1956 (Ho 1965). As previously noted, the agency responsible for this task is FELDA, which aims at settling as many families as possible on new land schemes (FELDA 1963: 42).[9] Many arguments have been put forward to explain government involvement in pioneering settlement in the mid-1950s. At first, in order to provide land for the landless, land reform was proposed, especially in areas where the problem was particularly acute. However, such a proposal was unacceptable as it would have involved a takeover of developed land, much of which was foreign-owned. Moreover, such a step would have violated the spirit of the compact between the British administrators and the newly elected government. A smooth transition in the transfer of government and the stability of the Malayan economy were of paramount importance. In addition, those who had political power themselves had vested interests in the productive assets based on land and were therefore most reluctant to pursue a policy of land reform.

The large tracts of undeveloped land presented at least a partial solution to the problem of landlessness. Second, because of uncertainty over government policies, especially immediately after independence, there was little or no expansion of foreign investment. The absence of the necessary infrastructure in the more remote areas of the country discouraged private enterprise from expanding cultivation there. Finally, the recommendations of a government Working Party on Land Settlement in 1956 indicated a real need for planned and co-ordinated land development to ensure that economic development and social development progressed in tandem. The same Working Party recommended the establishment of FELDA as a statutory authority (Malaya 1956b: para. 91). The Land Development Ordinance no. 20 of 1956 provided the initial legislative framework, although it contained deficiencies that had to be rectified at a later date.

In general FELDA schemes involved the physical transfer of participants to new agricultural settlements. The schemes on average were larger than 1,600 hectares, with a central village providing a relatively high standard of facilities and services (see Figures 3.3 and 3.4). Public investment and subsidies were quite high and these were underwritten by the federal government. There was very close supervision by FELDA at all stages, from land clearance through to the marketing of produce.

Uneconomic sized farms and poorly managed state and federal schemes came within the sphere of the Federal Land Consolidation and

Figure 3.3. Malaysia: Central village layout plan for a FELDA scheme

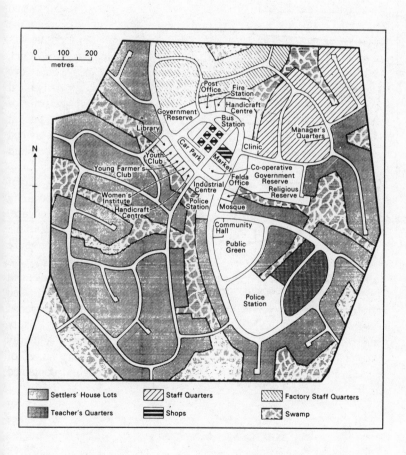

Source: *Tunku* Shamsul Bahrin and Perera (1977: 72).

Figure 3.4. Malaysia: Pattern of development of a FELDA scheme

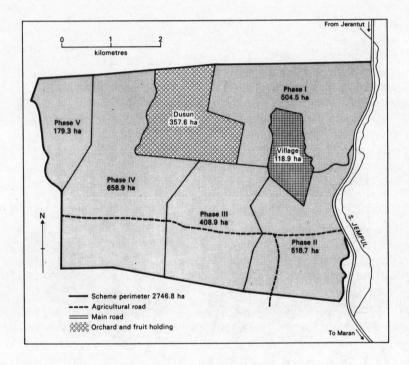

Source: Tunku Shamsul Bahrin and Perera (1977: 33).

Rehabilitation Authority (FELCRA). In contrast to either FELDA or FELCRA schemes, state land or youth schemes received a lower degree of public financing and supervision. The state government provided the funds and some schemes did not involve the settlement of participants. Fringe Alienation Schemes (FAS) involved the opening of land in the vicinity of existing agricultural settlements with the intention of supplementing uneconomic holdings (see Jackson 1963: 261-2). Thus the various models of land development - state land development, fringe alienation, youth, and FELCRA schemes - differ from one another in the scale and degree of financing and investment, facilities provided, scale of operations, role of participants, and the presence or absence of settlements (Hashim 1979: 64).

During its early years, FELDA had to tread very carefully since state governments were particularly sensitive over issues concerning land, which was a state matter. As a result, the legislation setting up FELDA reiterated its role as one of providing financial and technical assistance to state land boards and corporations. This meant that the state government had to undertake the planning and execution of the projects. It was no wonder therefore that progress initially was very slow; by 1960 only about 5,900 hectares had been developed. These were principally based on rubber since it offered higher prospects of settler income (Alias 1975). This unsatisfactory situation was redressed by amendments to the legislation when FELDA's role was redefined and its function as a loans board changed to that of an executing agency.

Under FELDA large tracts of suitable virgin jungle were prepared by private contractors and planted with high-yielding rubber and fruit trees and food crops (*dusun*). Each family received a holding of about 4 hectares in area of which about 3.2 were planted with rubber and 0.8 with a subsidiary crop. FELDA undertook to provide financial assistance to settlers which included an allowance until the rubber trees matured, and all necessary economic and social services on the scheme. Settlers were selected by interview on a point system with priority going to landless young married Malays who had farming experience. When the newly planted rubber matured, settlers were expected to repay their FELDA loans by instalments. FELDA's aim was to establish remunerative and productive land settlements based on rubber smallholdings.

The introduction of FELDA was initially greeted with widespread enthusiasm on the part of farmers and, especially, landless Malays since it offered an opportunity to move into comparatively high income-generating rubber smallholdings. Yet the expected rush did not materialize. Some states, protective of their constitutional jurisdiction over land matters, declined to co-operate with FELDA in favour of persisting with their established padi-orientated programmes. In its early period FELDA had to persuade people to participate in these land settlement projects. 'Apparently to many the known insecurity of their livelihood was preferable to the unknown security that the government projects offered' (Alias 1975: 6). However, in a survey of FELDA schemes between 1957 and 1971, Wikkramatileke (1972: 85) concluded that 'one cannot escape the feeling that this particular facet of land development in West Malaysia had begun to snowball'.

High-yielding rubber remains the basis of many schemes although since the *First Malaysia Plan* similarly remunerative crops such as oil palm, coffee, and cocoa became available to smallholders on FELDA schemes. It is significant that income generation was used as the sole criterion for the development of schemes.

In the early phases of FELDA settlement, participants arrived at virtually ready-made smallholdings, bypassing the truly pioneering stage. This was a radical departure from practices in other parts of South East Asia such as the transmigration programme in Indonesia, where settlers were given only the necessary tools for jungle clearing and a bag of seeds (MacAndrews 1982). Perhaps because the smallholding was more or less a going concern, settlers on FELDA schemes tended to neglect the 0.8 hectare subsidiary crop holding since they treated this in the same way as they had treated their *dusun* (fruit orchards) in their previous *kampungs*. FELDA had intended that these subsidiary plots would provide supplementary income for participants. Variations in standards of main-tenance were partially solved by the *gotong-royong* (co-operative) method in which settlers were not allocated their individual lots until they had worked in conjunction with a group for about four years. During this time training in crop husbandry, maintenance standards, and general agricultural practices were imparted and, more importantly, 'laggards' were pulled into line by peer group pressure.

It is also significant that FELDA very quickly realized the need to switch from merely giving out money as a free government grant or allowance to that of a subsistence credit. These cash loans enabled settlers to purchase basic subsistence requirements until the rubber trees reached maturity and yielded income. The loans were given on the basis of satisfactory performance in maintaining their smallholdings. However, the collection of these debts later became financially burdensome to the FELDA organization. In the early period, for the sake of immediate development, the actual profitability of FELDA schemes was relegated to the future without undue concern for interest or for capital repayment (Rudner 1970: 89). By the 1970s, however, the position had changed. But FELDA still found it extremely difficult to collect loan repayments from the settlers. In order to prevent the surreptitious sale of rubber by settlers so that income would escape the notice of the administration, FELDA adopted a repayment scheme based on the price of rubber with a set minimum payment per month.

With experience gathered over the initial years, the role of FELDA was enhanced by the provisions of the Land (Group Settlement Areas) Act of 1960. This act enabled state governments to appoint FELDA as the development agency for a particular piece of land and vest the rights in the land to FELDA. Participants were regarded as 'occupiers' in anticipation of title. The act also provided for collective ownership through some form of co-operative society. Such a change also came about with a switch in the main crop grown. The introduction of oil palm as a major crop in FELDA schemes, a crop that hitherto was solely an estate crop unsuited to smallholding operations, provided the need for co-operative effort. Collective ownership meant therefore that large areas of oil palm could be planted and cultivated by smallholders working collectively. There also remained the possibility of incorporating crops other than rubber in FELDA schemes. Since 1970, all four hectares of a settler's land have been devoted entirely to the main crop.

By the end of 1985 a total of 360,000 hectares of new land was developed by public sector agencies, of which FELDA was responsible for 161,000 hectares (45 per cent). About 68 per cent of FELDA schemes were planted with oil palm, 23 per cent were in rubber, about 4 per cent in cocoa, with the remaining 5 per cent taken up by village settlement. The choice of the main crop to be grown was guided by prevailing market demand and outlook as well as agronomic suitability in each scheme. Table 3.1 shows a summary of progress in land development for the period 1971-85.

A total of 9,400 families have been resettled, involving nearly half a million people. The average development cost of resettling a family in FELDA schemes increased from $37,500 in 1980 to $53,000 in 1985 as a result of rising costs in material inputs and higher labour costs, compounded by the fact that newer schemes were located in remoter areas. During the period of the *Fourth Malaysia Plan* the average annual income of FELDA settlers ranged from $6,000 in rubber schemes to $14,700 in oil palm schemes (Malaysia 1986: 306).

During the period of the *Fifth Malaysia Plan* new land development will continue to be emphasized, with FELDA scheduled to develop a further 175,500 hectares. The major areas of concentration will be in Pahang (36 per cent), Sabah (33 per cent), Johor (13 per cent), Kelantan (7 per cent), and Perak (5 per cent). In order to equalize incomes between settlers in schemes planted with different crops, a system of share

Table 3.1. Malaysia: Land development, 1971-85

Agency / Programme	Achievement		Fifth Malaysia Plan target
	1971-80	*1981-85*	*1986-90*
Federal programmes	*527,531*	*202,470*	*175,500*
FELDA	365,587	161,600	175,500
FELCRA	60,729*a*	31,100	-
RISDA	101,215*b*	9,770	-
State programmes	*233,724c*	*158,000*	*93,700*
Joint venture / private sector	*134,615*	*57,100d*	*17,500*
Total	*895,870*	*417,570*	*286,700*

Sources: Malaysia (1981: 270; 1986: 306).

Notes: a Excluding rehabilitation schemes and existing *kampung* consolidation schemes.
    b Block new planting schemes only.
    c For programmes of regional development authorities and state schemes.
    d Refers only to land development in areas under Regional Development Authorities.

ownership will be implemented. Under this system, each settler, irrespective of type of scheme, will be given a share equivalent to about 4 hectares. This arrangement differs from the existing system in which settlers are given outright ownership of land once settler debts and development costs have been repaid.

The aim is to plant new FELDA schemes with oil palm (65 per cent), cocoa (16 per cent), and rubber (13 per cent) while the remainder (6 per cent) will be used for village settlement. It is expected that these projects will involve a further 33,800 settlers. State programmes under RDAs, SADCs, and SEDCs will develop a further 84,100 hectares while in Sabah and Sarawak about 9,600 hectares will be developed by state land development boards and the Sabah Rubber Fund Board (Malaysia 1986: 320-1).

Problems and Prospects

Despite the impressive record of FELDA's achievements there have been expressions of concern about the efficacy of the FELDA model. A report by the Food and Agriculture Organization (FAO) and the World Bank (1975) critically questioned past resource allocation decisions between land development and existing agriculture. For example, since the *Second Malaysia Plan* more than 50 per cent of public sector development expenditure on agriculture has been allocated to land development. While this expenditure has had a substantial impact on the economic growth base of Malaysia, it has benefited only a small number of the rural population. This has meant that in order to speed the impact of development expenditures to more people living in rural areas, an acceleration of the development of agriculture on existing traditional smallholder farms of padi, rubber, coconuts, coffee, cocoa, pineapples, and other *dusun*-type enterprises will be required. To this end, the various micro-scale projects incorporated in the IADPs through to large-scale drainage and irrigation schemes and RDAs have been designed to spread the reach of the country's development efforts.

The narrowness of this reach may be illustrated by the following. Since 1956 FELDA has been responsible for resettling 94,000 families, an average of about 3,100 families per year. In 1984 there were about 483,300 households in poverty in Malaysia (Malaysia 1986: 7); thus, given the current record of achievements by FELDA, it would probably take about 150 years to settle the population that are currently living in poverty. Furthermore, if the present allotment of 4 hectares per household is pursued, about 1.9 million hectares of suitable agricultural land will be required. Yet in peninsular Malaysia there is an estimated reserve of undeveloped suitable land of only about 2.6 million hectares (World Bank 1980: 55), leaving little for any other sort of development. Thus land development and settlement *per se* will be unlikely to solve the problem of rural poverty (see also Mehmet 1982a: 357).

It is clear that while FELDA schemes provided a good example of successful land development, the costs of these achievements have been high in terms of financial investment and technology. Other costs have, however, also become apparent. The problem of environmental degradation in its most serious form has been the destruction of tropical rainforest and its replacement with an ecological system of commercial tree crops that are less well adapted to the existing ecological and pedological conditions. The ecosystem of rubber trees and oil palm estates of FELDA are so different from that of natural vegetation that inevitably there will be some imbalance in the physical environment. According to Goh (1982: 4) there are an estimated 7,900 species and 1,500 genera of seed plants in peninsular Malaysia. Of these about 2,500 of the species are trees. Such richness of plant species reflects the complexity and productiveness of the rainforest ecosystem. Rainforest vegetation plays a crucial part in the development of deep soils. It keeps soil porous while allowing deep percolation even on steep slopes, and runoff is minimal. But while the luxuriance of forest may imply great soil fertility, studies have demonstrated this to be a myth (Finck 1973). There are few mineral nutrients because of severe leaching, and organic content is low. Deforestation for agriculture inevitably causes disruption to the natural ecosystem, leading to soil deterioration.

The effects of changing land use and logging activities have diminished the area under primary forest in the country. A 1966 survey of forest resources in the peninsula showed that about 9.1 million hectares of a total land area of 13.2 million hectares were under primary forest cover. By 1978 the area had decreased by about 15 per cent. It was estimated that between 1971 and 1976 the average area of forest logged was about 3 per cent per year. Thus, given the current rate of timber exploitation and land development activities, it would be unlikely that the lowland *dipterocarp* of peninsular Malaysia could last until the end of the century (Goh 1982: 5). The natural environment as a dynamic system is in delicate balance to the extent that any economic activity that is imposed will ultimately result in damage to the total environment. While legislation in Malaysia is in place[10] to avert the dire consequences of economic exploitation, '[l]essons from the past have shown that laws concerning land-use have been honoured more in their breach than in their compliance' (Goh 1982: 14).

Rambo's (1982) examination of the adaptive strategies of the Orang Asli (aboriginal groups) in peninsular Malaysia illustrates the complex and efficient methods of the Orang Asli in dealing with their local environment. These strategies have been ignored by development planners in Malaysia, and as a consequence the primeval environment is being destroyed by the introduction of land schemes. The knowledge of the Orang Asli in adapting to their environment is being lost although they could be of great benefit to planners in Malaysia in designing more effective strategies for use in the future.

From a social point of view Meade (1976) has found that human health problems in land development schemes, such as the incidence of disease, have in many instances been higher than expected. While physiological problems are curable the question to ask is whether there are ready medicines to cure social problems. Robertson (1975: 31) considered that while 'economic and technical interests have been comprehensively represented ... attention to human relations has only recently been given any emphasis'. The emergent social ills include unemployment, inequality, and so-called 'second generation' problems of out-migration,[11] questions of traditional laws of inheritance that threaten to exacerbate the problem of land ownership, tenure, and settler development, and the management of modern agriculture (Ali 1975).

The failure to create new FELDA societies in areas of settlement has been a cause of concern since some settlers were intent on hanging on to old ties that link them to areas or *kampungs* of origin and to particular state and linguistic affiliations. This is manifested in the remittance of money to parents and relatives in their former *kampungs*, annual visits 'home' during *Hari Raya* (Muslim New Year) and the feeling among some settlers that their life in the FELDA scheme was a temporary sojourn with the hope of retiring to their former *kampungs*. A major problem among the children of settlers is their disinclination to pursue farm work (Hashim 1981). This has partly been explained by Massard (1984) who believes that it reflects the stringent work rules imposed by FELDA to the extent that the settlers were in fact collectivized labour units. Whether the view expressed is accurate or not, it is believed that whatever the strategies adopted, they should make settlers neither too dependent nor too antagonistic to change (MacAndrews 1982: 23).

FELDA settlement schemes have been conceived within a free market framework on the assumption that the settlers themselves, as entrepreneurs, will pursue goals to their own economic advantage. De Koninck and McTaggart (1987: 353) believe that the premise is entirely unrealistic since the lack of market information precludes settlers from participating as informed actors. Moreover, poor linkages such as the lack of infrastructural facilities or being tied to particular crops has made the production unit unresponsive to market fluctuations, especially during periods of depressed conditions. A more accurate description of the FELDA settlement scheme was that it brought about a uniformity of product and probably a uniformity of producer to the extent that the scheme as a whole lacked social and biotic diversity. Settlement projects in Malaysia have been described as centrally directed work-camps (de Koninck and McTaggart 1987: 354). This critical view is, however, seemingly directed to the more fundamental question of whether the agricultural settlement schemes served the interests of the settler, the state, or the international consumer of the scheme's product (Sutton 1977: 80). A model of ecological imperialism has been proposed by Palmer (1974). Where production was geared to the international economy, then national development was secondary to all else and the interests of the individual farmer received scant attention. These policy questions require resolution at a macro-level in which the primacy of either the settler, the commodity, or the state will have to be resolved. Such fundamental issues have yet to be addressed.

That the various land schemes have involved a relatively high proportion of public development expenditure is undeniable. More importantly, they have yielded little or no benefit for the most impoverished groups and have also tended to intensify inequalities amongst the rural population (Tan 1981: 221). FELDA settlers may be considered the *nouveau riche* of the rural populace in Malaysia. Yet analysis has shown that states with the highest incidence of poverty have not been given an equitable share of settlement opportunities. The pace of development and the amount of land currently allotted to settlers militate against the settlement of a greater number of poor families (Tan 1981). While the results of cost-benefit analyses have been variable, there is doubt as to whether the returns have really justified the outlay (de Koninck and McTaggart 1987: 343).

In terms of income, however, the question has been asked as to whether FELDA schemes have been instrumental in raising settlers' incomes and whether the income levels of people living in neighbouring areas have similarly been increased. On FELDA schemes, land holding has little or no effect on income disparities among households because settlers were allotted similar sized holdings. Variability in production and therefore income may have come about either through poor management and/or poor soils on which to grow crops. Field surveys of FELDA schemes in Johor Tenggara and West Johor provide affirmative answers to both questions (Iwasaki *et al.* 1979: 19). No discernible differences are found in income levels between areas inside development schemes and those outside. As well, land development schemes have created employment opportunities in areas adjacent to them (see also Cheong *et al.* 1979: 204ff). Similar findings have also been reported elsewhere (Blair and Noor 1983: 43). FELDA settlers have been reported to have received incomes which were about '143 per cent of the national Malay average for both rural and urban areas combined' (Blair and Noor 1980: 19). Unfortunately, there are no data for other rural areas that are not part of or adjacent to FELDA schemes so that comparisons of the type conducted here may be made.

For the immediate future, it appears that the FELDA model of land development will be pursued with some modification. The idea of a share-ownership system rather than title to land promises an equitable solution to a related problem of land inheritance, especially among the Muslims. The Muslim law of inheritance specifies the exact division of property between heirs so that with the passing of generations, land parcels progressively become smaller (Ibrahim 1965; Ali 1975).

Under the share ownership system each settler is given a share equivalent to four hectares of land and in this it differs radically from the previous method in which settlers were given outright ownership of land. This is very similar to the FELCRA 'share system' in which settlers hold equal shares in the whole and are jointly responsible for the development and operation of the scheme with profits distributed among settlers. However, on the basis of cost-benefit analysis Mehmet (1982a) has found that the costs of resettlement on FELCRA schemes were much higher as compared with FELDA schemes ($40,000 compared to $27,000 in 1980 respectively) and that the benefit-cost ratios were above unity for FELDA schemes. Moreover, income levels of FELCRA settlers were generally lower than those of FELDA settlers. Clearly the results are inconclusive and much more needs to be done in this area before one or the other method is adopted as the standard model.

The switch from rubber to oil palm as the main crop has paid dividends, as have ventures using cocoa as a crop. More significantly, FELDA's direct marketing of primary commodities like palm oil and rubber either in its raw or semi-processed form produced from FELDA's own mills and factories appears to provide the much-needed outlet for production as well as a control over marketing mechanisms. During the *Fourth Malaysia Plan*, for instance, FELDA sold about 3.5 million tonnes of palm oil and about 367,800 tonnes of rubber, representing about 18.6 per cent and 4.9 per cent of total Malaysian output respectively. The FELDA crop earned a total of about $3.5 billion and $854 million from crude palm and kernel oil, and rubber respectively (Malaysia 1986: 313). Moreover, the possibility of FELDA becoming an integral link in the marketing chain for non-FELDA and unorganized rubber and oil palm smallholders would radically alter traditional methods of disposal of primary farm products. These marketing activities would not only stabilize farm incomes of FELDA settlers, but could also bring about a reduction in poverty in rural areas through the competition and presence of FELDA *vis-à-vis* customary marketing channels for primary produce.

However, while there are improvements in income and expanded opportunities in employment two problems persist: the high cost of settling a family (estimated at $53,000 in 1985) and the small number of settler families that have participated in FELDA schemes. One facet of this problem is the recovery of some development costs from settlers. These costs are amortized over 15 years when the crops mature (that is, after about 4-5 years from initial settlement) at an interest rate of 6.25 per cent at 1977 value. The repayment includes the costs of development of the agricultural holdings, house, and the settler's subsistence allowance. The typical monthly settler obligation for a 2.8 hectare rubber holding was about $80 and for a 4 hectare oil palm holding it was $260 in 1977 (Bahrin and Perera 1977: 83). The differences stem from higher costs of development of the latter, larger parcels of land, and in the case of rubber, repayments were linked to the prevailing price of rubber. Moreover, settlers on oil palm schemes were better able to afford larger repayments because of good prices for palm oil and higher outputs from their holdings. Yet it is estimated that such repayments make up only about 60 per cent of government investments (Alias 1975: 20). Whether these high costs will finally lead the government to abandon this form of land settlement in favour of lower cost programmes involving more people is a moot point. The alternative of full cost recovery, however, cannot be seen as a politically viable solution, although in the long run the shortage of available land might force the decision in that direction.

Of course, there are other problems which FELDA has to solve, such as the management of these schemes once title to land has been passed over to the settlers, and social issues such as attitudes, political awareness, and work skills. Larger questions include the loss of political patronage. Successive previous governments have adopted land development as a necessary step towards economic and social growth. The question is whether support for it will be forthcoming once the country has been developed. Another issue concerns the lack of suitable land to be developed by FELDA. All these questions will force FELDA to assume new roles and to design strategies that are as yet untried to meet future needs of resettlement and redevelopment of land in Malaysia. Land development *per se* may not have provided the much-needed solution to rural poverty, as the following section will show.

RURAL POVERTY AND UNEVEN DEVELOPMENT

In discussing poverty and uneven development there appear to be two sources of contradiction. First, there is the apparent conflict between distribution and growth. Second, there are incompatibilities between traditional and modern values in so far as the adoption of economic policies is concerned. Taking the first issue, there is a continuing debate over the role of regional development in relation to the objective of income distribution on the one hand and economic growth on the other. At a theoretical level, the neoclassical theory of growth assumes that there is no incompatibility between growth and distribution and that the price mechanism will take care of the distribution among regions (Hirschman 1958).

'Trickling down' effects such as the movement of capital and the migration of labour from depressed regions will ultimately dominate so that in the long run income differentials will be eliminated. This is sometimes known as the Kuznets hypothesis (1955), which postulates that income distribution tends to become more equal once a certain threshold of per capita income is passed. Against this background are the negative or polarization effects such as the migration of labour out of depressed regions and the outflow of capital.

On the other hand, those subscribing to the theory of cumulative causation believe that, as growth occurs, disparities in income will increase progressively (Myrdal 1957). The concentration of economic activities in certain areas will cumulatively give rise to economies of scale or agglomeration (both internal and external) and encourage further innovation and development in these centres. In this way income differentials between rich and poor regions will tend to widen.

A variant of this is the Williamson hypothesis (1965) which states that regional income differences tend to grow larger during the early stages of economic development, then level off, only to decline again with the growing maturity and spatial integration of the economy.[12] This hypothesis is usually cited in support of inherently inegalitarian spatial policies. In the Malaysian context, the question of trickling down of wealth and evening out of income levels and cumulative causation has been approached obliquely. For example, after examining empirical evidence Cheong et al. (1979: 249) conclude that both opposing theories have some applicability but at different levels of income. Thus, income inequality initially rises with income growth, reaches a peak, and then declines with further growth of per capita income. The critical question in this relationship between distribution and growth is at what level of income this turning point will occur.

The second issue concerns the conflict between traditional and modern values in the process of development and the improvement of the economic well-being of poor farmers within the traditional structure of Malay rural society. On the one hand, to retain Malay culture (with its roots in rural life), to maintain the strengths of Islam, and to preserve the generally conservative voting habits of politically significant constituencies entails that the broad structure of Malay society will have to remain unchanged. On the other hand, the desire for economic development and income growth through the introduction of technological and economic policies in the capitalist mould, shaped by European colonization and post-independence external relations, is incompatible with the objective of preserving the *status quo*.

For example, in the padi sector Malaysia's policy was to achieve both self-sufficiency in rice production and the reduction of absolute and relative poverty among padi-growing households. One mechanism was the maximization of output in conjunction with certain controls over pricing, for example, the government's attempts at a guaranteed minimum price. But evidence suggests that the mechanism has been less successful in reducing poverty (Courtenay 1983: 27). Technological advances that have made possible considerable increases in productivity have themselves contributed to growing inequality. By their nature, such advances as required labour shedding, land aggregation, and higher cost structures, all part of the logic of capitalist agriculture, have contributed to the apparent paradox. Indeed, survey data from Kemubu RDA show that many householders must seek off-farm employment to supplement household income in order to cross the poverty income threshold (Chew and Shand 1984: 11).

These dilemmas highlight the need for flexible policies to accommodate new situations. For example, in the case of land development in general and FELDA in particular, the provision of infrastructural and social amenities has contributed to the well-being of the settlers and their families. However, the provision of these benefits is highly selective and this has produced a new gap in that those who are not part of the settlement scheme remain poor, further exacerbating the differences among individuals and ethnic groups. It is apparent that the concentration of benefits has produced two distributional effects: first, an increase in relative inequality, and second, an increase in absolute poverty. The latter is seemingly an almost universal feature of the capitalist mode of production. With public investment directed towards the pioneer fringe, the much-needed funds to uplift the more depressed peasant economy will either be unavailable or, where available, only in diminished quantities. Public investment is thus crucial to initiate development impulses in the peasant economy. Moreover, a high concentration of investment may also mean that benefits tend to be localized.

The suggestion here is that the nature of the interaction between the evolving economic system and the Malaysian socio-political institutional setting in the development process may have produced very uneven growth and has helped to increase spatial imbalance. In the early years of post-colonial government, planned development followed closely the growth-oriented paradigm. While impressive growth rates were achieved, rural-urban imbalances as well as class and ethnic ones began to increase. It took a catastrophic event such as the May 13 incident for economic planners to realize that growth alone was insufficient to ensure harmony and economic development. Thus the NEP was premissed on growth with redistribution, that is, a restructuring of employment and redistribution of ownership among ethnic groups in the various sectors and locations within the context of a growing national economy. In order that such a strategy be implemented, growth in the economy has to be assured. But there is the ever-present danger that there could be no growth in the economy. In that eventuality, it is doubtful if restructuring and redistribution would go ahead nevertheless.

In this study the major concern is with the spatial impact of uneven development of the economy, which may cause further imbalances in the growth of areas and regions. A poor region will suffer out-migration, leading to labour shortages and consequently a negative image in attracting foreign investment. It seems that once a downward spiral is in motion there can be no growth in this particular region in the short term until rectified by purposeful direct action by some government planning agency.

Regional imbalance in Malaysia has long been recognized (Ward 1968) and can be a problem to regional planning either by way of per capita development funding or of overall strategies. The record so far suggests that there has been limited success in stemming the growing concentration of economic activities in some states of peninsular Malaysia to the extent that this over-concentration threatens to leave behind states such as Kelantan, Sabah, and Sarawak in the quest for economic development. As spatial imbalances may have produced extreme economic polarities, they are being offset by the creation of new investment opportunities in the less developed states.

Yet, however effective the rural development programmes have been, it appears that uneven development and consequently poverty will persist in the urban-rural context. The explanation given by Salih (1981: 110) is that the underdevelopment of backward areas was due not so much to neglect, as claimed by many, as to their 'peripheralization'. As capital investment expanded and was fostered by the colonial state, the linkage of peripheral areas to the centre similarly became stronger but did little to increase local productivity and total production. The transitional processes to peripheral capitalism and its social formations are 'all germane to the problem of poverty and inequality at the local level in Malaysia' (Salih 1981: 128).

In the context of a Third World country there can be no single concept of income since there may be sources which are difficult to quantify in monetary terms, for example, personal services and payments in kind. In the *Third Malaysia Plan* a poverty-line income concept was used. It defined poor households as those whose total income was below the minimum necessary to sustain the household's basic level of living, taking into account nutritional and other non-food requirements (Malaysia 1976: 160). While the actual poverty-line income remains unspecified in official government publications, it is generally taken to be between \$150 to \$200 per month for each household.

The degree of income inequality in Malaysia was quite high by international standards and intra-group and intra-regional disparities accounted for much of this inequality (Anand 1983). To tackle these problems, specific target groups within regions or within ethnic groups need to be identified. An indiscriminate approach to regional development may increase overall inequality since the incidence of inequality appears to vary directly with levels of income and the degree of urbanization (Cheong *et al.* 1979: 248). There is a further development dilemma (Chan and Richter 1982: 77) in deciding whether to attempt to provide better income-earning opportunities in poor regions or to provide such opportunities in regions that are endowed with a comparative advantage. This problem arises from the observation that poor regions are poor because they are disadvantaged and suffer some form of economic constraint. The more successful regions can expect to develop faster and hence become the target area for in-migrants. The question is whether this pattern sets the scenario for future strategies aimed at a restructuring of society and redistribution of wealth.

RURAL REGIONAL DEVELOPMENT PROJECTS

Public sector response to the problems of growth, redistribution, and poverty has been both systematic and purposeful. Poverty groups and poor regions are given favourable weightings when resources are allocated. Furthermore, the emphasis has been shifted in favour of the restructuring of society rather than the purely growth-oriented approaches adopted previously. Since the *Third Malaysia Plan*, efforts to modernize and improve the productivity of all sectors of the economy have intensified. One major thrust is through rural regional development on a massive scale, including the setting up of new growth centres in rural areas to modernize the economy of the region in order to bridge rural-urban socio-economic imbalances (Ghani 1981). In addition, to manage these giant development schemes Malaysia has set up commercial corporation-type RDAs to implement resettlement schemes and to achieve swiftly the national objective of reducing regional disparities.

Project Bias

An analysis of the data presented in Table 3.2 shows that between 1965 and 1975 there was a spate of urban and regional studies. Apart from the Muda Irrigation Scheme, which was begun in 1961, regional studies have been conducted either to examine the potential for resource frontier development of land or as a solution to the socio-economic problems of the regions. Feasibility studies for drainage and irrigation projects, agricultural, and land development projects predominated whilst those directed towards urban and industrial development were more limited. Apart from the massive size of each of these study areas, it is to be noted that all studies were state- or district-based (see Figure 3.5). None of the studies appears to traverse state boundaries, and because they have been prepared in isolation, problems of double-counting of potential sources of settlers, labour, and resources have arisen, particularly when attempts at integration were made. The setting up of the Ministry of Land and Regional Development was intended to solve the lack of co-ordination between those agencies entrusted with the task of implementing regional master plans.

The large number of regions suggests that to a certain degree *ad hoc* decisions have been made in the course of these studies. Apparently caught up in the zeal to develop regions, each state commissioned particular studies to help solve 'special' problems within its own boundaries. It is no wonder that it was virtually impossible to integrate these regional plans into a total national scheme. Such piecemeal approaches inevitably resulted in competition for scarce resources such as skilled workers, settlers, and administrators. Moreover, rapid development in the surrounding region, or within the region itself, and

Table 3.2. Malaysia: Urban and regional programmes, projects, and studies

Region	Area ('000 ha)	Year of study	Type of development	Name of regional development authority
Muda	105	1961-63	Irrigation	MADA
Jengka Triangle	121	1965-66	Land	JENGKA
Terengganu	1295	1967	Land	-
Johor Tenggara	304	1969-71	Land	KEJORA
Pulau Pinang	103	1969-70	Urban	PERDA
Melaka	166	1970	Urban-industrial	-
Pahang Tenggara	1006	1971-72	Land	DARA
Kemubu	19	1972	Irrigation	KADA
Klang Valley	316	1972-73	Urban	-
Kelantan	1505	1973	Agricultural	KESEDAR
West Johor	148	1973	Agricultural	-
South Johor	300	1973-74	Urban	-
Negri Sembilan Timur	102	1974	Land, urban	-
Kuantan	63	1974	Urban	-
Terengganu Tengah	445	1974	Land	KETENGAH
North Perak	1263	1974-75	Land	-
Outer Klang Valley	505	1974-75	Agricultural	-
Trans-Perak	478	1975-76	Land, irrigation	TRANS PERAK
Bintulu, Sarawak	-	1979	Land	-
North Malaya	-	1981	Land, agricultural	KEDA

Sources: Abdullah and Mohamad (1982: 4); Higgins (1982: 162-3).

Figure 3.5. Peninsular Malaysia: Location of regional development
authorities and areas covered by various master plan studies,
1985

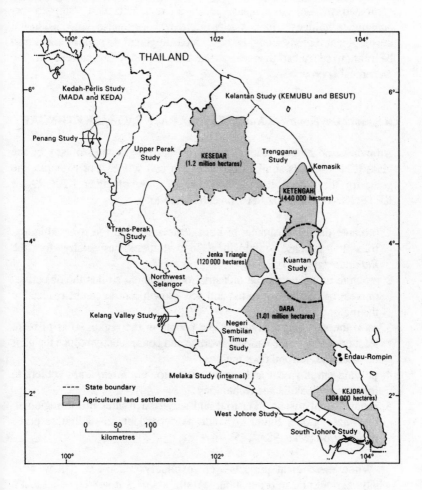

changes in national government policy have been left out at the implementation stage because of the inherent rigidity of the master plan itself. Abdullah and Mohamad (1982: 9) have suggested the abandonment of state-based regions for a system in which the regions are computed by objective means, such as regionalization using factor-analytic techniques. In this way, areas which hitherto fell outside the development regions would be developed. Regional disparities could also be minimized rather than exacerbated as they are by current *ad hoc* piecemeal approaches.

Regional Development Authorities: DARA, KEJORA, KETENGAH

An evaluation of the various objectives and programmes of any of the giant RDAs reveals similarities in content and scope. For example, the goals for the DARA RDA are similar to those of either KEJORA or KETENGAH RDA. DARA's objectives are to:

1. promote the establishment of large-scale agro- and forest-based industries to increase employment opportunities, especially for the *Bumiputeras*
2. promote urbanization and industrial development so that the objectives of creating rural urbanization and new growth centres can be realized in the region
3. raise the standard of living of the people in the region so as to be at least on par with the national average and consequently reduce the gaps between the rich and poor regions
4. provide employment and opportunities for the *Bumiputera* settlers to improve their skills and technology
5. promote and sustain industrial and service activities in the region so that the region's future will not be dependent on natural resource exploitation (Mat 1983: 135).

While these giant projects were explicitly ethnic-based, they were wholly agricultural in orientation. From Table 3.3 it will be noted that a large proportion of the land area is devoted to agriculture. Much of this area was planted with oil palm, with rubber having a secondary role. Apart from differences in geographical area, the heavy concentration on primary commodities suggests that these RDAs were no different from FELDA schemes in terms of their economic base. It also suggests that these RDAs were exposed to the vicissitudes of the international market

Table 3.3. Peninsular Malaysia: Selected regional development
authorities, area, and emphasis

Regional development authority	Area (000 ha)	Phasing to completion	Popn. at compl. (000s)	New towns (no.)	Major township	Scheme emphasis
Jengka Triangle JENGKA	121	1970-78	85	23	Jengka	Oil palm (85%) rubber (13%) village (2%)
Johor Tenggara KEJORA	304	1971-90	300	28	Bandar Tenggara Penawar	Oil palm (58%) rubber (23%) and livestock (19%) tourism
Pahang Tenggara DARA	1,006	1972-90	500	36	Bandar Muadzam and *Tun* Abdul Razak	Oil palm (82%) rubber (11%) livestock (7%) tourism and mining
Terengganu Tengah KETENGAH	261	1974-95	?	6	Durian Mas	Oil palm (90%) rubber (7%) and fruits (3%) and mining

Source: Various master plan studies.

for the sale of these crops, thereby introducing an element of instability into the system.

Medium- and small-scale industries to be established in these RDAs included those that were resource-based, such as timber mills, sago, tapioca, and fruit processing, as well as those industries serving local consumption needs such as beverages, furniture, footwear, and transport. However, as noted by the *Fifth Malaysia Plan*, the creation of non-agricultural employment opportunities was slow and inadequate in these RDAs. Within DARA and KETENGAH more than 80 per cent of the working population was involved in agriculture in 1984 (Malaysia, 1986: 183).

The pattern of settlement recommended for DARA was unique in that its aim was to establish population concentrations in a few intermediate-sized towns rather than in many small villages. This, it was hoped, would assist in building an urban structure within the region that would fill a niche between the primary growth centres at one end of the scale and the small villages at the other. Moreover, the government's strategy of rural urbanization was designed to regroup existing villages to form urban nuclei. Such villages would have populations of about 2,500 people and would benefit from the provision of co-operative farming, basic infra-structure, and social services at reduced public cost. However, to date in JENGKA, KEJORA, DARA, and KETENGAH, less than one-third of the population resides in towns. The new townships had only a marginal impact in upgrading the quality of life and generating employment for the hinterland population (Malaysia 1986: 183).

Weak linkages between identified development poles and the regional development areas meant that the 'spread effects', which appeared so enticing in theory, did not take place. For instance, Kuantan, the designated pole for DARA, failed to generate the expected growth for the region. Instead, DARA's orientation shifted towards developing strong links with the richer western and southern parts of the peninsula. Nor did Kuantan help alleviate poverty and unemployment in Kelantan and Terengganu, the economically lagging northeast region (Wong 1987a: 16). In sum, the lack of sufficient co-ordination between macro-, regional, and sectoral planning as a whole is responsible for the non-attainment of goals.

The agricultural schemes in the KEJORA RDA are managed different-ly from those in the FELDA model. KEJORA schemes are run on an 'estate' basis by which settlers are employed on a wage contract. Field surveys indicated that settlers in the KEJORA area had lower incomes than those in FELDA schemes. However, settlers on public estates tended to have higher household income than workers on private estates. This suggests that public land development schemes on the KEJORA model may contribute to the amelioration of income distribution among poor households so long as the management of the estates is efficient (Iwasaki *et al*. 1979: 23).

KESEDAR and KEDA

KESEDAR, the development authority for South Kelantan (1978), and KEDA, the development authority for Kedah (1981), are two very different RDAs in that they were set up to redevelop and to increase the productivity of undeveloped land within their jurisdiction (*Haji* Husin 1981). In these two regions there was a paucity of large areas of potential agricultural land, particularly in the more densely settled Kedah Plains. The problem of unemployment and underemployment, brought about by efficiency in production methods and indirectly through the Muda irrigation project, had made the situation more acute.[13] Unlike other RDAs discussed above, KESEDAR has no master plan but instead has a broad development brief. KEDA's task was to work within an amalgam of recommendations, policy guidelines, and strategies derived from various socio-economic surveys and studies of the area.

The KESEDAR model is radically different in other ways. KESEDAR operated within the constraints of small, potentially agricultural land for development and limited financial resources. Another major difference was that while scheme participants were given land, agricultural implements, and seed, the land that they were allotted had neither been previously prepared nor in any way developed - a policy diametrically opposed to the FELDA model. But in the final analysis, the idealism of self-reliance has had to give way to practicalities because land settlement was unsuccessful. In the event private contractors were engaged to clear the jungle and prepare the land, using settlers as a paid workforce. But as costs rose because of inaccessibility and poor management of contract work, the RDA has taken over the task of subcontracting the phased development of land in 40 hectare blocks. As the areas being developed were on the borders of existing villages and settlements, the RDA also undertook the rehabilitation and resettlement of villages in an effort to provide basic infrastructural facilities and amenities as well as the improvement of the economic base.

KEDA RDA encompasses nearly three-quarters of the state of Kedah. Known as the 'rice bowl' of the country, padi growing provides the main source of income. MADA was responsible for raising the levels of income of a majority of farmers with access to irrigation water. This may have inadvertently caused large differentials in income between MADA farmers and non-MADA farmers. In an attempt to remove regional disparities KEDA was set up to oversee the development of projects throughout the state, which included MADA. This unprecedented overlapping of two RDAs has meant the running-down of the role of MADA. Moreover, as a statutory body MADA's legislative brief ran only for 20 years with the option of renewal. Two implications can be derived. First, subsuming MADA under the KEDA RDA meant the possibility of bringing about a truly regional area-wide development. This would rebut criticisms of the *ad hoc* and piecemeal approaches discussed previously. Second, the relatively short life span will not allow the development of long-term programmes so that the present project-oriented strategies will continue to be prevalent.

KEDA's major projects included village rehabilitation and redevelopment which involved the entire population of the state. Rural growth centres were identified on the basis of small-scale agro-resource based cottage industries. Once developed, other socio-economic projects were undertaken with the twin objectives of income growth and an increase in living standards.

It is perhaps in recognition of political realities that two very different strategies have been pursued. On the one hand, the Kelantan state government was until 1974 ruled by a party different from the one in power at the federal level. On the other hand, because Kedah's development was virtually serviced by two statutory authorities, the state government has insisted that the executive head also assume the role of chairman of KEDA's board of directors. A more likely explanation is the fact that particular methods have been adopted in recognition of geographical realities. In these two examples the realities of a small, densely settled state (Kedah), and of two very poor regions whose economic base has been founded on a subsistence crop (padi), have moulded the methods used.

Evaluation of Selected RDA Projects

Commercial corporation-type RDAs have been set up to organize development and the management of agricultural estates as business concerns. While this form of business organization is not new to the private sector, similar forms in the public sector are of recent origin. Under this method RDAs were established as public corporations and had the capacity to form subsidiary companies under the Malaysian Companies Act (1965) either as wholly owned or as joint enterprises with private bodies. This form of organization offered several advantages since government equity participation could be flexible depending on circumstances. The enterprise could develop its own management policies based on commercial principles and not be unduly influenced by political interference, and the enterprise could obtain investment funds from private as well as government sources. In the light of such developments some RDAs have entered into joint ventures to establish and manage commercial agricultural projects.

The following discussion is based on Puthucheary and Milne's (1984) assessment of joint enterprises in the agricultural sector in Malaysia. Our reliance on this source is due to a dearth of published information. Moreover, the growing importance of RDAs has made it imperative to make some assessment so as to gauge the efficacy of this form of rural regional development in Malaysia.

Joint enterprises include the participation of government and the private sector. Both partners contribute more or less equally to capital assets, share in management, and participate jointly in the full risks of the enterprise. The FELDA model has demonstrated the advantages of large-scale centralized management of plantations when compared with smallholding agriculture. But when these plantations are subdivided and apportioned to individual smallholders on repayment of their loans for development costs, problems may be created in the future management of the estates. In the newer, commercially run agricultural projects, especially those in RDAs, no transfer of ownership of individual plots of land was envisaged. Instead, profit sharing, better housing, and near semi-urban living have been introduced. The workers in such schemes eventually come to own shares in the agricultural company. The design of such projects also ensures that no income differences from FELDA schemes would result.

In theory modernization of the agricultural sector through the plantation system and through the concept of owning shares would take place. Both developments accorded with the NEP goals of restructuring society and the redistribution of wealth. Joint enterprises were expected to accumulate profits for reinvestment and for payment of bonuses to the workers. In time the companies were to be turned over to Malay individuals and firms, thereby creating a Malay commercial entrepreneurial class.

The data for the following analysis was obtained from a survey of 26 enterprises of which six were wholly owned government companies. Ten of the joint enterprises were owned by RDAs (KEJORA five, DARA five, KETENGAH three) and another ten by state economic development corporations (SEDCs) and Food Industries of Malaysia (FIMA). The main activities of these enterprises were in industrial crops. Of a total area of 99,415 hectares owned by the 26 enterprises, 60 per cent were in rubber and oil palm cultivation, 30 per cent in sugar, fruit, and other plantation crops, while 9 per cent were for poultry and cattle farming. In terms of paid-up capital, of $206 million, the government's share was about 56 per cent (see Table 3.4).

In using the reported financial performance of these joint enterprises, Puthucheary and Milne (1984: 9-10) give a word of warning. The data may not provide a complete picture of the financial performance of these enterprises. Second, the balance sheet may not reflect the true financial situation of the enterprises because of under-reporting either in order to conceal profits or to avoid paying taxes or dividends. Finally, production and sales data may be smaller than actual performance as a result of leakages from the system arising from unrecorded sales by corrupt personnel within the organization. The performance of the joint enterprises noted therefore gives an 'order of magnitude' and establishes some baseline data for future comparisons.

Only two out of 26 enterprises earned income before tax and interest payments and only one was clearly making profits after deducting all expenses. The only financially successful enterprise was poultry farming, with a paid-up capital of $2.5 million. The net losses for all 26 enterprises in 1980 amounted to $40.4 million, with a cumulative loss of $123 million - an amount almost equal to the government's total contribution in equity capital. Losses have been sustained mostly on the sugar cane projects although rubber and oil palm shared a similar fate. However, the performance of the latter two crops was to be expected as the projects had yet to reach maturity. Thus if profit maximization was the sole objective of the investment, it appears to have failed.

The causes of these enterprises' poor financial performance have been categorized under the broad headings of high development and operating costs, poor management, high financial expenses, labour problems, and external factors. These are discussed next.

HIGH DEVELOPMENT AND OPERATING COSTS

Development costs in joint enterprise estates were about $3,750 per hectare as compared with $3,500 for FELDA and $3,410 for private sector estates. The longer distances from towns, relatively small size of estates, and nature of the activities carried out resulted in higher costs. Moreover, these public enterprises seemed not to be cost-conscious. For example, managers were unaware of comparative costs for goods and services or used high-cost couriers for communication in areas where

Table 3.4. Peninsular Malaysia: Financial performance of selected joint enterprises by activity, 1980 ($000s)

Activity	Paid-up capital	Total net income before tax and expenses	Total net income after tax and expenses	Cumulative income
Rubber and oil palm				
KEJORA (2)	12,017	-1,503	-2,955	-5,893
DARA (3)	18,000	-2,134	-2,820	-6,432
KETENGAH (3)	29,600	-1,428	-1,548	-2,105
SEDC (3)	6,782	-2,323	-2,351	-4,730
Sugar-cane				
SEDC (3)	93,500	-20,278	-29,385	-91,262
Other crops				
SEDC (7)	27,786	-1,055	-1,272	-3,943
Cattle farming (3)	14,489	-1,008	-1,121	-8,223
Poultry farming (2)	4,225	+1,128	+1,035	-548
All enterprises (26)	206,399	-28,601	-40,417	-123,136

Source: Puthucheary and Milne (1984: 12).

Note: - Denotes a loss.

telephones were unavailable. It also seems that private enterprises were willing to participate by buying and selling goods and services either to or from the enterprise but were reluctant to participate on a profit-sharing basis. Their reluctance to do so stemmed from a fear of political interference in the maximization of (private) profits.

POOR MANAGEMENT

A lack of adequately trained managerial and technical staff constrained the performance of joint enterprises. Some projects were undertaken without adequate feasibility preparation or assessed without adequate information, with the result that alternative informed decisions could not be made. For instance, after several years of losses, independent assessors concluded that some of the projects were not financially viable and should never have been started in the first place.

HIGH BORROWING COSTS

Insufficient equity necessarily resulted in operations being financed from loan capital. Most RDAs and SEDCs obtained development loans from the federal government to finance a large part of their investments. These loans could be described as 'soft loans' granted with a 15-year grace period before interest accrued and at a generally low interest rate. Paradoxically, this has led to problems of over-borrowing, resulting in a high gearing ratio (debt to capital ratio). Naturally, there were severe cash-flow problems and unsound financial structures. Only five of the 26 enterprises appeared to be in a financially strong position to meet their loan liabilities.[14] The rest had to depend on financial assistance from the government.

LABOUR PROBLEMS

Joint enterprises were at a disadvantage against FELDA schemes when competing for labour since potential workers preferred to become FELDA settlers rather than work in the plantations. Joint enterprises were also in a poorer position to provide social amenities and other benefits when compared with private estates. Labour problems in joint enterprises were further compounded by poor attitudes to work, lack of discipline, and unwillingness to be trained, which together affected overall productivity. From a management viewpoint there was little or no control over the workers since many lived outside the plantations. Apart from security for the plantations, workers also insisted on regular hours of work as they were experiencing transport difficulties getting to and from work. Ironically, this may be a problem of modernization and the first signs of a social transformation taking place as evidenced by job security and regulated hours of work. But the reality is that the ideal time for tapping rubber trees is before dawn and poultry and cattle require feeding early in the morning. These activities cannot wait for the arrival of workers at 8.00 a.m., neither do agricultural activities cease with the siren at 4.30 p.m. Cattle still need to be herded at dusk.

EXTERNAL FACTORS

There is no doubt that some blame can be laid on the price of commodities in the international market for the poor financial performance of joint enterprises. Public policy goals of self- sufficiency, for example, in beef production and the policy of spreading development may have unduly influenced joint enterprises in making decisions concerning what and where to plant. Frequently these industries were located in remote areas lacking basic infrastructure and supporting services.

SOCIO-ECONOMIC OBJECTIVES

Schemes in regional development areas do not seem to have had much success in attracting people. In the DARA area the master plan provided for an estimated population of 380,000 by 1980 and 500,000 by 1990. At the end of 1980 the settler population was less than 44,000. On the whole Malays have not been attracted to work in commercial plantations; their preferences lie either in owning land or in FELDA-type schemes. Studies of KEJORA and DARA have revealed discontent among workers because of remoteness, inadequate facilities, and poor conditions generally. According to Chan and Lim (1981: 440),

[i]n the KEJORA context, even the first generation appears dissatisfied with conditions in the scheme, particularly with the lack of land ownership. Even the first generation have expressed some desire to leave, if possible, for FELDA schemes.

In addition, in the context of KETENGAH,

[u]nless incentives are attractive and compelling enough in comparison with incentives and pull factors of other areas, it is unlikely that Terengganu Tengah can attract any hold on to the

workers and settlers. This is especially pertinent and serious in the private sector agricultural projects and estates where the workers have no land ownership rights

(Ling 1977: 18)

The lessons drawn from the above discussion are that the opportunity cost of the use of land seldom enters into the appraisal of public enterprise investment projects. There should be more effective controls to ensure proper investigation and feasibility studies before the final decision is taken to set up new enterprises. Proper investment criteria are also required in the light of commercial realities and market conditions. In that event, there would then be little need to impose bureaucratic controls because in an avowedly capitalist system, the price mechanism of the market place would guide decisions and shareholders in the enterprise would demand accountability.

RURAL DEVELOPMENT IN SABAH AND SARAWAK

The problems and resources of Sabah and Sarawak are very different from those of peninsular Malaysia and thus require separate treatment in this chapter. The themes of rural regional development, its objectives, and the organization of land and other development will be given special attention. Before this examination, however, the objectives of rural development and settlement in these states will be stated to highlight the major thrusts of the respective state governments.

In Sarawak the first objective of development was to increase employment opportunities in rural areas through resettlement, and second to increase the productivity of farmers by providing them with economic holdings, high-yielding varieties of crops, improved technology, and better marketing facilities. Finally, improvements were sought in the quality of life of farmers through the provision of housing, social amenities, and services (Lian 1980: 1). A basic feature of the programme was the 'development area' concept in which efforts were concentrated on schemes to achieve maximum effect with the limited resources available (Sarawak 1963: 27-32). But the existence of customary land tenure is an impediment that may undermine these plans. The rationale of the concept was based on the premise that the most satisfactory way of developing agricultural land was through planned, block settlement. In this way indigenous agriculture could be improved through better yields, for example, from hill padi. Moreover, the most cost-effective means of providing social services and amenities was to locate them in areas of dense population concentration.

In Sabah, rural economic development was based on the RED Book concept, used in peninsular Malaysia in the 1960s. Agricultural productivity was to be raised through the mobilization of local labour and capital in the production of cash crops and through the adoption of modern techniques of farming. A second component of agricultural development was directed at subsistence farmers and smallholders to facilitate better use of available land near settlements. These minor agricultural schemes were established by the Department of Agriculture.

The above objectives accorded with the broad aims of rural development for the country as a whole. The plan was to modernize, that is, 'to stimulate the adoption by the agricultural community of improved practices and patterns of production' (Malaysia 1965: 105) and to increase the area under cultivation, expand production, and provide employment opportunities. However, the emphasis and the mechanism used to achieve these objectives were different. For instance, under the *Fifth Malaysia Plan,* Sabah was allocated development expenditure for economic projects of about $2,146 million and Sarawak $1,907 million, making up about 9.1 per cent and 8.1 per cent respectively of the total allocations under the economic sector. Of the amount allocated to Sabah, about $993 million (46.3 per cent) was to be spent on agriculture and rural development, as compared with $587 million (30.8 per cent) for Sarawak.

Within this sectoral allocation for agriculture and rural development, Sabah will spend about 83 per cent on land and regional development and only 11 per cent on agriculture. Sarawak will spend slightly over half its development allocation on agriculture (50.8 per cent) and only about a little more than a third (35.6 per cent) on land and regional development (Malaysia 1986: Appendix A). Why and how these different emphases have come about may be understood by a separate examination of each state.

Sabah Government's Development Policy

Consistent with trends in Malaysia in the 1980s the Sabah state government not only makes policy, but is also heavily involved in its implementation. Successive state governments have given priority to rural development for various reasons. First, the political imperatives of the rural sector are too costly for a state government to ignore if it is dependent on the rural vote. Second, infrastructural developments alone do not necessarily ensure improvements in the economic status of the rural population. Indeed, with the spectre of 'leakages' of rural income and 'escape spending' in nearby towns,[15] it appears that with improvements in accessibility, a townward movement of people occurs in the form of daily trips or more permanent migrations. Finally, any hoped-for improvements through spontaneous colonization and pioneering of the interior may not take place without concurrent investment and heavy capital outlay by the public sector. Moreover, past experiences have indicated that the opening up of land by individual farmers on an *ad hoc* basis gave rise to haphazard colonization of land and uneconomic holdings. High rates of failure and subsequent abandonment were common as were the low incomes and productivity that have characterized most pioneer settlements (Voon 1981: 54-5).

The organization of rural development in Sabah is hierarchically structured, as it is based on the RED Book programme. The JKKKK (*Jawatan Kuasa Kemajuan Keselamatan Kampung*, or Village Development and Security Committee) was responsible for implementing planned schemes and projects. The District Action Committee provided the link between the JKKKK and the State Development Office. Thus there was a two-way flow of information, with instructions flowing downwards and suggestions moving up the chain of communication. Yet even with this highly organized structure, some targets have not been achieved.

In 1980 there were about 200 minor agricultural schemes in Sabah involving a total of 32,376 hectares of coconuts, wet padi, rubber, and some areas of cocoa, coffee, and oil palm. Voon (1981) has suggested that many of these schemes failed because development involved group rather than individual effort, thus detracting from total commitment and an individual interest in its successful outcome. The physical isolation of the schemes, insufficient financial assistance to farmers involved with the schemes, and 'political' motivations for initiating the schemes rather than economic considerations have provided a recipe for failure. Other agencies that were involved in economic development included statutory authorities, corporations, and quasi-government bodies. Table 3.5 summarizes some of these agencies.

SABAH LAND DEVELOPMENT BOARD (SLDB)

The SLDB, established in January 1969, aims at the development of large blocks of land in relatively unpopulated areas. Consequently, a large number of its schemes were concentrated on the north and east coast Residencies of Sandakan and Tawau. Sabah has had a long history of 'planned' land development and settlement. From as early as 1910 there

Table 3.5. Sabah: Agencies and statutory authorities involved in economic development

Agency	First estab.	Recons- tituted	New agency name
Sabah Rubber Fund Board (SRFB)	1950	1965	-
North Borneo Electricity Board	1957	1963	Sabah Electricity Board
Radio Malaysia Sabah	1963	-	Radio TV Malaysia Sabah
Sabah Railways	-	-	-
Sabah Foundation	1966	1970	Yayasan Sabah
Sabah Ports Authority	1968	-	-
Sabah Padi Board	1968	1979	Lembaga Padi dan Beras
Sabah State Housing Commission	1968	1979	State Housing and Town Development Authority
Sabah Land Development Board	1969	-	(SLDB)
Sabah Economic Development Corporation	1971	-	(SEDCO)
Sabah Forestry Development Authority	1976	-	(SAFODA)
Sabah Rural Development Corporation	1976	1977	Korporasi Pembangunan Desa
Sabah Credit Corporation	-	-	-
Sabah Sports and Cultural Board	1976	1980	-
Yayasan Bumiputra Sabah	1979	-	-
Sabah Energy Corporation	1982	-	-
Sabah Economic Planning Unit	-	-	-
Department of Agriculture	-	-	-
Fishery Department	-	-	-
Public Works Department	-	-	-
FELDA	1956	-	-

Source: Sullivan and Leong (1981).

has been official assistance in populating certain localities and in settling the shifting cultivators who lived in the interior (Lee 1965a; Voon 1981: 60). Most activities concerning land development in the initial years were undertaken by the Department of Agriculture but since the formation of SLDB, the Department's task has been relegated to minor agricultural projects.

In 1969 the SLDB began developing some 4,047 hectares of land in 15 agricultural schemes. By 1978 it had established 29 schemes covering a total planted area of 32,500 hectares mainly under oil palm but including rubber, cocoa, and coconuts in a minor role. Settlement, however, has lagged behind physical development as only half of the schemes have a permanent population - about 2,405 families. The SLDB has also purchased derelict rubber plantations for redevelopment; seven were purchased in 1980 with an aggregate area of 14,164 hectares and were redeveloped as oil palm estates (Voon 1981: 60; see also Figure 3.6).

OTHER AGENCIES

As noted earlier, the Department of Agriculture took charge of integrated minor agricultural schemes of between 40 hectares and 400 hectares. The schemes catered for landless farmers as well as those with uneconomic-sized holdings, giving settlers proximity to their previous villages and land holdings. Other public agencies that also developed land include the Rubber Fund Board, the Padi Board, *Koperasi Pembangunan Desa* (KPD, Rural Development Corporation), and the federal agency, FELDA. FELDA is poised to play an even greater role in land development not only because of the vast areas available in the state, but also because of its reputation and experience in this sphere of activity. During 1981-85 it developed about 37,200 hectares in Sabah (Malaysia 1986: 171). The KPD, previously a farmers' co-operative, was transformed into a development agency in 1977 to help subsistence farmers and smallholders. The projects undertaken were either joint ventures with local farmers or simply developing under-utilized land. Such *in situ* projects vary in size from 4 hectares to 400 hectares and can involve one to 190 landowners. In 1979, there were 32 such joint ventures covering 2,213 hectares of land owned by 1,016 farmers. The farm activities in these projects included subsistence crops and a variety of cash crops such as maize, soya beans, temperate vegetables, pepper, groundnuts, and cashew nuts (Voon 1981: 59). The Rubber Fund Board assists rubber smallholders in replanting with high-yielding varieties with subsidies of $1,236 per hectares for new planting and $2,224 per hectares for replanting (see Figure 3.7). During 1981-85 this agency replanted

Figure 3.6. Sabah: Sabah Land Development Board schemes, 1978

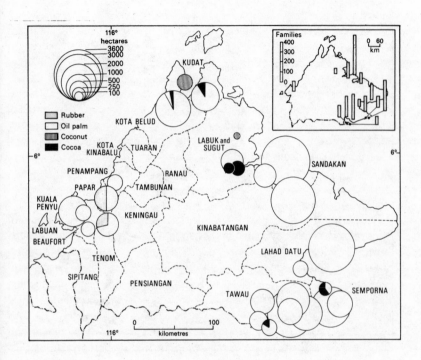

Source: Voon (1981: 61).

Figure 3.7. Sabah: Pre-planned smallholder scheme areas and areas reserved for agricultural development by various government agencies, 1979

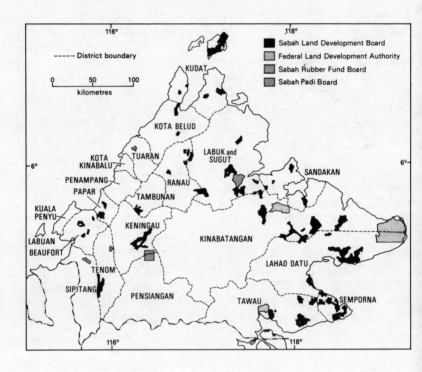

Source: Voon (1981: 62).

67,000 hectares of rubber involving 4,140 smallholders (Malaysia 1986: 308).

PROBLEMS OF DEVELOPMENT

As elsewhere in Malaysia, the state government has had to contend with problems of development. While it might be possible to apply lessons learnt in peninsular Malaysia, especially in terms of the technical and managerial aspects, the Sabahan 'problem' emphasizes a different and more dramatic dimension. The relocation of rural communities into planned agricultural settlements has produced socio-cultural problems. On the one hand, the shifting cultivators' way of life was to move from area to area in search of sustenance. Strident objections have been raised not only to their sedenterization but also to their being uprooted from ancestral lands on which they have foraged for generations. Thus, this problem is more than just that of adaptation or of 'belonging to a place'. Even if the psychological barriers are overcome, having to adapt to a new way of life in a new environment in the company of people from diverse ethno-linguistic backgrounds and experiences can be a traumatic encounter. In some SLDB schemes up to ten different groups may be found.

Moreover, as land development can be a costly affair in Sabah (averaging about $38,000 per family; Voon 1981: 64) the question has been raised as to whether it is

> morally justifiable to make a people [such as the Muruts, for example] hitherto with no debts in the pursuance of their livelihood, admit to loans, however small, which they are committed to repay, thereby in effect creating a whole group of people in debt.
>
> (Khoo and Cho 1973: 92)

The development of existing rural areas can be a complex process. In view of the dispersion of the population and socio-economic diversity of rural communities, the public sector can do no better than to begin by building on and adapting social structures at the grass roots and using the village headman as the 'prime mover' of development. Life in the *kampung* community, where interpersonal contact was most important, can be a very powerful tool for the process of development. Thus, rather than foisting a large, overbearing bureaucratic development machinery on such societies and thereby perhaps unwittingly creating a 'dependence mentality' among the rural population, the preservation of rural society as far as is practicable will ensure social stability and progress. As Voon (1981: 66) has observed, any rural development programme may be assessed as successful if the rural population can be made to sustain the process spontaneously.

The technical problems of development, such as enviromental damage through improper planning, poor management and inefficiency in the public service, and the shortage of experienced and qualified personnel, may be overcome.[16] However, one of the difficulties is the need to reconcile conflicting notions of 'time' in the implementing agencies on the one hand and traditional society on the other. Time, for traditional societies, is relevant only in terms of cycles of planting and harvesting. This comes into conflict with the concept of phased development in which time is imperative and the lack of progress at one stage can prevent other stages and activities from being implemented. To the bureaucrat, this lack of time consciousness appeared as apathy on the part of rural society as much as a lack of readiness to change and a distrust of innovation. But how does one go about persuading rice growers to adopt a new cropping system when the whole fabric of their society is imbued with customs, taboos, and the invocation of spirits to protect their crops? (Burrough and Jamin 1972). This remains the challenge of rural development policy in Sabah.

Agricultural Development in Sarawak

Over half of the economically active population in Sarawak is engaged in agricultural pursuits for a livelihood. Three-quarters of the land suitable for agriculture is under shifting cultivation (Malaysia 1986: 181). It is no wonder therefore that there was an emphasis on agriculture in the form of integrated agricultural programmes and large-scale land development. While land development began in 1964, it was only in 1972 that it became organized with the establishment of the Sarawak Land Development Board (SLDB). By 1977 it had established 16 schemes covering a total developed area of 41,364 hectares along similar lines to those in peninsular Malaysia (see Figure 3.8).

Another agency, the Land Consolidation and Rehabilitation Authority (SALCRA), established in 1976, was charged with the task of consolidating and developing unused, idle land in rural areas, especially 'native land'. The Authority does not purchase the land but helps the owner to develop the holding. Between 1981 and 1985 SALCRA

Figure 3.8: Sarawak: Location of established land development schemes, 1977

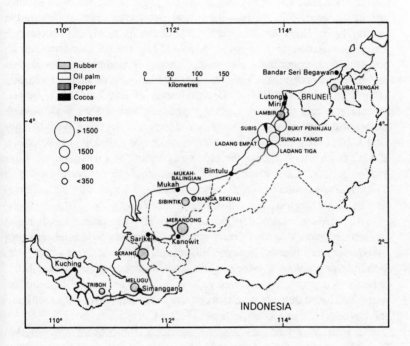

Source: Lian (1980: 2-3).

rehabilitated about 3,220 hectares of oil palm, 2,730 hectares of cocoa, 1,460 hectares of rubber, and 200 hectares of tea smallholdings (Malaysia 1986: 310).

A particular problem in Sarawak is that posed by Native Reserves and Customary Land, a category which covers about a quarter of total land area in the state.[17] In the past these lands were created by the felling of virgin jungle. However, these are rights of the user only (usufructuary) and cannot exceed the area that may be used by the holder or retained if that person or community moves elsewhere. Transference outside the community is prohibited. There are sizeable amounts of such land in the Second Division, the Rejang Delta, Bintulu District, the Miri-Marudi Bekenu area and the lower Limbang Valley. 'Mixed-zone land' covers almost a tenth of Sarawak, mostly in the First and Second Divisions, the Sibu Sarikei area, the middle courses of the Rejang, and the coastal zone of Mukah District. This is the sole category of land that Chinese may own or occupy. Land classification and tenure therefore remain a basic problem, the solution to which must precede any large-scale agricultural development (Jackson 1968: 74-6; Lee 1965b: 27-9).

SALCRA's efforts at developing Native and Customary Lands have met with mixed success. In early schemes, its policy was to absorb the land owners as settlers. However, this resulted in the inclusion of persons with little or no interest in the projects who consequently contributed little or performed poorly. An alternative method that was tried in the Sibintik scheme included outright purchase and the exclusion of owners as settlers, and has also been unsuccessful (Lian 1980: 1).

As with other land development agencies, the problems which the SLDB has faced include the reluctance of potential settlers to be uprooted, the inability to recruit workers for scheme preparation, and poor accessibility. The structural employment problem has partially been solved by contracting Indonesian labourers. However, the problem of accessibility (for example, in the oil palm scheme at Mukah Balingian) has significantly increased the costs of development; such costs are not recouped as they are not imputed to loan accounts of the settlers (Lian 1980: 4). While settlers may be carefully selected, as in FELDA schemes, many come from conservative communities with strong traditions and customs. Radical change may not be readily forthcoming, desirable, or acceptable. Whole communities will need to be recruited into settlement schemes rather than individual families (Senftleben 1978: 225). But the question still remains as to whether land development was the most suitable way of developing the rural economy. Despite noble objectives and policies, rural populations were unwilling to move out of their traditional areas (Lian 1980: 7-9). Thus from the point of view of affecting only some people in the rural areas, the rural development programmes have been successful only in a limited way. Shifting cultivators living in remote areas either may not have been affected by development efforts on the part of the government or have chosen not to participate in these programmes. Such an observation thus introduces the intractable problem of bringing about human development as part of the development and modernization process.

GROWTH, REDISTRIBUTION, AND HUMAN DEVELOPMENT

Dudley Seers (1977) summed up the unsatisfactory results of the First Development Decade by identifying two streams of thought about growth and development. The first chose to stay within the neoclassical structure but with a shift from a pure growth centre strategy to other measures such as export orientation. The second involved 'self-reliance' and 'basic needs' as the best strategy to combat poverty and reduce inequality. Self-reliance does not mean economic self-sufficiency (autarchy) because in some contexts it is based on neoclassical growth paradigms. For example, regional development theory and practice were almost exclusively based on the growth paradigm (Taylor 1981: 266).

The importance of the principle of self-help has been recognized by the Malaysian government. In the *Second Malaysia Plan*, for instance, the government sought to cultivate the spirit of self-reliance *(berdiri-kari)*[18] and a positive attitude among people to participating in socio-economic development programmes (Malaysia 1971: vi). A further programme was also recommended in the *Mid-term Review of the First Malaysia Plan* (Malaysia 1969: 1, 48). The *Jayadiri* programme initiated in 1968 was aimed at supporting and developing self-reliant farm communities throughout the country. Under this programme concerted efforts were made to meet the needs of more rapid development in areas at a take-off stage while providing other areas with key infrastructural elements to aid development. The programme was seen as an integration of all activities towards greater agricultural productivity in all areas. However, the preoccupation of the *Third Malaysia Plan* with poverty eradication and the restructuring of society stifled further attention to this principle of self-help.

This chapter has focused on the Malaysian government's efforts at rural regional development. In doing so, it has highlighted the project bias of the strategies in agricultural or land and regional development. The strategy of growth with redistribution has been in the forefront of development planning at least since the *Third Malaysia Plan*. Two outcomes can be seen.

First, the emphasis on economic growth or growth-related activities in the long term necessarily entails a preoccupation with technical success to the exclusion of everything else. One of the results of this emphasis relates to what has been called 'the revolution of rising expectations'. As modernization takes place everywhere, with the pressure of attaining yet higher living standards, the question of poverty and comfort becomes a relative one. Moreover, the *Bumiputera* farmers and rubber smallholders look increasingly towards the government as the 'godfather' of development in supplying capital for starting businesses, tractors for the farms, or finance to subsidize the replanting of rubber trees, thereby building up a 'dependence syndrome'. This attitude can negate the entire objective of development since economic progress becomes a matter of political bargaining and putting pressure on the local member of Parliament (Ghani 1981: 291).

The second outcome is the lack of any participative role for the people because development is directed.[19] For, to paraphrase Hashim (1979: 70), 'the central figures in development are the people themselves. They are not only the reason for development but also the means of development.' The pressing need for human development in the pursuit of physical and economic progress is thus apparent where there are large numbers of adult rural farmers, fishermen, labourers, and estate workers who cannot understand why there is a form to fill in for everything when dealing with bureaucrats in the local Land Office. This group of rural people cannot be allowed to live in a perceptual world of their own when everything around them is changing rapidly. What is required is a 'new kind of Malaysian' (Robertson 1975) although the morality whereby

> the Muruts [of the Nabawan Valley Scheme] will have become a people with no particular distinguishing mark with regard to their activities or way of life

> (Khoo and Cho 1973: 93)

would need to be severely questioned. The term 'new' reflects Lerner's (1963) *Passing of the Traditional Society* in which there is a change in value orientation, with indicators such as positive and rational attitudes, achievement orientation, and control of one's environment. A modern society is a participant society and a good indicator of its success is active participation in socio-economic as well as political activity. These may be achieved without abandoning the value systems of rural people because not everything is wrong with traditional institutions. For instance, the 'work group' (*kumpulan kerja*) should be used in preference to the 'work committee' (*jawatankuasa kerja*) since the word 'committee' connotes the holding of meetings but no work (*Haji* Omar 1979: 189). Human development in terms of social and economic behaviour should also be a part of the rural regional development programmes that have thus far been characterized and evaluated solely on the basis of technical success and economic growth. The costs of insufficient attention in this area can be politically ruinous for the country as a whole as uneven development, non-growth, and maldistribution will be perpetuated.

In conclusion, a comment needs to be made regarding the overall thrust of the development effort. Thus far, all planning has been premissed on the assumption that the restructuring objectives of ethnic identification with economic function, and the redistribution objective of eliminating poverty groups will be achieved with economic growth. As the mid-1980s have shown there can be negative growth, that is, no increase in the GDP has been achieved. In that situation, the question is: what then? Will the plans be carried out nevertheless? Will some alternative plan be put in place either by compromising the stated objectives or by abandoning those objectives totally and starting afresh? These are interesting questions but their discussion must be postponed until the final chapter, after a discussion of the prospects of urban and industrial development.

4
CITIES AT THE CROSSROADS: GROWTH AND TRANSFORMATION

It has been suggested that there are five principal ways in which one may view a city. As a social system, the city produces intensive interaction and interdependence among its residents and institutions. The city is also a spatial system in that the pattern of interactions among its residents is spatially bounded. Further the city is a subsystem of society where it is part of an encompassing whole. As a space-organizing subsystem the city functions as a central place (within a hierarchy of central places) to organize surrounding and sometimes distant areas into economic, social and cultural spaces. Finally, as a redistributive centre the city has control over dependent areas and spatially dispersed populations for appropriating and redistributing surplus production for mutual enrichment (Friedmann and Wulff 1976: 6-7). The city may also be considered a major production system, for example, through its manufacturing and industrial output.

Such a view of the city implies that as a space-organizing system it is not self-sufficient. Its interdependence with the hinterland and its service functions such as markets, commerce, and transport play an important role in the well-being of the state or region of which it is a part. In this chapter, an examination is attempted of the process of urbanization in Malaysia and the growth of cities. The transformation of Malaysian cities demographically, socially, and economically has brought about challenges as well as opportunities. A description of the various responses by the public sector, on the one hand, and the urban residents, on the other, gives an impression of how these problems of growth and transformation are being met.

In Malaysia before European colonization, the notion of an urban system was non-existent in concept and in fact. Before the coming of Europeans, cities for the most part took the form of ephemeral 'orthogenetic' cult entities. In general this meant that settlements were conventionally made up of groups of people led by some prince, warlord, or warrior. Examples of riverine settlements and inland agglomerations with no particular *raison d'être* were quite common before European settlement. However, the urban system after European settlement was the imposition of an imported 'alien' European phenomenon upon the customary settlement system (Lim 1977). The pattern of contemporary urban development therefore dates from European colonization, beginning in the sixteenth century with the Portuguese settlement of Melaka. Urbanization in Malaysia may be considered an 'alien phenomenon, tacked on to a rural background' and is associated with Chinese, Indian, or European enterprise or a combination of all three (Aiken and Leigh 1975: 546). The evolution and transformation of this urban system are examined next.

URBAN TRANSFORMATION

The path to modernization and developmental change is a long, continuous and complex process. On such a journey there will be all kinds of changes. Friedmann (1961) has argued that an urban transformation has occurred or is in the process of occurring where there is a national integration of social, political, and economic space. Such a process may take place via spatial diffusion mechanisms down the urban hierarchy and from urban centres to inter-urban peripheries. But the problem with such a model is that the transference down the urban hierarchy may be affected by institutional structures so that as well as urban to rural transference of ideas and commodities, there is also a cityward movement of people. This then raises two general issues of a social character.

First, an ecological relationship exists between town and country. Keyfitz (1965) and others have suggested that the countryside has always provided a food surplus for the city in return for industrial goods. But where the productivity of secondary industries remains low and other economic sectors fail to provide the growth dynamism, then the city is 'parasitic' and becomes a burden to the country. A social problem surfaces because 'under such conditions frustrated individuals are likely to take on anomic and pathological attitudes and behaviour' (Yeung 1976: 296).

The second general issue is the question of widespread urban poverty. The income distribution in the urban area may be such that only a few people are able to sustain a relatively high standard of living. Such differentials may lead to a situation of widespread urban poverty among the indigenes. The group with economic power is invariably blamed for all the ills of the city. Perversely, this group is made up of immigrants. Thus, Dwyer (1972b) and Osborn (1974) have predicted the possibility of future confrontation between these two groups of people drawn along ethnic lines. The city can therefore be a source of potential tension, political conflict, and extremist behaviour.

However, the social change that was envisaged by the theorists has not affected the masses. There is an absence of wide-ranging revolutionary changes in life-styles, behavioural patterns, and social stratification. McGee (1969: 16) has suggested that the persistence of a pluralistic society and a larger than expected 'bazaar' sector, as opposed to a modern firm-type sector, has constrained rapid social change similar to that which has occurred in the west. In fact, McGee has reiterated elsewhere that

> in the context of the majority of Third World countries, it seems that a theoretical framework which regards the city as the prime catalyst of change must be disregarded. And further, that to understand the role of cities properly, one must investigate the condition of underdevelopment which characterizes these countries, of which the cities are only a part.

> (McGee 1971a: 31)

In Malaysia it has been observed that social mobility may be observed to take place horizontally among regions and vertically among occupational sectors. This mobility is 'closed' according to ethnic and other attributes of the people (Salih and Young 1981: 142). Thus, it is not merely an urban-rural differential but also an intra-urban occupational differential which may determine whether or not social change takes place.

That urban transformation is only at its incipient stages may be observed from the slow pace of change in the economic structures. In the west economic structures have had to be dismantled to accommodate urban transformation. The western city has had to absorb huge numbers of workers from rural areas who were displaced by rapid increases in farm productivity and mechanization. New forms of business organization had to be devised to tap the labour supply. The critical point to note is that it is not possible to separate urban transformation from agrarian transformation - one is a part of the other. In the case of the Green Revolution in South East Asia the promised rewards did not materialize because the farm inputs required to boost production were either absent or used ineffectively through poor management (Gibbons *et al.* 1980; Jacoby 1972). Yet there was still a cityward movement of migrants seeking employment. There was also no contemporaneous change in the organization of industries or occupations, some of which were only a little different from those existing before the Green Revolution.

There were minimal changes in the structure of the economy. Agriculture was still the largest contributor to GDP with industrialization yet to become prominent. In short, the dualistic nature of the economy, in which a traditional and a modern sector coexisted, remained a central feature of developing countries in South East Asia.

Many of these features persist in the Malaysian economy except for those cities described as being at the crossroads of modernization. Kuala Lumpur, Georgetown, Ipoh, Johor Bahru, and Petaling Jaya are in this category. Yet even in these cities marginal occupations still abound. The labour force is growing at an alarming rate but the pace and nature of industrialization afford only restricted employment opportunities. Unemployment and underemployment have become major problems in these cities (Ooi 1975). The nature and form of urban transformation in Malaysia thus reflect first its incorporation into the monetary economy through time, and second, the pattern of contemporary development.

As a means of grappling with this issue of urban transformation, a working definition of urbanization similar to that proposed by Friedmann and Wulff (1976) is adopted because certain elements in the definition bear directly on the question of a transformation.

Urbanization may be thought of as the concentration of formerly dispersed populations that were primarily engaged in farming into a number of settlements whose main activity is to provide services, trade, markets, and manufactures. In addition, urbanization refers to an urban mode of production in which the life-styles, way of thought, and production of goods in these agglomerations are spread to outlying towns and rural populations. Any study of urbanization must therefore describe changes which take place, evaluate their significance, and attempt to understand the social and economic processes which have brought them about. Also, these studies should be

> concerned about their pathology - the famine, overpopulation, immiseration, dependency, unemployment, and poverty that accompany the spatial transformation - and with the policies that are addressed to these conditions

(Friedmann and Wulff 1976: 4)

The need therefore is to examine the nature and extent of the urban transformation with respect to changes in the demographic, social, and economic structures of cities. In addition, there is a need to place urban transformation in the context of social transformation so as to make sense of the former.

Lampard (1969: 5-6) has proposed a statistical yardstick to measure the demographic dimension. A country is said to be approaching an urban transformation when 40 to 50 per cent of its population is concentrated in urban areas or, alternatively, when between 25 to 30 per cent live in large cities with populations of 100,000 and over. In 1980 the urban population accounted for only 34 per cent of Malaysians. At the same time only about 22 per cent lived in urban areas larger than 100,000 (Khoo 1982a). On both counts therefore it seems that Malaysian cities have yet to approach such an urban transformation. However, two general qualifications need to be made.

First, the cut-off values that have been used are approximations and as such have to be taken in the context of the social and economic development of the country concerned. Simply having a high ratio of urban to total population may be either indicative of a preference for city lifer or due to the nature of the population distribution of the country. A more plausible explanation could be found in the threshold used to distinguish urban from non-urban agglomerations.

Second, it is contended that even if the difficulties of definition have been overcome, the differences between the Malaysian data and the suggested cut-off values are only minor. It can be said that there is an incipient transformation of Malaysian urban centres. Alternatively, it could be argued that if the data on Malaysian towns were disaggregated and presented as state-wide data, then it would be shown that three states (Pulau Pinang, Selangor, and Terengganu) and Kuala Lumpur have 40 per cent or more of its population defined as urban. When the data on towns above 100,000 people are used, states such as Perak and Negri Sembilan are added to the list under the first criterion; thus a total of five states and one territory now fulfil Lampard's second criterion. These observations suggest the theme for the next section since the size and distribution of large urban centres are inextricably tied to the broader questions of urban growth and urbanization in the country. Thus, a detailed discussion of the implications of the transformation of cities will have to be postponed pending an examination of urban patterns and processes.

URBANIZATION: SPATIAL PROCESSES AND SPATIAL PATTERNS

This study takes as its starting point the pattern of urbanization associated with socio-economic development following independence. After a brief discussion of what is considered urban in the Malaysian context, the twin themes of levels of urbanization and rates of urban growth are described. Then the implications of a rank-size distribution are considered, together with the ethnic pattern of urbanization, especially those of the Malays. As urban employment and unemployment are critical issues, an evaluation is attempted of efforts to transform the balance of the mix of occupations from the primary to the secondary and tertiary sector. The policy implications of this discussion, including a national urbanization policy, conclude this chapter.

Definition of Urban

There is a wide variation in the definition of what is urban in Malaysia. Different census definitions have been used in the past so that in 1970 a threshold population of 10,000 was adopted instead of the 1,000 figure used in the 1947 and 1957 censuses. This threshold figure is important as it appears that levels of urbanization since 1970 have been lower than in previous censuses. A review of past studies of urbanization reveals that there is no accepted threshold among social scientists for distinguishing which centres are urban. Ooi (1975) uses the 10,000 threshold, Pryor (1973: 61) prefers 20,000, while Sendut (1962; 1965) has at various times used 1,000, 2,000 and 5,000 thresholds. Lee (1977) has suggested 5,000 as a compromise threshold figure with the proviso that there should be a 'perceivable urban form', that is, some contiguity in the urban physical fabric and a recognizable dominant centre.

In Sarawak, the 1960 census had no definition of the term 'urban'. A close reading of the Census Report suggests that 3,000 was taken as the threshold figure (Jackson 1968: 64-5). In Sabah, Jones (1966: 138-44) reported that 'urban' was interpreted liberally in 1960 so that, for example, Sandakan was an 'extended' town that included areas intended for future development despite a lack of urban characteristics. The data on urban centres for Sabah may thus be unreliable in detail owing to the lack of comparability of urban areas in the two censuses.

Rather than become embroiled in this issue (and the cumbersome reference to settlements as rural-urban or metropolitan-rural) the definition given by the Department of Statistics, Malaysia is used. It states that

> [t]he term 'urban' refers to gazetted local authority areas with a population of 10,000 and over; all other areas are classified as rural.

(Khoo 1982a: viii)

This definition describes a 'statistical town' rather than an 'urban area'. It also postulates a 'legal town' such that people living outside the gazetted local authority area either have no status (are illegal?) or are classified as rural even though they live virtually within the shadow of the town boundary. Thus the definition may underestimate the degree of urbanization of some areas simply because some residents in the vicinity of the urban area are excluded as they have no legal status. This can happen in very large urban areas such as Kuala Lumpur, Georgetown, Ipoh, Kelang, and where there are large peripheral areas that fall outside gazetted boundaries. In one sense therefore the discussion centres around the phenomenon of a 'statistical' urbanization since the reclassification in 1970 of gazetted areas would have excluded some that in 1957 were defined as urban.

In the Malaysian context the urbanization process has proceeded with a shift of people from rural to urban areas as well as of the balance between urban to urban movements. There has been some 'leakage' with the movement of people from urban to rural areas, especially those residents of large New Villages who moved back to the rural areas and into agrarian occupations (Saw 1972; 1976). Natural increases also added to the urbanization process although these were counterbalanced by migration overseas. Peripheral villages were also swallowed up in the physical expansion of urban areas. Both Pryor (1973) and Hirschmann (1976) have shown that natural increase rather than migration was the main demographic process behind urban growth and hence the degree of urbanization. The urbanization process arising from a shift of people will be useful in helping to describe and explain the patterns that emerge.

Urban Population Growth

The dynamic forces that fuel the urbanization process can be reduced to four factors that have at various times been responsible for shaping the growth of Malaysian cities. Traditional sources of growth arising from natural increase and migration have been the major contributors to the urbanization process. Warfare and insurgent activities have also been responsible for driving people into towns, as for example, during the Emergency (1948-60) in Malaya. City boundary expansion, the spatial growth of the urban area, and continual census redefinitions of the urban threshold populations have led to visible urbanization.[1] To these may also be added the broad processes of structural transformation associated with the 'capitalization' of agriculture, industrialization, and the creation of administrative functions to oversee city and international growth.

The demographic components of the urbanization process in South East Asia are different from those in western countries at comparable stages of development (McGee 1971b: 164). The difference lies in the high fertility and mortality rates of western cities which permitted rural to urban shifts; in South East Asia the phenomenon was one of 'pre-industrial fertility and post-industrial mortality' (Davis 1971, quoted in Yeung 1976: 293) so that high birth rates and low child mortality rates combined to produce high natural increase rates. Davis's description of the problem, however, does not accurately depict the Malaysian situation. For example, the period 1980-83 saw a continuation of the declining trend in overall fertility in Malaysia although the differentials in natural growth between ethnic groups were maintained.

In peninsular Malaysia there was an upward trend in fertility among the Malays in the early 1980s resulting from an increase in third, fourth, and fifth births. In 1983, for example, the total fertility rate for Malay women was 4.53 children, as compared with 4.47 children in 1980. By contrast, Chinese and Indian fertility rates have fallen from 3.14 and 3.38 to 2.72 and 3.00 children respectively between 1980 and 1983 (Malaysia 1986: 131-2). The reasons for such patterns include the maintenance of a large family among later-marrying Malay couples and the low level of acceptance of family planning among the Malays. The decline in Chinese and Indian fertility stems from a rising first marriage-age, the increasing use of contraception, and the desire for a smaller family than in the past. Some decline in fertility among all ethnic groups in Sabah and Sarawak has been recorded although fertility among indigenous groups in these states was higher than among Malays in the peninsula. In Sabah, indigenous women had on average six children while those in Sarawak had five.

Infant mortality per thousand live births in peninsular Malaysia was 17.5 in 1984, as compared with 23.9 in 1980. Again, infant mortality was highest among Malays (20.1 per thousand live births) and lowest among Chinese (10.5 per thousand live births) in 1984. Comparable data for Sabah and Sarawak are unavailable because of the poor quality of vital statistics arising from a high degree of under-registration of births and deaths (Khoo 1983: 48-56). However, significant improvement in mortality rates in these two states is expected, owing to improvements in nutrition and family hygiene, lower incidence of diseases, and general improvement in socio-economic conditions.

To better appreciate present-day patterns of urban growth, it has been suggested that the process be viewed as one of three waves. This 'wave hypothesis' is a tacit recognition of the interplay of both historical and socio-political processes impinging on urbanization. Hence, in this case one may observe socio-political processes manifest in the spatial patterns of urban areas. According to Salih and Young (1981), the first wave occurred in the period between 1785 and 1930 with the colonial economic and political penetration of the Malay States. This intervention served to direct the pattern of economic production and to establish selected pre-eminent 'nodes' for exports of local produce. In addition, this period witnessed the immigration of non-indigenous labour that helped to keep the investment of capital productive. The second wave of urban growth was the period between 1947 and 1970 and included the Emergency resettlement scheme. This created the New Village as a counter-insurgency measure to deny communist insurgents food, aid, and material support. During this period there was also the urbanization of rural areas as a result of the establishment of planned settlements in 'frontier' regions by the Federal Land Development Authority. Finally, the third wave, beginning in the 1970s, was the product of a policy of promoting basic Malay urbanization. Under the New Economic Policy of the *Second Malaysia Plan* it was felt that the promotion of Malay urbanization would hasten the correction of imbalances in Malaysian society.

But it is to be noted that these three waves applied to peninsular Malaysia only. In the case of Sabah and Sarawak, it is arguable that the 'middle' wave did not take place. Instead, the first wave began with the period of the British North Borneo Company in Sabah in 1882, with a brief interlude between 1942 and 1945 during the Japanese occupation, and ended with the formation of Malaysia in 1963. Sarawak developed similarly as a result of successive concessions by the Sultan of Brunei; the period of rule by the 'White Rajahs' of the Brooke family from 1840 to 1942-45 (Japanese occupation) and then to the formation of Malaysia marks the first wave of urbanization. Thus the second wave may be considered to have begun with the formation of Malaysia, which heralded the period of conscious planning for the development of towns and new settlements.

The identification of the various phases of urban growth is useful because it provides a convenient temporal point of reference. An examination of urban centres with a population in excess of 10,000 will show distinctive features through time. Most urban centres experienced a fairly steady growth in size since 1947. However, the level of urbanization accelerated only during the last two census periods (1970 and 1980). There has been a doubling of the urban population and a still larger increase in the number of urban centres since 1947. As noted previously, these reflect definitional changes from a low threshold of 1,000 (1947 census) to that of 10,000 (since the 1970 census). The New Village resettlement programme, natural increase, rural-urban migration, and government policies have been responsible for both the pace and the level of urbanization. Five authors (Pryor 1973; 1975a,b; Ooi 1975; Hirschmann 1976; Salih and Young 1981) have given particular attention to the study of urbanization in peninsular Malaysia while four others (Lee 1977; Sidhu 1981; Rimmer and Cho 1981) have assessed the ethnic variable in the urbanization process.

Level of Urbanization

The level of urbanization and the number of urban centres in each of the states of Malaysia are shown in Table 4.1 and Figure 4.1. The level of urbanization varied from 9 per cent in the case of Perlis to 47 per cent in Pulau Pinang and 43 per cent for Terengganu through to 100 per cent for Kuala Lumpur. Only one urban centre in Perlis crossed the 10,000 population threshold (in 1970 Kangar, the largest town, had a population of only 8,700). Pulau Pinang had six urban centres accounting for 47 per cent of the urban population. But Terengganu had only three centres, which accounted for about 43 per cent of the population. The implication is that the urban population in Terengganu is more highly concentrated in the larger towns than is the case in Pulau Pinang. Wilayah Persekutuan includes Kuala Lumpur, the country's major conurbation.

Although Johor has the largest number of urban centres, its level of urbanization is much lower than those of Pulau Pinang and Terengganu. It may be noted that about two-thirds of the population of Malaysia lived in four states and a territory although these accounted for only about half the number of urban centres (34 out of 67) in the country.

The steady increase in the number of settlements with a population of 10,000 or more in the period 1911-70 is illustrated in Table 4.2 and Figure 4.2. The number of urban areas has increased from eight to 36 for states in the former Federation of Malaya; since the formation of Malaysia it has increased from 55 to 67. The largest gains during the intercensal periods were those between 1947 and 1957 (not including Sabah and Sarawak).

Table 4.1. Malaysia: Distribution of urban population, 1980

State	Total popn. (000s)	No. of centres	Total popn. (000s)	% of total population
Johor	1,645	12	585	36
Kedah	1,121	3	163	14
Kelantan	898	6	250	28
Melaka	467	2	110	24
Negri Sembilan	576	4	189	33
Pahang	802	5	212	26
Perak	1,812	8	590	33
Perlis	149	1	13	9
Pulau Pinang	958	6	455	47
Sabah	1,055	5	211	20
Sarawak	1,351	4	238	18
Selangor	1,522	7	524	34
Terengganu	543	3	234	43
Wilayah Persekutuan/ Kuala Lumpur	981	1	981	100
Malaysia	13,880	67	4,755	34

Source: Khoo (1982a).

Figure 4.1. Malaysia: Distribution of urban centres, 1980

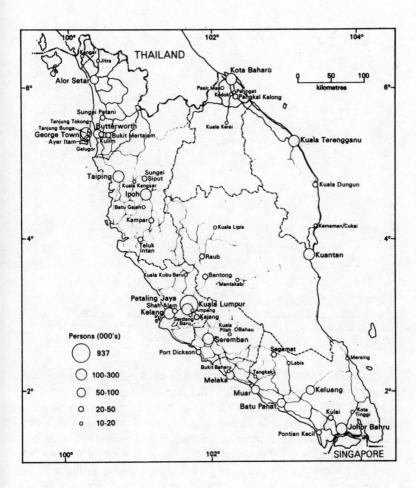

Figure 4.1 (cont.)

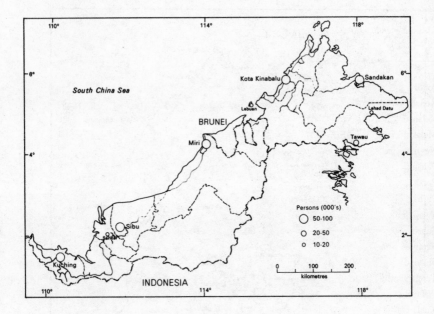

However, when the two eastern states of Sabah and Sarawak are included, the largest increase was in the intercensal period between 1957 and 1970. Only two states recorded large gains in the number of urban centres - Johor and Sabah. However, one state (Terengganu) showed a decrease in the number of urban settlements from five in 1970 to three in 1980. The reason for this anomaly was the redrawing of the gazetted areas of the municipality of Kuala Terengganu, which resulted in the absorption of the previously separate local council areas of Kuala Terengganu Tengah and the neighbouring Kuala Terengganu Manir.

A significant feature of these gains is that they occurred in states which experienced the most intense efforts at regional development. Thus the east coast states of Kelantan and Terengganu and the central states of Pahang, Negri Sembilan, and Johor showed the effects of the penetration of developmental influences. Lower-order towns such as Mentakab

Table 4.2. Malaya and Malaysia: Number of urban centres with a population of 10,000 or more, 1911-80

| | Census year | | | | | | |
| | *Malaya* | | | | | *Malaysia* | |
State	*1911*	*1921*	*1931*	*1947*	*1957*	*1970*	*1980*
Johor	-	2	3	4	5	7	12
Kedah	-	1	1	2	3	3	3
Kelantan	1	1	1	1	1	5	6
Melaka	1	1	1	1	1	2	2
Negri Sembilan	-	1	1	1	2	3	4
Pahang	-	-	-	-	4	4	5
Perak	3	4	4	4	9	8	8
Perlis	-	-	-	-	-	-	1
Pulau Pinang	1	1	2	4	4	5	6
Sabah	-	-	-	-	*	3	5
Sarawak	-	-	-	-	*	3	4
Selangor	1	2	2	2	5	7	7
Terengganu	1	1	1	1	2	5	3
Wilayah Persekutuan / Kuala Lumpur	-	-	-	-	-	0	1
Malaysia	8	14	16	20	36	55	67

Sources: Malaya and Malaysia *Population Census 1911; 1921; 1931; 1947; 1957; 1970; 1980;* Sabah and Sarawak, *Population Census 1960*.

Note: * Sabah and Sarawak had three urban centres in the 1960 census.

Figure 4.2. Malaysia: Number of settlements with populations of 10,000 or more, 1911-80

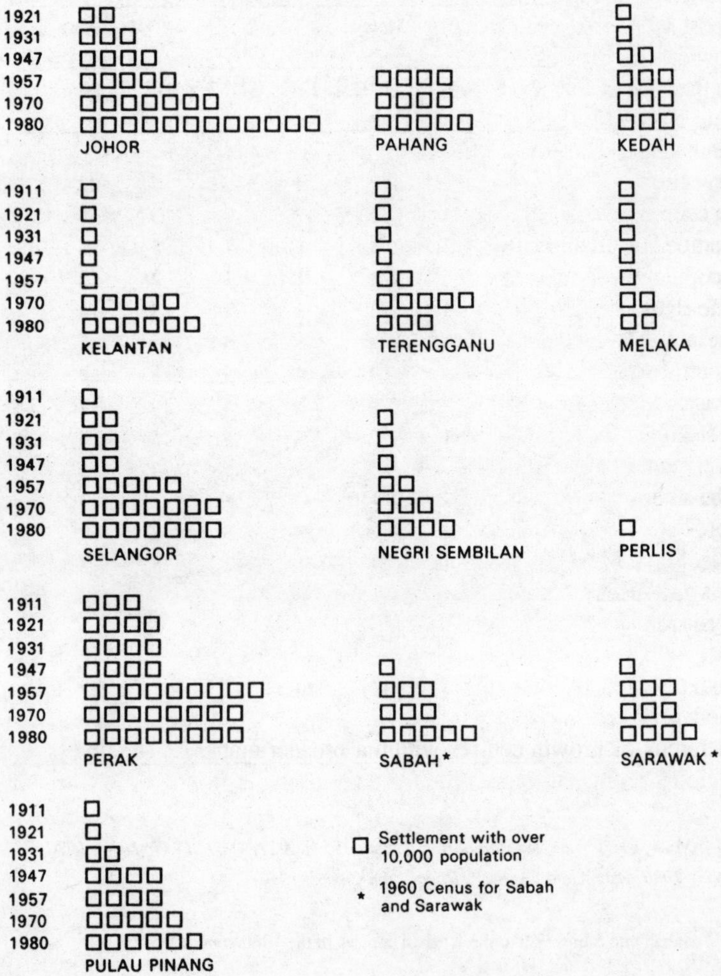

(Pahang), Kota Tinggi, Tangkak, Labis (all Johor), Kuala Pilah, and Bahau (both Negri Sembilan) have broken the 10,000 threshold since the 1980s, no doubt as a result of benefits flowing from the respective regional development areas within the orbit of these towns.[2] It is apparent that inland towns such as Kuala Kerai, Kadok (both Kelantan), Jitra (Kedah), and Kangar (Perlis) have grown because of improvements in transport infrastructure, particularly as these towns lie in the economic shadow cast by the East-West Highway in northern peninsular Malaysia.

In the case of Sabah the port functions of the five major urban centres of Kota Kinabalu, Labuan, Lahad Datu, Sandakan, and Tawau in exporting timber and other local produce have elevated these to the level of an 'urban centre'. However, in Sarawak only Sarikei was added to the list of urban centres above 10,000 people, between 1970 and 1980. In general, the number of urban centres in each state was in direct proportion to the total population and the size of the state.

The discussion so far suggests that urbanization was concentrated in the western states of peninsular Malaysia, with rapid growth in the eastern and central southern states of the peninsula and only in parts of Sabah and Sarawak. Indeed, as observed by Ward (1968) and McTaggart (1972), and confirmed by Pryor (1975a: 20), urbanization in peninsular Malaysia was very uneven and confined to two or three central western states. It may be added that in Sabah and Sarawak the 'flat' urbanization surface was broken by minor peaks located at the coastal port towns of Kuching, Sarikei, Sibu, Miri, Kota Kinabalu, Sandakan, Lahad Datu, and Tawau. Pryor's (1975b: 30) multivariate analysis and description of peninsular Malaysia applies equally to the country as a whole:

> both the vertical complexity and horizontal spread of urbanization and modernization, and the resultant statistical surface suggests a hierarchy of growth centres within a broader matrix of rurality or, in regional economic terms, within the periphery.

Growth Rates of Urban Centres

The distribution of the urban population of Malaysia, given in Table 4.3, shows that in both 1970 and 1980 censuses the largest number of urban dwellers were found in Perak and Selangor (which also included Kuala Lumpur). Perlis did not register any urban population in 1970 because there was no centre above the 10,000 threshold criterion. Data for 1985 shows that the pre-eminence of Selangor and Kuala Lumpur was maintained except that Johor had overtaken Perak in total number of

Table 4.3. Malaysia: Distribution of urban population by state, 1970-85 (000s)

| State | 1970 | | 1980 | | 1985 | | Ave. annual urban growth | |
	Urban	Total	Urban	Total	Urban	Total	1970-80	1981-85
							(%)	(%)
Johor	336	1,277	565	1,601	731	1,854	5.2	4.5
Kedah	121	955	159	1,102	184	1,211	2.7	2.5
Kelantan	103	686	246	889	306	1,026	8.7	4.0
Melaka	102	404	106	453	114	493	0.4	1.5
Negri Sembilan	104	481	183	564	233	625	5.7	4.2
Pahang	96	505	207	791	254	999	7.7	3.6
Perak	432	1,569	574	1,774	637	1,935	2.8	1.6
Perlis	-	121	13	147	16	165	-	4.3
Pulau Pinang	395	775	431	912	566	1,050	0.9	4.4
Sabah	108	653	207	1,003	289	1,280	6.5	6.6
Sarawak	150	976	228	1,295	296	1,543	4.2	4.4
Selangor	733	1,631	508	1,475	833	1,822	-	9.8
Terengganu	109	405	232	542	299	637	7.5	4.9
Wilayah Persekutuan/ Kuala Lumpur	-	-	938	938	1,153	1,153	-	3.2
Malaysia	2,789	10,438	4,597	13,486	5,911	15,793	5.0	4.4

Sources: Khoo (1982a: 95); data for 1985 from Malaysia (1986: 184).

Notes: 'Urban' refers to gazetted areas with populations exceeding 10,000 people.

Average annual growth rate has been calculated as follows:

$$r = 1 / n \log_e P_n / P_o$$

where: r average annual rate of growth
   n exact number of years between P_o and P_n
   P_o population in initial year
   P_n population in the later year.

urban dwellers, reflecting a faster growth rate through both natural increase and in-migration.

In terms of relative proportions of urban dwellers to total population, the picture was somewhat different. Pulau Pinang and Selangor showed the highest proportions of urban population since the 1970 census and this was maintained through to 1985. On the basis of the data for 1985 Perlis, Kedah and Sarawak have the lowest number of people living in urban centres. The number of persons living in urban areas in Malaysia has grown steadily: it was 27 per cent in 1970 and rose to 34 per cent in 1980 and 37 per cent by 1985.

The fastest growth rates of urban centres during the intercensal period of 1970 to 1980 have been recorded in the east coast states of Kelantan (8.7 per cent), Pahang (7.7 per cent), and Terengganu (7.5 per cent), with Sabah showing a growth rate of 6.5 per cent. However, except for Sabah, these rates of growth fell off between 1981 and 1985. In the case of Sabah the growth rate was 6.6 per cent, and for Selangor the growth rate was 9.8 per cent, by far the largest rate of growth recorded over the last 15 years under consideration.

The accelerated growth was common to almost all states except Melaka, due to its small areal extent and relative lack of development. The levelling off and some slight decline in rates of urbanization for all states except Melaka and Perak for the period 1981-85 were indicative of the beginnings of the process of stabilization and consolidation of existing urban centres. It also suggests that the Kuala Lumpur conurbation may be attracting many more in-migrants than can be accounted for by additions to the population through natural increase. For the country as a whole it also meant that more people were living in a smaller number of large metropolitan centres.

To confirm this hypothesis of urban concentration, it will be necessary to study the growth trends of the largest towns in Malaysia. The 1970 Population Census offers a convenient cut-off since it defines metropolitan towns as those with more than 75,000 people. Using this criterion it was found that in 1970 there were eight such towns, whereas by 1980 the list had increased to 14 (see Table 4.4). Kuala Lumpur occupied the top rank in size of population in both 1970 and 1980. In fact, the dominance of Kuala Lumpur was very evident as it had three times as many people as the next largest town, Ipoh, and nearly four times as many as that of the third-ranked centre, Georgetown. The expansion of the city area of Kuala Lumpur in 1974 from 93 to 243 square kilometres at the time of the declaration of its Federal Territory status also confirmed

Table 4.4. Malaysia: Metropolitan towns, 1970 and 1980

| Town | Size | | Absolute change | | Average annual change 1970-80 |
| | 1970 | 1980 | 1970-80 | | |
	(000s)	(000s)	(000s)	(%)	(%)
Kuala Lumpur	452	938	486	108	7.3
Georgetown	270	251	-19	-7	-0.7
Ipoh	248	300	52	21	1.9
Johor Bahru	136	250	114	84	6.1
Kelang	114	196	82	72	5.4
Petaling Jaya	93	218	125	134	8.5
Melaka	86	88	2	2	0.2
Seremban	80	136	56	70	5.3
Kuala Terengganu	53	187	134	253	12.6
Kota Baharu	55	171	116	211	11.3
Taiping	55	149	94	171	9.9
Kuantan	43	137	94	219	11.6
Sibu	51	87	44	86	5.3
Butterworth	61	77	16	26	2.3

Sources: Malaysia (1972: 207-83); Khoo (1982a: 92-4).

Notes: In the 1970 census of population and housing, metropolitan towns were defined as those having a population 75,000 or more.

Average annual growth rate has been calculated as follows:
$$r = 1 / n \log_e P_n / P_o$$
where: r average annual rate of growth
n exact number of years between P_o and P_n
P_o population in initial year
P_n population in the later year.

the city's status as the nation's most important political, economic, and social urban centre (Leong 1981: 261).

A second feature of growth trends among metropolitan towns was the rate at which some towns have been growing relative to others. One indicator of this dynamism in the system was the change in ranking between 1970 and 1980 (Figure 4.3). Except for Johor Bahru (fourth rank) and Sibu (thirteenth rank), all other towns experienced a change in rank; four towns experienced a fall in rank and six improved their positions.[3] Leinbach (1971: 83) has suggested that despite the fluctuations in position, rank correlations between the five censuses 1911-57 indicate a degree of temporal stability. A similar analysis by Pryor (1973: 59) confirmed the earlier findings and added that there was temporal stability for the period 1957-70.

Such changes in rank positions are closely linked to the average annual rates of change. It will be seen that Kuala Terengganu (12.6 per cent), Kuantan (11.6 per cent), and Kota Baharu (11.3 per cent) have experienced the most rapid growth over the 1970-80 inter-censal period, partly accounting for the improvements in their rank positions. On the west coast of the peninsula only Petaling Jaya and Taiping showed high growth rates (8.5 per cent and 9.9 per cent respectively). Georgetown recorded a relative decline in population. However, this was somewhat illusory because the apparent loss of population was included in the newly established local government authorities of Ayer Itam, Tajung To'Kong, Gelugor, and Tanjung Bunga. These local authority areas were contiguous with the municipality of Georgetown but had at least 10,000 people. It should be noted also that in the list of metropolitan towns only the east Malaysian town of Sibu in Sarawak is featured. Other large towns in Sabah and Sarawak, such as Kuching, Miri, Sandakan and Kota Kinabalu, would have been included if the metropolitan town threshold were lowered to 50,000. In the event, these towns have been excluded on statistical grounds. However, this does not mean that they were unimportant; by legal, administrative, or commercial criteria they may be more significant than some metropolitan towns in peninsular Malaysia.

The distribution of the urban population by size of urban centre is shown in Table 4.5. Slightly less than a fifth of the urban population lived in towns of 10,000 to 50,000 people. Nearly two-thirds lived in towns larger than 100,000 inhabitants. The total number of people living in urban centres in 1980 was about 4.6 million. Thus one in three persons in Malaysia lived in an urban area, and most probably could be found in the three largest metropolitan areas of Kuala Lumpur, Ipoh, and

Figure 4.3. Malaysia: Rank order of metropolitan towns, 1947-80

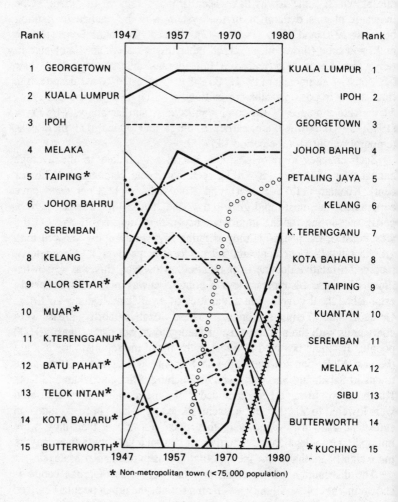

* Non-metropolitan town (<75,000 population)

Table 4.5. Malaysia: Distribution of urban population by size of urban
centres, 1947-80

Size of urban centre	Population (000s)				Average annual growth (%)		
	1947	1957	1970	1980	1947-1957	1957-1970	1970-1980
Above 100,000	518	884	1,330	2,933	5.5	3.2	7.9
50,000 - 100,000	293	418	607	768	3.6	2.9	2.3
30,000 - 50,000	64	114	167	242	5.9	3.0	3.7
20,000 - 30,000	64	132	172	297	7.5	2.0	5.5
10,000 - 20,000	87	224	286	358	10.0	1.9	2.3
Malaysia urban population	-	-	2,562	4,598	-	-	5.0
Peninsular Malaysia Total population	4,909	6,279	8,810	11,188	-	2.6	2.4
Malaysia Total population	-	-	10,440	13,486	-	-	2.6

Sources: Malaya/Malaysia *Population Census 1947; 1957; 1970; 1980.*

Notes: Average annual growth rate has been calculated as follows:

$$r = 1/n \log_e P_n / P_o$$

where: r average annual rate of growth
n exact number of years between P_o and P_n
P_o population in initial year
P_n population in the later year.

Georgetown. This pattern will probably continue in the future since these metropolitan areas are growing about one-and-a-half times faster than the national rate of urban growth and three times faster than the population growth of the country as a whole.

This account of urban growth has excluded some smaller centres from consideration as only settlements with more than 10,000 people were examined. Nevertheless, it can be concluded that urban growth and development have been distributed unequally across the states of Malaysia. The unequal distribution of urban growth was clearly related to the spatial variations in economic activity. In addition, some cities were already large, thus tending to account for a much faster relative growth. It is not surprising therefore that there are differences in the rates of growth of urban centres among the states just as much as there are differentials in the recency of such growth.

The increase in the number of urban settlements was most dramatic in the intercensal period 1947-57 and this trend has continued for the subsequent census periods of 1957-70 and 1970-80. There are now eight times as many urban settlements as there were at the start of the century.

But there have been suggestions that the pace of urbanization slackened in the intercensal period between 1957 and 1970 (Saw 1972; Pryor 1973; Hirschmann 1976: 448). The slower pace of urbanization appears to have continued in the period between 1970 and 1980. Salih and Young (1981: 131) have suggested five reasons for this slackening in the urbanization process:

1. rural development has succeeded in retaining potential rural-urban Malay migrants in the cities and prevented them from 'voting with their feet' and relocating
2. the bulk of the rural-urban in-migrants are Malays who are easily absorbed into the government sector. This sector consists of two streams, a smaller group of new graduates and educated elites joining the civil service, and a larger group, the majority of which are absorbed into the expanding 'protective services' - army, police, and other paramilitary forces
3. rural migrants to Sabah and Sarawak and contract labourers to Singapore and Saudi Arabia accounted for the slowing down of urbanization
4. since urbanization in Malaysia is measured only in terms of gazetted areas, it ignores rural migration to peripheral areas of large towns. These migrants therefore are undetected in the official 'urban' data yet they make up an important component of the total population

5. improved transport infrastructure has opened the way for long-distance commuting which has effectively slowed down rural-urban migration, for example commuters from Seremban to Kuala Lumpur.

Such a fortuitous circumstance of low levels of urbanization may provide planners with the opportunity to manage urbanization in a way that could aid in achieving the government's policy of restructuring society. Restrictions on urban development in already congested centres, redirection of migration flows from rural areas to settled regional areas and other administrative devices may help produce a pattern of urbanization which coincides with the aspirations of government policy.

The slow pace of urbanization in Malaysia is unexceptional (Hirschmann 1976: 458), at least when compared with neighbouring countries. However, Jones (1975: 99) suggests that Malaysia's rapid economic development encourages an equally fast rate of urbanization. The question is how to reconcile these divergent viewpoints and how to account for the rapid physical growth of individual urban centres. It is suggested that the answer to these questions lies in the concept of primacy and in how one defines 'urban', because a low urban threshold figure may suggest apparent rapidity of change as compared with a more realistic threshold. The key therefore is an understanding of the broad processes associated with urban growth.

The Urban Hierarchy

When Malaysia's 25 largest towns are plotted on a log-normal graph showing their respective sizes and ranking, a rank size distribution is apparent.[4] Figure 4.4 shows that the distribution is uniform although there have been internal changes within the ranks through the various censuses. The minor shifts in rank position have occurred because of the tendency towards a stabilization of growth rates. Greater variability in growth rates has occurred in urban centres below 10,000 people and the growth rates of medium-sized towns are much higher than those of metropolitan towns.

Pryor (1973) used the concept of primacy to assess the degree to which the largest settlement in a state is 'super-eminent' in size in relation to other cities in the region. In disaggregating the data on the basis of each state, he measured the degree of dominance of the largest city in relation to the next four largest cities in that state. On the basis of this method, Kuala Lumpur produced the second lowest primacy index, while Johor Bahru and Alor Setar dominated the states of Johor and Kedah respectively to a very high degree. There was no causal relationship between the relative dominance of the largest city and the tendency for a given state to have a population that was predominantly urban-based. Seremban and Kuala Terengganu increased their primacy between 1957 and 1970 while Melaka and Johor Bahru experienced the largest reductions in primacy in their respective states over the 13 years under consideration.

The significance of this discussion is that primate cities tend to dominate economic activity in particular areas and, in general, the larger they become the more dominant they are. This self-generative pattern of growth affects development and urbanization processes in a positive way. The pattern of primacy may be indicative of the pattern of economic development.

Another index was devised in Pryor's study to measure a region's degree of urban concentration since it was recognized that the percentage of population in a given settlement-size class bore a direct relationship to the population as a whole. A modified index of urban concentration[5] measures the ratio of high urban population (20,000 and over) by the ratio of rural population (less than 1,000). On this basis Pulau Pinang and Selangor have indices two and a half to three times the degree of urban concentration of their nearest rivals. Perlis could not be assessed because of an absence of settlements of the required size, while Kelantan, Kedah, and Terengganu characterized the lower end of the scale. The highest increases in urban concentration were in the states of Pahang and Perak. These results have led to the hypothesis that an inverse relationship should obtain between primacy and urban concentration because high primacy occurs with one large city and a largely underdeveloped settlement pattern at the lower end. However, Pryor concluded that no such statistical correlation existed in peninsular Malaysia to confirm the hypothesis.

Statistical Summary

The Malaysian urban structure in the decade of the 1980s was in a state of flux, as evidenced by the discussions above. There is a movement closer to adherence to the rank-size rule as time goes by. However, there is an absence of cities in the 250,000 to 500,000 category as well as of cities between 10,000 and 30,000, not dissimilar to the 'missing link' in the mid-range sized cities in Melanesia (Ward and Ward 1980). Urbanization, though slow in the poorer states in peninsular Malaysia and in Sabah and Sarawak, has gathered pace in the 1970s and 1980s. It is not

Figure 4.4. Malaysia: Rank-size distribution of the 25 largest towns, 1911-80

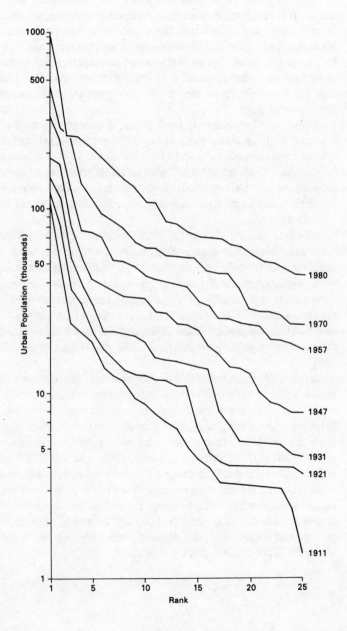

clear from available evidence why poorer states have slower rates of urbanization. A probable reason may be that as income opportunities are unavailable in urban areas owing to low levels of economic activity, the expected inflow of labour from rural areas is staunched.

There is also a close relationship between urbanization and GDP per capita. It is submitted that because transport, commerce, government, and other services are urban-based there will be a high positive correlation between urbanization and these sectors of the economy, and conversely a high negative correlation with non-urban-based activities. Moreover, the secondary and tertiary sectors of the economy may be expected to generate higher levels of income than the primary sector of agriculture, forestry and fishing.

In terms of the urban informal sector, it may be expected that urban migrants will be ambivalent since there are marginal differences in income levels in both rural and urban locations. It is not clear, however, how income levels compare between urban informal sector activities and those engaged in the rural cash-crop export sector. The expectation is that the rural export sector has a firm grip on farm labour so as not to impel it towards the city.

However, it is clear from Table 4.6 that some of these hypotheses may have some basis. Correlation analyses between the proportion of urban population to the GDP per capita and all other sectors show significant association except for the sector comprised of mining, manufacturing, construction, and utilities. The correlation coefficient between the urban population and GDP per capita yielded 0.91 (significant at the 95 per cent level) and the correlation of the urban population with agriculture yielded the expected negative association of -0.78 (significant at the 95 per cent level).[6]

A general statement from these analyses is that high levels of urbanization on a state-wide basis are correlated with high levels of GDP per capita. This describes the group consisting of Kuala Lumpur, Selangor, Terengganu, and Pulau Pinang. A second observation is that there are a large number of states which have moderate levels of urbanization and are associated with average levels of GDP per capita. Kelantan stands out only because it has average levels of urbanization and a low GDP per capita. This suggests that there may be other explanatory variables that need to be considered. It could be perhaps that the ethnicity of towns and cities may provide some understanding of the processes of growth and decay and the relative well-being of urban centres in Malaysia. This aspect is discussed next.

Table 4.6. Malaysia: GDP per capita, sectoral shares of the GDP, and urbanization, by state, 1985

State	GDP per capita ($)	Index	Sectoral shares of the GDP (%)			Urban share of population (%)
			A	M	S	
Johor	3,324	88	29	32	39	39
Kedah	2,358	63	48	14	38	15
Kelantan	1,740	46	39	15	46	30
Melaka	2,765	74	18	32	50	23
Negri Sembilan	3,846	102	28	37	35	37
Pahang	3,495	93	45	20	35	25
Perak	3,194	85	22	39	39	33
Perlis	2,604	69	42	19	39	10
Pulau Pinang	4,120	110	5	46	49	54
Sabah	3,572	95	34	34	32	23
Sarawak	3,085	82	21	49	30	19
Selangor	4,963	132	11	53	36	46
Terengganu	4,719	126	19	58	23	47
Wilayah Persekutuan / Kuala Lumpur	7,783	207	*	23	77	100
Malaysia	3,758	100	21	36	43	37

Source: Malaysia (1986: 174-5, 185).

Notes: * Less than 1 per cent.

A Agriculture, forestry, and fishing.

M Mining, manufacturing, construction, and utilities.

S Transport, commerce, government, and other services.

ETHNICITY AND URBANIZATION

In Malaysia the Emergency of 1948-60 boosted the urban population from 16 per cent in 1947 to 26 per cent in 1957, a surge that saw the relocation of the rural Chinese communities into new urban villages. This emergency helped crystallize an existing situation by hastening the pace of Chinese urbanization (Dobby 1952: 172). The Emergency after May 13, 1969, marked the beginnings of accelerated Malay urbanization by policy design within the context of a slowing down of the national urbanization process. As a consequence of this phenomenon, any discussion of future urbanization of the country must pay particular attention to the question of Malay urbanization brought about by the NEP. The rise of a Malay (*Bumiputera*) commercial and industrial community will necessarily be concentrated in urban areas since this is where most secondary and tertiary sector activities are to be found. Moreover, given that the rural component is predominantly Malay and that future urban population increases will result from rural-urban migration, any acceleration of urbanization will mean predominantly Malay urbanization.

The shares of the various ethnic groups in urban areas for peninsular Malaysia between 1947 and 1980 are shown in Table 4.7. Attention is directed to the peninsula because the question of ethnicity is much more pressing here than in the Bornean states and also because the dichotomy between Malays and non-Malays is much clearer in so far as efforts to implement the NEP are concerned.

A distinctive feature of ethnic urbanization in Malaysia is that the immigrant communities have always been a highly urbanized group. This is in part explained by the nature of their economic activity as well as by their settlement patterns. Such a statement applies equally to the Chinese and Indians in peninsular Malaysia as well as to Chinese, Indians, and Malays in Sabah and Sarawak.

The Chinese are by far the most urbanized. Particularly in the post-war period, they have become increasingly concentrated in urban areas. The resettlement of Chinese rural squatters into New Villages involved nearly half a million people. In 1980 some of these New Villages crossed the rural-urban threshold to become urban centres in their own right, for example, Serdang Baru and Ampang, both in Selangor. Many smaller urban areas are overwhelmingly Chinese in character. Nearly 56 per cent of all Chinese in Malaysia live in urban areas.

The pattern for Indians (and Pakistanis), as well as for other ethnic groups such as Europeans and Eurasians, shows a similarity to the Chinese pattern except that the degree of urban concentration is much lower. Even so, these groups have also become more urbanized since the

Table 4.7. Peninsular Malaysia: Degree of urbanization, by ethnic group, 1947-80

Ethnic group	Total population in urban areas (%)				Average annual growth rate (%)
	1947	*1957*	*1970*	*1980*	*1970-80*
Malay	7.3	11.2	14.9	25.4	6.3
Chinese	31.1	44.7	47.4	55.9	2.9
Indian	25.8	30.6	34.7	41.2	3.2
Other	46.2	49.3	40.8	41.6	4.5
Total urban	*15.9*	*26.5*	*28.7*	*37.5*	*4.3*

Sources: Malaya and Malaysia, *Population Census 1947; 1957; 1970; 1980.*

post-war period, the proportion rising from a quarter of the total Indian population to about two-fifths. The urban proportion of other groups, however, has fallen from 46 per cent in 1947 to 42 per cent in 1980.

Since 1947 the basic ethnic structure of urban areas in peninsular Malaysia has remained largely unchanged. There are, however, signs of a greater percentage of Malays living in urban areas, as witnessed by the jump from only 7 per cent of total Malay population just after the Second World War to about one-tenth at independence and to about a quarter in 1980. In fact, the average annual growth rate of urban Malays between 1970 and 1980 was 6.3 per cent, about twice that of the other two major ethnic groups and nearly one and a half times faster than the growth of the total urban population in peninsular Malaysia. However, the share of the

Malay urban population was still below its proportion in the total population. The growth of the Malay population in urban centres has been attributed to the rise of Malay nationalism, the penetration of the monetary economy into rural areas, and to government policy.

In a study of Malay urbanization and the ethnic profile of urban centres in peninsular Malaysia, Lee (1977) used a diversity index devised by Lieberson (1969). This index measures the degree of homogeneity or heterogeneity along a continuum. In the Malaysian context all urban populations were analysed with regard to a single polynomial of four terms: Malay, Chinese, Indian, and 'others'. The index, which is between zero and one, gives a measure of diversity, with values closer to one indicating greater diversity or less homogeneity in the urban area in terms of ethnicity. Diversity indices were computed for each of the urban areas in 1957 and 1970 and Lee (1977: 231-3) concluded that on the whole the trend was towards greater ethnic homogeneity. Malays were becoming an important component in the population of metropolitan areas such as Seremban, Kuala Lumpur, Petaling Jaya, Kelang, Georgetown, and Melaka. Furthermore, Malay urbanization was directed not only towards urban areas but also to those which were essentially Malay. The directional bias of Malay migration towards larger urban centres was also confirmed by regression analysis of the same data.[7] There is nothing to suggest that the patterns identified by Lee using the 1970 census data will change dramatically when the same method is applied to the 1980 census data.

The hypothesis of 'negative coexistence' proposed by Lee is largely validated: urban centres are likely to continue along the path of ethnic polarity in either the Chinese or the Malay direction. Such a conclusion, however, appears to be diametrically opposed to current thinking among policy planners. The policy is to encourage more Malays into cities and into urban secondary and tertiary activities. Accelerated Malay urbanization may, however, result in the displacement of non-Malays in the workplace. This displacement is inconsistent with the basic tenets of the NEP, which is premissed on shares of an expanded national cake rather than on 'disruptive redistribution'.

Salih and Young (1981: 141) have suggested that the mode of production may need to be changed in terms of choice of techniques. One way could be to mobilize the informal sector because of its labour-absorptive capacity. Malaysia was fortunate in that urban growth *per se* was not a real problem. The problem was one of urban restructuring in a pluralistic milieu so that the internal components of urban growth and development could be reorganized to reflect the aspirations of Malaysian society. A lack of understanding of rural-urban processes, as well as ineffective and inappropriate policies which themselves are based on partial understanding, may exacerbate existing problems. The aims of urban social restructuring may thus go unmet (Salih and Young 1981: 143).

RURAL-URBAN MIGRATION

The 1980 census provided for the first time data on inter- and intra-rural and urban migration flows. Persons who stated that they had previously lived in a place other than their birthplace were classified as 'urban' if that place had a population of more than 10,000 and if it was a gazetted area. All other localities were considered rural. Four types of flows may thus be discerned: urban-urban, urban-rural, rural-urban, and rural-rural (Kwok and Singh 1983; Khoo 1983).

Table 4.8 shows that in Malaysia the major form of migration was from rural to rural areas. This accounted for 45 per cent of total internal migration (involving about 1.2 million people), a statistic attributable to rural development and to land development schemes. It is possible, however, that there may be over-reporting of rural-rural migration and an under-reporting of urban-urban migration. Rural migrants to fringes of metropolitan towns were classified as rural if they settled outside the boundaries of these gazetted areas. Similarly, urban migrants moving to the fringe of urban areas and beyond the boundaries were deemed to be urban-rural migrants. Caution is thus required when interpreting internal migration data. Rural-urban migrants constituted only 10 per cent of all migrants between 1970 and 1980, amounting to about 410,000 persons. When the data are disaggregated by region, rural-rural migration is dominant, with 44 per cent of the total number of internal migrants in peninsular Malaysia, 57 per cent in Sabah, and 54 per cent in Sarawak. However, some differences are apparent because in Sabah and Sarawak urban-rural migration was the second largest stream whereas in peninsular Malaysia, urban-urban movements were next in importance. Intra-urban migration in peninsular Malaysia overall was much greater as a consequence of the higher degree of urbanization.

The data were subjected to statistical analysis to ascertain whether there were any differences between the origins and destinations of these migration streams. The question was whether there was a movement bias towards either urban or rural destinations depending on origins. A two-by-two chi-squared test was used to show that there were significant differences between urban or rural origins and urban or rural destinations

Table 4.8. Malaysia: Rural and urban migration (during the ten years preceding the 1980 census), 1980* (000s)

Area of origin	Area of destination		
	Urban	Rural	Total
Malaysia			
Urban	544	477	1,021
Rural	410	1,169	1,579
Total	954	1,646	2,600
Peninsular Malaysia			
Urban	518	417	935
Rural	364	1,005	1,369
Total	882	1,422	2,304
Sabah			
Urban	15	25	40
Rural	19	78	97
Total	34	103	137
Sarawak			
Urban	12	36	48
Rural	27	86	113
Total	39	122	161

Source: Khoo (1983: 77-8).

Note: * Excludes migrants from Sabah and Sarawak to Peninsular Malaysia and vice versa. Migrants with unknown urban or rural origin have also been excluded.

in all cases except one. In the exceptional case, in Sarawak, there was no difference between origins and destinations.[8]

The migration streams for each of the ethnic groups are shown in Table 4.9. For Malays and Indians, intra-rural migration was the predominant form of movement. This is not unexpected since a majority of Malays resided in rural areas and there was a tendency for Indian estate workers to move from one rural area to another rather than to urban centres. However, in the case of the Chinese the predominant form of migration was intra-urban, reflecting the relative strength of numbers of Chinese living in urban areas. Again, chi-squared analysis was performed and, apart from the 'others' category, there were significant differences between the origins and destinations of the three major ethnic groups.[9] This conclusion may be explained in terms of the larger than expected stream in one cell of the matrix which could have influenced the outcome of the statistical calculations. Nevertheless, the implications are quite clear that while intra-rural migration predominated, rural-urban migration among the Malays and other indigenous groups was becoming important. Population projections given by the *Fifth Malaysia Plan 1986-1990* showed that Malays and other *Bumiputera* in urban areas would register the highest rate of growth (6 per cent per annum), compared with 2.5 per cent for the Chinese and 3 per cent of the Indians. As a consequence, the Malay urban population is projected to increase from 2.2 million to 3 million during the plan period. Malays and other *Bumiputera*, therefore, will constitute the largest ethnic group of the total urban population in peninsular Malaysia by 1990 (Malaysia 1986: 133).

As a result of rural-urban migration and urban growth, a particular problem that arises is the lack of employment opportunities. More accurately, there is a mismatch between employment creation on the one hand and the combination of the rate of in-migration and natural increase on the other. Urban employment and unemployment therefore are seen as a necessary concomitant of urban growth. How Malaysian urban centres have responded to increasing numbers of people seeking work is discussed in the next section.

URBAN EMPLOYMENT AND UNEMPLOYMENT

One of the principal goals of economic development is the reduction of open urban unemployment as well as hidden unemployment and underemployment in rural areas (Paukert *et al.* 1981: 9). The prime concern here is to examine the urban side of the equation. This focus has been chosen because the relationships between urban in-migration,

Table 4.9. Malaysia: Rural and urban migration (during the ten years preceding the 1980 census), by ethnic group, 1980* (000s)

Area of origin and ethnic group	Area of destination		
	Urban	Rural	Total
Malays and other indigenous			
Urban	242	279	521
Rural	280	905	1,185
Total	522	1,184	1,706
Chinese			
Urban	236	141	377
Rural	98	154	252
Total	334	295	629
Indians			
Urban	62	54	116
Rural	30	106	136
Total	92	160	252
Others			
Urban	4	3	7
Rural	2	4	6
Total	6	7	13

Source: Khoo (1983: 79).

Note: * Excludes migrants from Sabah and Sarawak to Peninsular Malaysia and vice versa. Migrants with unknown urban or rural origin have also been excluded.

unemployment, and urban growth are important considerations when devising programmes to restructure urban society. Basically, it is a question of whether the urban economy is able to absorb new additions to its population and workforce given natural increases, in-migration, and a lagging rural sector. However, there is an inherent contradiction. It has been theorized that the greater the growth of employment in a city, the higher would be the in-migration rate and the higher its unemployment level (Todaro 1981: Ch. 9).

The question that arises first is whether or not such a theory is tenable and, second, whether it is applicable in the Malaysian context. Even if it can be persuasively argued in the affirmative, there is still a need to verify its applicability. For example, economic policies containing programmes that have a large labour absorptive capacity, particularly those relating to the informal sector, would have to be devised. In addition, if this strategy were to succeed, there should also be no differentials between urban and rural areas in terms of job opportunities. This would help staunch the flow of rural in-migrants. These issues need to be further explored.

As the issues of employment and labour force participation rates have already been discussed in Chapter 1, attention here is switched to the issue of unemployment, particularly the urban-rural differential. The argument is that where unemployment rates are higher in rural than in urban areas, in-migration will most likely take place.

Where the transfer of the unemployed to the city has already taken place, there may be out-migration and a reverse flow to the rural areas. However, this is thought to be unlikely because it is expected that employment creation, apart from land development schemes, will be more rapid in urban than in rural areas. In any event, recent census data suggest greater unemployment in the rural areas.

A basic difficulty of studying unemployment is to enumerate those who are apparently without jobs and are not seeking work. The practice of the Malaysian Department of Statistics is to classify those inactively unemployed (for various reasons) as unemployed, in addition to those who were seeking work during a 'reference week'.[10]

Of the 4.6 million persons aged 15-64 who were in the labour force in Malaysia in 1980, 6 per cent were unemployed. In regional terms the highest unemployment rates were recorded in Sabah (8 per cent) compared with 6 per cent and 5 per cent respectively for peninsular Malaysia and Sarawak (see Table 4.10). On a state-wide basis, the less industrialized states of the east coast registered the highest rates of unemployment (Terengganu 8.7 per cent and Kelantan 8.1 per cent). The more advanced and modern industrialized economies such as Selangor and Kuala Lumpur reported the lowest rates of unemployment. The

Table 4.10. Malaysia: Number of unemployed persons and unemployment rates of the labour force aged 15-64 years by state and stratum, 1980

State	Unemployed persons (000s)	Unemployment rate (%)	Unemployed persons	
			Urban (%)	Rural (%)
Johor	31.5	5.8	5.3	6.1
Kedah	27.1	7.2	6.5	7.4
Kelantan	23.7	8.1	8.3	8.1
Melaka	9.9	7.0	6.4	7.2
Negri Sembilan	11.3	6.1	4.9	6.7
Pahang	14.0	5.2	4.8	5.3
Perak	39.3	6.9	5.7	7.4
Perlis	4.3	7.8	6.1	7.9
Pulau Pinang	17.9	5.5	5.2	5.9
Sabah	27.0	8.0	6.2	8.3
Sarawak	24.2	5.0	6.7	5.1
Selangor	25.8	4.8	3.7	5.5
Terengganu	14.9	8.7	10.1	7.7
Wilayah Persekutuan/ Kuala Lumpur	14.7	3.8	3.8	-
Malaysia	*285.6*	*6.2*	*5.3*	*6.6*

Source: Khoo (1983: 122, 124).

differences between unemployment rates are associated with urban-rural differentials, age groups, and sex composition. It will be observed from the table that rural rates of unemployment were higher than urban rates for all states except Kelantan, Terengganu, and Kuala Lumpur. In the case of Kuala Lumpur no rural data are recorded. However, for Kelantan and Terengganu, the high unemployment rates for urban areas suggest that the drift into urban centres has already begun. It implies that the rural areas have been unable to absorb new additions to the labour force. Interestingly, the degree of urbanization in Terengganu was fairly high (43 per cent) as compared with the national figure (34 per cent). Both Terengganu and Kelantan had two of the highest average annual rates of urban growth between 1970 and 1980, 7.5 per cent and 8.7 per cent respectively.[11] The primary cities in these states recorded two of the fastest rates of growth among all urban centres in Malaysia.[12]

Table 4.11 shows the distribution of unemployed persons by age and stratum. Unemployment was heavily concentrated among young persons who were first-time job seekers. In 1980, about 64 per cent of the unemployed in Malaysia were in the 15-24 age group. In general, for most age-group categories the rates of unemployment were much higher in Sabah and Sarawak when compared with peninsular Malaysia, probably because those states contain a much smaller and less dynamic secondary and tertiary sector. Such a pattern replicates itself when urban-rural data are tabulated.[13]

Thus, contrary to past trends, data from the 1980 census indicated that unemployment rates were higher in the rural areas than in the urban areas for all states with the exception of Terengganu, Kelantan, and Sarawak.[14] Part of the reason for this difference was a more rapid decline in the urban unemployment rate. For example, in peninsular Malaysia in 1975 the unemployment rate in urban areas was 7.2 per cent, compared with 6.4 per cent in the rural areas. However, by 1980 the corresponding rates were 5.1 and 5.9 per cent respectively (Khoo 1983: 122). Trend analysis shows that the unemployment rate for urban areas declined nearly four times faster than that for rural areas. A plausible explanation of the faster decline in the urban unemployment rate was the rapid expansion of employment opportunities in the urban sector. Unemployment in rural areas increased because of a slower pace of job creation and the reduced absorptive capacity of agricultural activities.

A further explanation was that because of the changes in the way in which unemployed persons were categorized, it is possible that the degree of underemployment, especially in informal sector activities, may have increased relative to those who were unemployed, thus hiding the real rate of unemployment in urban areas. Thus, whether the percentage of the

Table 4.11. Malaysia: Percentage distribution of unemployed persons by age group, region, and stratum, 1980 (%)

Region and stratum	Age group							
	15-19	20-24	25-29	30-39	40-49	50-59	60-64	15-64
Peninsular Malaysia	40	27	9	8	6	6	4	6.1
Sabah	28	23	12	14	12	8	3	8.0
Sarawak	30	22	10	12	10	10	7	5.0
Malaysia	*38*	*26*	*9*	*9*	*7*	*7*	*4*	*6.2*
Urban	16	7	3	4	4	8	8	5.3
Rural	19	10	4	5	5	9	9	6.6
Total	*18*	*9*	*4*	*5*	*5*	*9*	*9*	*6.2*

Source: Khoo (1983: 122-3).

workforce in the informal sector had increased and a greater proportion were earning subsistence-level incomes will be difficult to estimate, let alone collect information as regards its prevalence and incidence.

The data used above are too generalized to verify Todaro's hypothesis. Apart from the unavailability of data by urban centres, the 1980 census definitions for the various categories of employment and unemployment are different from those used in the 1970 census. Consequently, it would be nearly impossible to estimate the growth of employment in cities with the available published data. In addition, while data tell us about in-migration over the 10 years prior to the census in 1980, finer-grained time series data would be required to estimate growth rates for each individual urban centre. However, a major conclusion is that the unemployment problem was more acute in rural areas for every age group and for females than in urban areas.

SOCIAL ISSUES AND URBAN DEVELOPMENT

The previous sections on ethnicity, rural-urban migration, and employment in urban areas have directed the discussion towards residual issues which show that Malaysian cities are highly similar to those in other parts of South East Asia. The provision of housing, the rehabilitation of squatter settlements, provision of basic services, and the eradication of poverty and social inequality are foremost in government urban development programmes.

A conventional means of meeting housing needs has been public housing programmes. Under the various development plans, especially the *Fourth* and *Fifth Malaysia Plans*, the public sector concentrated mainly on building low-cost houses and provided sites and services. The private sector provided medium- to high-cost housing in urban areas. During the *Fourth Malaysia Plan* the public sector constructed 201,950 housing units, meeting nearly 50 per cent of the planned target. Of this, about 35 per cent were low-cost units built in urban areas as walk-up high-rise flats. These units were either sold outright or rented out with an option to purchase by those who had rented for a minimum period of ten years. Of the 204,200 units constructed by the private sector, only about 9 per cent of the houses were low-cost, as compared with about 42 per cent in the medium-cost category. The *Fifth Malaysia Plan* demonstrates a need for about 835,500 units to cater for population growth and replacement throughout the country. Of this, nearly 75 per cent will be required in the low-cost category (Malaysia 1986: 521-7).

It is evident that investment in urban housing has been insufficient to meet demand, especially for the low-cost units. Invariably, the newly created housing stock has served the better-off segments of the urban population. To counter this, Bank Negara introduced the Special Housing Loan Scheme in 1982 to reduce speculation in the housing market and to dampen excessive demand for housing. In addition, to accelerate housing development the government promoted the use of prefabricated systems of construction, the establishment of one-stop agencies, and reviewed and updated legislation and regulations to standardize these among the states. The government also continued to develop housing projects jointly with the private sector. This had the dual effect of reducing the financial burden on the public sector and increasing private sector participation, especially in constructing low-cost houses.

The scarcity and high cost of urban land are seen by many as an obstacle to greater participation by private developers in providing low-cost accommodation. Sometimes this is cited as justification for greater government participation in urban land markets. Probably a more cogent reason is the incidence of squatters, illegal settlers on public and private land, in major metropolitan areas throughout the country. In Kuala Lumpur alone, it has been estimated that in 1980 there were about 240,000 inhabitants (22 per cent of the population) who lived in squatter settlements. About two-fifths of these squatters were Malays and *Bumiputera*. More than three-quarters of these people were newly arrived in-migrants from surrounding areas (Leong 1981: 273).

In so far as the issue of squatters and squatting is concerned, the government has neither a coherent national policy nor a consistent programme for tackling the problem. The most obvious mechanism has been the use of legislative powers such as the National Land Code, 1965, and its amendments in 1974, and the Clearance of Squatters Regulations, 1969. Their common theme is squatter eradication and the measures include the demolition of dwellings, eviction, fines, and imprisonment. The Code specifies a fine of $10,000 and/or one year's imprisonment for squatting. Yet despite these measures, one estimate suggests that there is an average in-migration of about 1,000 persons per week into metropolitan Kuala Lumpur, making it difficult for city administrators to cope with, or check, squatter development (Chan 1983: 503).

The framing of policies and programmes to help squatters and solve urban squatting will involve more than physical resettlement and legal controls. Checks on rural-urban migration by attacking the root cause of such movement, the availability of urban employment, and addressing issues of urban 'dualism' are all required. Together these variables produce a mixture of social effects. On the one hand, there is a group of privileged wage-earning urban residents who live a life-style totally different from that of the less privileged. On the other hand, the latter group is wholly made up of people in the informal sector. Their numbers continue to grow and there is fear that frustration and continued deprivation may induce violence and open confrontation (Dwyer 1972a). In combination with the ethnic variable, the impact on urban areas can be catastrophic if left unchecked.

The provision of urban services may be seen as a principal component of housing supply in urban areas. Public sector investment in the operation and maintenance of water supply, electricity, rubbish removal, drainage, and infrastructure will do much to help expand the supply of urban housing. It will also help restrain increases in land prices for residential development and stimulate private investment in shelter.

One group of fringe urban dwellers that will directly benefit from the provision of such social infrastructure and amenities is the 1.8 million people living in New Villages in 1985. While a majority were engaged in agriculturally based activities to supply urban food needs, others undertook trading and other business activities. Programmes for improving the quality of life of residents of New Villages will continue during the *Fifth Malaysia Plan*, with priority given to redevelopment of these urban centres. In addition, small industries will be created and promoted to turn them into economic centres (Malaysia 1986: 528).

Any discussion on managing the litany of urban social problems will be incomplete without mention of the provision of an accessible transport system in urban areas. Every urban transport system plays a central role in facilitating city growth efficiently and equitably. Here 'efficiency' is used in the economic sense of maximizing total welfare, while equity refers to the distribution and allocation of resources in a socially just way. Thus transport is seen as the means of providing the essential link between home and place of work, and between producers and consumers of goods and services.

Transport is also an important source of employment, particularly for the less skilled labour force. The example of trishaw pulling in some urban areas of Malaysia comes readily to mind; being highly labour-intensive, it provides an important source of employment (Rimmer 1982: 65). Other examples include car washers and car-park 'jockeys' who wash and clean cars and direct traffic to any available parking space in congested city centres.

Apart from marginal employment such as this, the urban poor are particularly dependent on transport services. These services determine the poor household's access to employment opportunities. Moreover, accessibility is an important determinant of whether other social and infrastructural amenities are provided in that part of the city. However, high rates of vehicle ownership, mixed traffic, and heavy volumes of all types of traffic have meant that congestion is quite serious in many metropolitan areas. Thus longer journeys to get to work preclude longer hours at productive work.

To overcome problems of access to transport, the introduction of the minibus to the transport system in Kuala Lumpur in 1976 showed that private enterprise could be relied on to provide a successful and profitable service. Within two years of its introduction, over 400 minibuses were operating in the city, providing a service that spread from Petaling Jaya in the southwest to Ampang in the northeast, a distance of approximately 40 kilometres. Yet despite this low-cost, low-capital operation, the government has been investigating the feasibility of a twin transit system of an 'aerobus' and light rail transit to solve some of Kuala Lumpur's transport problems (Specter 1984). It would appear that such a venture would be costly in capital investment and expensive for the average user, such as the minibus passenger. Moreover, the average Malaysian's love affair with the motor car is still as passionate as ever, given that the ownership of 'wheels' bestows social status, independence, and mobility.

URBAN MANAGEMENT AND PLANNING

A number of policy issues remain to be addressed. The first concerns the structure of urban settlements in so far as it impinges on society and economy. Then there is the broader issue of a national urbanization policy that will set the agenda for urban development in the next few decades. Many South East Asian cities have inherited from the colonial period social and economic structures that persist in the 1990s. Some of these cities continue to be ethnically diverse and most have yet to achieve any structural change. Thus the dualistic economy of a modern and a traditional sector (in Geertz's (1963) nomenclature, a firm-type and a bazaar sector) is characteristic of these cities. Much of the urbanization in South East Asia has been characterized by urban growth without either industrialization or marked economic progress. Various labels have been used to describe such patterns, for example, 'urban involution' (Armstrong and McGee 1968), 'pseudo-urbanization' (McGee 1967) and 'over-urbanization' (Hoselitz 1962). In other words, urbanization has been racing ahead independently of industrialization and economic growth.

There have been two consequences of this phenomenon. First, significant additions to the urban population are not absorbed into the urban industrial economy but either remain in the informal sector with low-productivity jobs or are openly unemployed. Second, urban growth becomes an impediment to economic progress since most of the rural-urban migrants have been marginalized and contribute little to economic production. For example, rather than producing new goods, people at the margins are only 'servicing' the transfer of goods from one party to the next as intermediaries. They may also be recycling goods to extend their economic life and perhaps thus defeating the planned obsolescence of such goods. Thus urbanization, rather than a sign of economic progress as suggested by the basic model, may connote an additional obstacle to economic development (Hirschmann 1976: 445).

In so far as Malaysia is concerned, the questions remain as to whether the dualistic urban economy persists and whether urban growth and urbanization have been accompanied by industrialization and economic progress. An immediate response to both enquiries is in the affirmative. Dualism persists hand-in-hand with industrialization and economic progress. In this sense Malaysian urban growth and urbanization are exceptional when compared with other South East Asian nations. But Malaysian urban centres are also at a crossroads; there are many paths, all laden with challenges, opportunities, and problems. The choices made will basically be policy choices and these need to be examined.

The dualism inherent in many Malaysian cities has been given particular attention. Modern sector activities have been accorded due regard under government policies to promote modernization and industrialization. For example, the modern sector has been given priority in infrastructural improvements. The weaker informal sector has been provided with some commensurate services but nowhere near what is required, given that it is the larger of the two sectors in terms of participants and that its potential labour absorptive capacity is much higher. However, by judiciously strengthening the informal sector, the government may go a long way towards reducing the unemployment problem in urban areas and indirectly the problem of urban poverty. For example, positive support has been provided to informal sector employment in urban areas in Malaysia. Informal sector activities have been encouraged by a

much more liberal licensing policy; the enforcement of law through education, not prosecution; the provision of loans and other inducements, particularly for the *Bumiputera* indigenous population;

and the recognition that hawking provides an important avenue for employment and entrepreneurial development.

(McGee and Yeung 1977: 49)

The disparity in income between the modern and the informal sectors is tending to widen and therefore there is an urgent need to tackle problems arising from this dualism in the urban economy. The starting points for achieving these ends may lie in concentrating on strengthening the links between the 'upper' and 'lower' circuits (Missen and Logan 1977) and in maximizing the output from this 'shared space' (Santos 1979).

It has been postulated that an emphasis on growth-oriented strategies will tend to produce increasing rural-urban disparities. Such disparities, it is thought, will result because inevitably the more successful and faster pace of growth will be generated in the urban areas (Prantilla 1981b: 4). In addition, urban growth without significant structural change in the economic and social aspects will lead to the persistence of dualism. As widespread urban poverty will become prevalent in the future, it has been advocated that 'cities for the poor will have to be consciously designed, rather than the poor fitted into cities basically designed for the convenience of the moderately wealthy and the rich' (Dwyer 1972b: 52). In the Malaysian context one suspects that this prescription for the design of cities may be neither acceptable nor applicable.

Thus it is necessary to revise expectations of economic growth to a level that offers a balance between growth and equity. 'If high growth standards are scaled down to reasonable levels, urbanization may not be accompanied by 'opulence, sophistication, and urbanity', but it can at least be graced by satisfaction, fulfilment and a sense of purpose' (Yeung 1978: 29-30). It may be noted that because the nature of the economic system is conceptualized in the capitalist mould, some of the postulates above do not address the root cause of the problem. That is, the capitalist development process itself may engender the persistence of the problems of dualism, an argument which radical theorists may wish to exploit.

Osborn (1974: 253) has concluded that an important consideration for the future development of the country is to reconcile the differentials in the levels of income and opportunity between the rural rich and poor and between the urban rich and poor, more particularly between Malays and non-Malays. He proposed an alternative approach to current patterns of development that calls for public investment in medium-sized cities below the so-called 'threshold of dynamism'.

These medium-sized cities within an urban system give another view of urban growth and urbanization, particularly in relation to changes in economic and industrial structures. The analysis can proceed along three dimensions: first, it may focus on the impact of a 'horizontal shift', such as inter-regional population movement with or without a 'vertical shift' (occupational mobility), on patterns of urban growth. Second, the differential impacts of agglomerated and dispersed industrialization on the functioning of the national urban system may need to be reviewed. Finally, the impact of non-spatial policies on the evolution of the urban system, and policies with an avowed or obvious spatial dimension, may need to be identified and analysed (Honjo 1981: 2-3).

In terms of the broader policy consideration of a national urban system, Malaysia can expect a relatively large proportion of its inhabitants to live in small rural settlements or as non-nucleated populations because of its transitional status as neither a truly 'developed' nor an 'under-developed' nation. It is also clear that the settlement system is much more complex than the simple centre-periphery construct suggests and that multi-nodality will feature prominently in it (Pryor 1973: 60-6). Rapid urbanization is thus of central importance in the national development process. As previously noted, the singular feature of Malaysian urban structure is its lack of urbanization. This circumstance is being reversed by appropriate political action. In proceeding along this path, Hirschmann's (1983: 11) warning that urbanization may be an impediment to economic development will also have to be heeded. For example, the lack of urban employment may force many into the less productive informal sector or may swell the ranks of the unemployed and be part of an unproductive sector. In this sense, greater urbanization may act as a 'drag' on economic development.

Malaysia has never had a deliberate urban development strategy to manage urban growth. Within this context a National Urbanization Policy (NUP) was initiated in early 1980. In accordance with the objectives of the NUP to ensure the orderly development of urban centres, structure plans were prepared to provide detailed proposals for the implementation of urban programmes and guidelines for development controls (Malaysia 1986: 183). Urban development also involves the strengthening of urban centres in less developed states and regions and the evolution of a network of towns in the regions so as to encourage a greater spread of urban development.

Under the *Fifth Malaysia Plan 1986-1990* a two-tiered approach was adopted for the evolution of a closely knit national urban system. At one level comprehensive programmes of satellite towns, infrastructure, and urban renewal for six regional growth centres (Kuala Lumpur,

Georgetown, Johor Bahru, Kuching, and Kota Kinabalu) are expected to enhance their roles in the respective regions. At another level secondary growth centres will be encouraged through programmes that will cater for increased growth and reduce urban diseconomies.

Furthermore, the strategy of concentrating industrial growth in selected urban centres is designed to take advantage of scale and agglomeration economies to generate employment and attract urban-bound migrants - the major component of urban population growth (Malaysia 1986: 196). Comprehensive urban development planning under the NUP will mean that the role and functions of urban centres will be more clearly defined. At a macro-level the economic function of urban centres and their linkages to metropolitan centres will be identified. At a micro-level, structure plans for all state capitals will be prepared and local plans will implement the programmes outlined in these structure plans.

Concurrent with the NUP is a National Spatial Plan (NSP). Such a plan will ensure that regional development programmes and projects will take advantage of the settlement system, the spatial distribution of resources and production capacity, and inter- and intra-regional economic linkages. Together these two plans will provide the basis for the integration of spatial planning at the macro-, sectoral, and project levels; and will take cognisance of plans already in existence, such as the Industrial Master Plan and the National Agricultural Policy strategy.

There is thus an observable policy shift in strategy from the purely sectoral-based attempts of the past to one that is highly integrative within a system of 'natural' regions of the country. Moreover, for the first time there is an explicit enunciation of what the government hopes urbanization will achieve, that is, the provision of better services and facilities for the rural population, thereby giving them a better quality of life (Malaysia 1986: 165). Finally, industrial and urban development will garner prevailing market forces and the economics of location to help foster the national urban system. In summary, it appears that Honjo's (1981) three-dimensional approach to altering economic and industrial structures has been adopted in varying degrees: through horizontal and vertical shifts of the people involved, through agglomeration of industries in which economies of scale dictate, and through aspatial policies that impact on the landscape spatially. This is a brave attempt to go past the crossroads and forge the growth and transformation of Malaysian urban centres in their physical, social, and economic dimensions.

5
PROMOTING INDUSTRIAL GROWTH

Malaysia has provided a fundamentally attractive environment for investors. The stability of government, the freedom in politics, the minimal interference of government, the ample availability of finances, the financial creditworthiness of the country, the substantial base of infrastructure and natural resources, the plentiful supply of relatively well-educated labor, the comparative honesty and efficiency of government administration - all these factors were significant in Malaysia's rapid industrial growth during the 1966-1975 period.

(Young 1980a: 84)

INTRODUCTION

The above quotation sets out some of the bases for the relative success of industrial programmes in Malaysia. In the process of industrialization various strategies have been dominant. For instance, import substitution was a primary source of growth in 1963-68 while domestic demand was more important in 1968-71 (Hoffman and Tan 1980). In the 1980s, industrial development has been assigned a central role in Malaysia's overall diversification programme. This sector is seen as a new source of rapid economic growth, greater employment opportunities, and as a means by which the *Bumiputera* can participate in the economic activities of the country. Moreover, this endeavour assumes a spatial dimension as there was also the need to reduce open urban unemployment, and hidden unemployment and underemployment in the rural areas.

In most developing countries the early phase of economic development is characterized by small household enterprises that involve the whole family. They supply the market with consumer goods like textiles, clothing, and shoes. With industrialization, faster growth leads to larger enterprises, the use of more capital-intensive technology, and world-wide markets for both consumer and capital goods. How Malaysia corresponded to this archetypal pattern of development and its policy response to these challenges occupies a greater part of the discussion in this chapter.

Before outlining the structure of this chapter, we will discuss briefly the conceptual framework within which the promotion of industrial growth is to take place. To begin with McGee's (1986: 35) notion of the world economy as a 'grid or lattice of places or locations which may be larger or smaller than the nation state' is eminently relevant. The grid is delimited by the interaction of six components: business organization, the human and physical resource mix, labour force structure, type of economic activity, class structure, and nation state. By changing the scale, this summary metaphor for the organization of global economic activity could be used as a framework for analyzing Malaysia's industrial growth. In this microcosm can be found all six of McGee's components.

There are three key elements which have determined the nature of Malaysian industrial growth. First, there is the conversion from an import-substituting strategy to one of export expansion. The switch occurred because the domestic market for consumer goods substitution had become saturated, while the attraction of assembly-type activity was too tempting to ignore. Moreover, given Malaysia's active participation in ASEAN, there was some prospect for regional industrial co-operation. However, the industrial base in Malaysia was narrow and difficulties were encountered in penetrating protected overseas markets. Moreover, neighbouring developing countries in Asia appeared to be moving along the same path in switching strategies from import substitution to export expansion so that in the final analysis it was a matter of 'who could do it better and probably cheaper'.

The second factor that has influenced Malaysia's industrial growth is the state's preoccupation with ethnic equity. Since the New Economic Policy there has been a determination to redistribute wealth and restructure employment in commerce and industry to ensure that poverty and employment will no longer be associated with ethnicity. While such a policy may be sound from an equity point of view, it appeared that there might be difficulties in achieving it efficiently. For instance, the policy was premissed on redistribution with growth. But what if there were no growth? Either it would take longer to achieve the equity objectives or they would have to be abandoned altogether.

The final factor is a spatial one. Conscious efforts are being made to disperse industry to areas away from the Kelang Valley. This over-concentration was deemed to be detrimental to other areas and regions.

What was needed was a more balanced distribution of industrial activity, with measures bringing about a dispersion to hitherto industrially poor regions. Thus, through direct policy devices such as locational incentive schemes, growth centre strategies, industrial estates, free-trade zones, and bonded warehouses, and indirectly through regional development planning, it was hoped that industrialization would spread throughout the country.

Export expansion, equity considerations, and the spatial redistribution of industrial plants interrelate and are being orchestrated by an increasingly active public sector participant in the economy. It appears that there is a two-stage government investment plan that entails on the one hand the growth of 'parastatal' sector investments in industries, consisting of public enterprises, and on the other, heavy reliance on private sources (local and foreign) to boost investment in the industrial sector. Thus the trend has been towards a rapid proliferation of public enterprises in many sectors of the economy characterized by varying degrees of success. Generous tax concessions and an equable investment climate have encouraged many multinational corporations (MNCs) and investors to set up branch plants in Malaysia in search of cheap unskilled labour and good returns on investment.[1] Unfortunately, the use of unskilled labour has resulted in the development of a secondary labour market dominated by low-wage female workers and rural migrants (Mehmet 1983).

The dilemma which the country faces lies in having to balance growth across the various sectors against the desire to expand industrial exports. For example, the manufacturing sector faces an exchange rate that was determined by exports of natural resources, particularly rubber, petroleum, tin, and timber. This places pressure on the exchange rate so that exports of manufactured goods become uncompetitive in the international market place. The trade-off seems to lie in policies that aim at bringing about equilibrium in external markets and those that promote domestic industrial growth. Added to this was the attempt to maintain the confidence of investors, especially from overseas. For example, the Petroleum Development Act, 1974, and the Industrial Co-ordination Act, 1975, were conceived as policy instruments to promote restructuring by legislative means. Many investors from overseas have interpreted these instruments as burdensome (Means 1983). However, there is evidence to suggest that the government is eager to be seen as flexible in implementing selected policy instruments. Such flexibility is vital since the government has to balance growth so that the *Bumiputera* can derive benefits from that growth while at the same time maintaining a bright, attractive, and dynamic environment for investors, with no legislative strictures to stifle rapid growth and profits for all concerned. The dangers inherent in such a process are considerable and it would be tempting to restructure and redistribute regardless of the state of economic growth.

Likely results will include a loss of confidence in the government and the flight of both foreign and domestic capital. Restructuring the industrial sector to reflect the ethnic composition of the country or redistributing shares in industries may indeed be feasible, but such short-run measures may rebound in the guise of unprofitable enterprises and retrogression because the industrial organization is unable to cope with the rapidity of the change. More ominously, there may be disharmony and disunity among the various ethnic groups as the measures might be interpreted as further evidence of government meddling in the economy and bringing about instability - a prospect the government does not wish to face. In view of this concern the requirement of a 30 per cent *Bumiputera* share in the economy set down by the *Outline Perspective Plan (Outline Plan)* for 1990 may be unrealistic.

After describing the pattern of industrialization in Malaysia since independence, attention is switched to examining the various strategies to promote industrial growth. Part two discusses the dualism resulting from rapid industrialization while part three assesses the role of public enterprises in accelerating industrial growth and drawing *Bumiputera* into the industrial sector. Part four evaluates the industrial future of the country.

INDUSTRIALIZATION: PATTERNS AND STRATEGIES

Industrialization in Malaysia in the 1970s was export-oriented and labour-intensive. However, in the 1980s it appears that the economy is moving away from this model. The change in emphasis was brought about in the light of the difficulties encountered in penetrating highly protected foreign markets, the uncertainties of growth prospects for the international economy, and adjustments required to overcome existing structural constraints within the industrial sector.

Thus in the 1980s much of the industrialization in Malaysia has been capital-intensive, providing fewer employment opportunities. The rate of labour absorption was low as compared with the rate of new additions to the labour force. This low rate was further exacerbated by the lack of integration between export manufacturing and the local small- and intermediate-scale industries, a structural problem brought about by rapid expansion of the industrial sector. It was also caused by the importation of high technology superimposed on domestic 'backyard' type industries.

The latter may have been unable to cope with the new demands put on their capacity and resources. Whether this lack of integration was the result of policy or a lack of planning, or a natural consequence of very rapid industrialization, is debatable since there can be many opportunities for building into this pattern of industrialization a concerted effort at 'forward' and 'backward' linkages (Hirschman 1958: 98-100).

While neither type of linkage can form the basis of a self-generating programme of industrial growth (Lim 1973: 248), it may be crucial to ask what have been the patterns of industrialization and what strategies have guided the future of this sector of the Malaysian economy.

Patterns of Industrial Growth

A specific feature of Malaysian industrialization was that although in the early years after independence import substitution played a significant role in some lines of manufacturing, for example, cigarettes, cement, soap, non-ferrous metals, and car assembly, export promotion was uppermost in the minds of the planners. In general, import-substituting industries were tooled from the start to serve both the domestic and international markets. Because of this latter need, the Malaysian economy was necessarily open to the international market with the consequence that the establishment of new export-oriented industries was foreign-driven. New plants were established by overseas investors and thereby under foreign control, and the use of capital-intensive methods and scales of production was transplanted from Europe and North America. Intuitively it may be said that such industries were not labour-intensive. However, they were expected to have a long-term effect on employment by the creation of new backward linkages, especially to areas adjacent to these export industries.

Available data for Malaysia up to the 1970s show three main patterns of industrial growth. Figure 5.1 shows the relationship between the growth of the manufacturing sector and the gross domestic product (1971-87). First, the modern sector of industry grew very rapidly while the traditional sector remained small and did not benefit from spill-over from modern industry. An indicator of such differences is to be found in the ratio of the self-employed to wage and salary earners. According to data from Paukert *et al.* (1981: 43-4) the proportion of self-employment to total employment in peninsular Malaysia was low (as would probably be the case in Sabah and Sarawak).

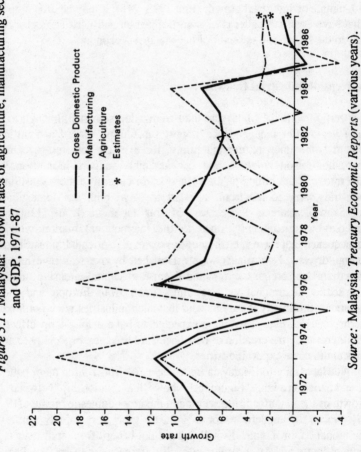

Figure 5.1. Malaysia: Growth rates of agriculture, manufacturing sectors and GDP, 1971-87

Source: Malaysia, *Treasury Economic Reports* (various years).

Second, small-scale industries with fewer than 20 employees have played an insignificant role in the Malaysian context. There were few or no small-scale industries in mining, and only a small number in manufacturing and construction (11 per cent and 7 per cent respectively of paid employment in 1971), with indications that these shares were falling in relative and absolute terms. The share of manufacturing output of large establishments employing over 100 workers increased from 39 per cent in 1957 to 66 per cent in 1971. However, employment growth has been rather less, with the share of manufacturing increasing from 6.4 per cent in 1957 to 10.5 per cent in 1970 (Hoffman and Tan 1980: 16, 276). Thus, with the diversification of manufacturing and the growing importance of large-sized firms, the data indicate that medium- and large-scale enterprises provided the driving force behind industrialization.

Third, foreign-controlled enterprises accounted for 80 per cent of the output of limited companies in mining, 62 per cent of output in manufacturing, and 58 per cent of output in construction in 1971. Foreign-controlled companies made substantial contributions to growth of output - about 21 per cent of GDP and 67 per cent of manufacturing during the 1968-71 period. But their contribution to employment growth was only about 33 per cent.[2]

Such a pattern of growth may provide classic evidence that producing internationally competitive exports leads to a reliance on foreign capital and to a development strategy unable to absorb labour that has been made redundant in the rural areas. It also necessitates an attractive domestic 'political climate' for foreign capital.

In sum, up to 1971 the programme to diversify the economy and the growth of the manufacturing sector in Malaysia had had mixed success in terms of the output, employment in, and growth of manufactured exports. Furthermore, these patterns have had a substantial spatial impact on economic development. This is discussed in a later section on the spread of industries.

Strategies for Industrial Growth

The strategies for industrialization adopted in Malaysia have included both import substitution and export promotion of labour-intensive industries. The shortcoming of this policy of import substitution (and, as a consequence, of high tariff barriers) was that domestic industry was not given a chance to 'grow up' by being pitted against foreign competition. Under import-substitution programmes local industry failed to develop competitively either because of tariff protection or disguised subsidies in the form of tax relief. Equally, an export-oriented strategy had its drawbacks. While cheap and plentiful labour could be harnessed to exploit comparative advantages, these export industries were inevitably exposed to the vicissitudes of the international market as well as the protectionist measures employed by some industrialized countries. Often such new export-oriented industry made use of imported capital. Such intensive use of capital and technology with low labour-absorptive capacity meant that appropriate intermediate industries were required to be developed in order to meet policy goals of employment. The industrialization pattern therefore reflected a choice between large enterprises on the one hand and small-scale labour-intensive family or sole proprietorship enterprises on the other. The industrialization programme in Malaysia has been buttressed by the export of industrial raw materials such as rubber, palm oil, tin, and petroleum. Moreover, the government has recognized that the strategy of import substitution was at an end and that 'increasingly the rate of, and stimulus for, industrial development will depend upon the expansion of exports' (Malaysia 1969: 75).

The key issue confronting the government after independence was to formulate an industrialization policy that took account of the effects on the rate of economic growth of protective tariff or import controls while at the same time maintaining Malaysia's attraction as an investment centre. This would also stem the flow of capital from the country. The immediate task therefore had to take account of the technical efficiency of domestic production, increasing exports and net capital inflow, while decreasing imports of consumer goods and capital flight so as to remove the foreign exchange gap. A study of the policy instruments adopted by the government provides valuable insights into the way the Malaysian government went about its task of industrializing the country.

In the *First Malaya Plan 1956-1960* the main increase in investment in the private sector took place in manufacturing. Gross fixed investment in manufacturing in 1958 amounted to $85 million, about 14 per cent of total investment. The establishment of Petaling Jaya as an industrial estate proved to be an important instrument for attracting industrial investment (Malaya 1961: 4). The government also provided substantial tax incentives under the Pioneer Industries Ordinance, 1958. Profits of enterprises which qualified as 'pioneer' industries were exempted from income tax for a period ranging from two to five years. A critical assessment of this Ordinance was undertaken by Lim (1973: 255-7). A major criticism was that the small fixed capital required for tax exemption and short time span of the exemption tended to encourage industries of a speculative nature. Moreover, a majority of pioneer firms did not benefit from investment incentives and therefore refrained from increasing their rate of growth. This was seen as a serious omission in the industrial promotion programme.

The *Second Malaya Plan 1961-1965* stated that the government's basic contribution to industrial growth was the preservation of a sound and stable monetary and financial climate. The pioneer industry policy was to be continued during the plan period (Malaya 1961: 20).

Close study of the *First Malaysia Plan 1966-1970* reveals that import substitution was an essential part of the growth strategy. Furthermore, manufacturing was seen as one way of reducing dependence on a few primary commodities and of achieving the diversification of the economy. In order to achieve a growth rate for manufacturing of 10 per cent per annum value added and 3.8 per cent per annum in employment, there would have had to be an increase in imports of capital goods and intermediate materials and a reduction of imports of consumer goods. This latter consideration was necessary to avoid the shortage of foreign exchange required to pay for the capital goods.

An analysis of the data on industrial growth rates derived from the Department of Statistics *Census of Manufacturing* for 1959 and 1968 reported by Lim (1973: Ch. 12) showed that the manufacturing sector recorded 17.4 per cent growth between 1959 and 1968. It estimated that the real growth of real value added for pioneer industries was higher at 57.5 per cent per annum because of tax concessions. There was also a change in the composition of net manufacturing output, a slowing down in the growth of processing of agricultural products, but rapid growth in newer industries such as chemicals and chemical products, non-metallic mineral products, base metals and metal products, and transport equipment - the so-called 'producer-oriented industries'. For example, the percentage share of processing activities in net manufacturing output declined from 28.9 per cent in 1959 to 10.5 per cent in 1968 while all producer-oriented industries recorded increases in their respective shares. There were modest increases of 1.7 per cent to 2.9 per cent in transport equipment, as well as large jumps, for example chemicals from 8.3 per cent to 11.2 per cent and non-metallic mineral products from 3.9 per cent to 8.2 per cent, over the same period.

According to Lim (1973) the ratio of the share of consumer-oriented industries to that of producer-oriented industries in total net manufacturing output may be taken as a rough indicator of the degree of industrialization of a country. Thus full industrial maturity is said to have been reached when the consumer-producer ratio approaches unity. In the period between 1959 and 1968 the ratio in Malaysia fell from 4.0 to 2.3 (Lim 1973: 249). Despite these indicators, the programme of industrial development tended to lack dynamism in that the inter-industry linkages did not provide the catalyst for more rapid growth. Consumer-oriented industries showed more growth than the producer-oriented industries, probably because of 'start-up' difficulties and the slow development of inter-industry linkages. Moreover, the pioneer industries were unable to sustain the momentum of growth, probably because of an intrinsic flaw in the conception of such industries and their role in industry growth, employment, and technology transfer. This gave rise to concern about the method and implementation of the pioneer industries programme.

In 1968, the Investment Incentives Act was passed to attract further industrial investment. The objective was to provide total or partial tax relief to companies investing in new enterprises or expanding existing ones. Eligibility for pioneer status was extended to include non-manufacturing industries on both locational and product criteria. Firms in designated development areas qualified for exemption, while priority products attracted further concessions. Priority products were those which could be used in other industries within the country and were substitutes for imported goods. The Federal Industrial Development Authority (FIDA) was reorganized in 1969. The Credit Guarantee Corporation was set up in 1970 to encourage commercial banks to extend loans to small business enterprises. The government-funded corporation guaranteed 60 per cent of the loans to small businesses. A Capital Investment Committee (CIC) was established to streamline administrative procedures for processing investment proposals. The Free Trade Zone (FTZ) Act, 1971, established FTZs and export processing zones (EPZs) in which facilities for the duty-free entry of materials and goods were provided.

An amendment to the Investment Incentives Act in 1971 offered tax exemptions based on the number of workers in each firm. Labour-intensive industries such as electronics were granted tax relief of four to seven years in an attempt to attract to the FTZs the 'footloose' industries seeking low-cost labour locations. Where these industries were set up in development areas and where either priority goods were produced or a specified level of local raw materials was used, additional periods of tax relief could be secured.

During 1960 and 1970 the average annual growth rate of manufactured exports from peninsular Malaysia was 14.2 per cent. Exports of manufactured products grew at more than twice the rate of total exports. Between 1960 and 1970 manufactured exports rose from less than 5 per cent of total exports to over 10 per cent (Malaysia 1971: Ch. X).

The *Second Malaysia Plan 1971-1975* encouraged the growth of a modern industrial sector in the belief that 'this sector ha[d] relatively favourable rates of labour absorption' (Malaysia 1971: 103). The plan also aimed at modifying existing industrial incentives so as to align the relative factor prices for land, capital, and skills more favourably to the use of labour. The setting up of industrial estates together with active public sector participation in the development of industrial plants combined with the further aim of creating a modern Malay business and commercial class. Labour as a factor of production was made much more attractive in relation to capital. Government assistance to industry took the form of direct income tax concessions, some protective tariffs, the provision of industrial credit, and industrial site development. Yet under this plan public expenditure on industrial development represented only 2.2 per cent of the total public development expenditure, while infrastructure absorbed about 39.8 per cent of total public outlay for development purposes.

At the end of this planning period the Industrial Co-ordination Act of 1975 and the Petroleum Development (Amendment) Act, 1975, were introduced. These pieces of legislation alarmed private sector investors as the Minister could now impose whatever conditions he saw fit in issuing a manufacturing licence. The amendment to the Petroleum Act required petroleum companies to give the National Oil Corporation (PETRONAS) a 1 per cent equity in the form of management shares. This opened the possibility of gaining effective control of any company's downstream activities without providing fair competition. Both acts had adverse effects on direct foreign investment and 'heralded a new and more ominous phase of Malaysian economic nationalism' (Gale 1981: 1138).

It has been recognized that the reservation of a wider range of activities for *Bumiputera*-only enterprises could seriously discourage continuing foreign investment in Malaysia and disrupt modern sector development in general. Moreover, although foreign investment has increased, its contribution to employment has been disappointing. Industries have also tended to concentrate around Kuala Lumpur and Pulau Pinang. The government reconsidered its 'managed industrialization' strategy and the administrative and regulatory requirements of the 1975 act have since been relaxed.

The Economic Planning Unit of the Prime Minister's Department has also commented on the weakness of the tax incentive system (Shepherd 1980: 190-1). First, tax holidays were perverse since they were worth more the higher the level of pre-tax profits, that is, the less they were needed. Second, the alternative investment tax credit is more attractive than the tax holiday only where the rate of return is very low in the long run. Third, the concession on labour use was attractive only if the projects had very low capital to labour ratios. There was a built-in bias against small investments and small-scale industry that was designed to encourage capital-intensive industries.

Yet despite the uncertainties engendered by the various acts, the period between 1971 and 1975 witnessed growth of around 11 per cent per annum in value added from manufacturing, and the share of manufacturing in the GDP rose from 12.2 per cent in 1970 to 14.4 per cent in 1975. Employment grew in manufacturing at a rate of 6.6 per cent per annum generating 108,300 new jobs, mainly in textiles, wood, chemicals, and transport equipment. The export performance of manufacturing between 1971 and 1975 grew by 29 per cent per annum in excess of the growth target of 15 per cent per annum (Malaysia 1976: 310-12).

In the *Third Malaysia Plan 1976-1980* manufacturing was again accorded a strategic role for achieving the goals of the NEP. The development of small-scale industries was integral to industrial growth, with an emphasis on labour intensity, use of domestic raw materials, and some measure of complementarity to larger industries. The participation of Malays and other indigenous groups was also made an important adjunct to industrial growth.

Data from the *Fourth Malaysia Plan 1981-1985* show that the share of manufacturing in GDP increased from 13.4 per cent in 1970 to 20.5 per cent in 1980 and that value added had grown by 12.5 per cent per annum between 1970 and 1980 (Malaysia 1981: 293). By all indicators, the industrial sector had become the leading growth sector in the economy. This was directly attributable to increased exports and rising domestic demand. The major industries that contributed to growth were oils and fats, textiles and clothing, and electrical machinery.

In retrospect, during 1970-80 there was a marked structural change in the industrial sector. Initially, there was an expansion of import-substitution industries. For example, food manufacture accounted for 15.3 per cent of manufactured value added in 1970, but by 1980 this had fallen to 9.3 per cent. There was then a shift to consumer durables such as household appliances, furniture, and clothing. This resulted from an expansion of the domestic market due to rising standards of living and faster-paced urbanization. During the latter part of the decade the shift was towards the development of export-oriented industries. The export of plywood, veneer, blockboard, and sawn timber increased at a rate of 12.8 per cent per annum and 9.4 per cent per annum respectively between 1970 and 1980 (Malaysia 1981: 294).

The rubber products industry became more diversified, moving into the production of household and surgical gloves, heavy duty tyres, and medical equipment. During the same period textiles produced for the domestic market increased by 9.9 per cent per annum while those for export rose by 26 per cent per annum. Similarly, electrical machinery grew at an average rate of 13.3 per cent per annum, reflecting a strong demand from overseas markets.

This growth in the production of consumer and intermediate goods overshadowed the production of capital goods. While the latter grew at an average rate of 9.7 per cent per annum over the same period, it accounted for a small proportion of the sector (less than 5 per cent) in 1980 and was confined to a narrow range of light capital goods, for example, transport equipment and light machinery. Greater diversification in the product mix of the capital goods industry had been encouraged but little change had occurred. In employment, the industrial sector generated 416,600 new jobs, accounting for 24.5 per cent of total new employment created during the 1970-80 period. People engaged in industry represented about 16 per cent of the workforce in 1980. In the next plan the industrialization strategy shifted towards the development of heavy industrial capacity.

The *Fifth Malaysia Plan 1986-1990* envisages that much of the overall economic growth for the nation will originate from the manufacturing sector, with the private sector playing a leading role. There is also a re-emphasis on the development of a more efficient and dynamic export-oriented industrial sector. While manufacturing overtook agriculture to become the largest sector of the economy during the last plan, this was not sustained because of poor export performance and low domestic demand. The growth of the sector accelerated from 4.6 per cent in 1981 to 11.6 per cent in 1984; by 1985 output from this sector had declined to only about 3 per cent. Similarly, employment in manufacturing also grew slowly during 1981-85 at a rate of about 1.9 per cent per annum, giving an overall increase of 72,900 new jobs.

The strategy of establishing certain heavy industries to foster linkages and an expansion of the industrial base was slow to be fully realized. The prospects for growth in the industrial sector are heavily dependent upon the economic performance of industrialized countries and rising protectionism.

According to the Malaysian Industrial Policies Study (MIPS) and the Industrial Master Plan (Malaysia 1986: 334), there is a need for changes in the direction of past policies and strategies. A reformulation, integration, and adoption of industrial incentives and measures to accelerate growth in the manufacturing sector are required. Under the

IMP four basic industries have been identified to broaden the industrial base: iron and steel, engineering, chemicals and chemical processing, and electrical - all having projected growth rates of between 7 and 12 per cent. In these endeavours, market penetration is a major factor in the export expansion strategy. The growth of manufactured exports would need to exploit Malaysia's comparative advantages in addition to economies of scale and a balanced incentive scheme that favoured competition and encouraged entrepreneurial initiative to facilitate the required change.

Industrial Policy Reform

The Malaysian economy has traditionally been heavily dependent on foreign investment. In 1983 it was estimated that 600 MNCs invested about US$1.3 billion in its economy (Chee 1985: 16). The favourable attitude of the government towards joint venture projects was an implicit recognition that they played a major role in industrial development and in helping to supplement capital resources and technical skills. While before 1975 controls on investment were directed towards the prevention of excess capacity in industries, after the mid-1970s the aim was in part to press new firms to comply with the objectives of the government under the NEP to increase *Bumiputera* participation. In part it was also aimed at fostering competition by granting licences to more than one investment in any given industry. This contrived move led to either a built-in excess capacity or the establishment of plants of less than optimal size.

Whatever the effects of such planned moves, it has to be borne in mind that the investment climate was changing. While previous investment decisions had hinged on labour cost advantages, in the 1980s labour costs were no longer the most important factor. This change has tremendous implications for industrial policy in general and labour or employment policy in particular. Industrial policy reform has therefore to be based on two important considerations. First, as Malaysia is still heavily dependent on the export of primary products, any industrial policy has to attempt to protect industries associated with the processing of these commodities. Second, protective tariffs may have resulted in a relatively inefficient import-substitution sector while the export expansion sector was relatively well-off in terms of growth and the utilization of capacity. In order to improve the performance of import-substitution industries, a re-examination of FTZs is required so as to allow production for the local market after payment of duties. In this way import-substitution industries may derive benefits in terms of scale of production, skills transfer, and some measure of competition. Policy must therefore be addressed to growth so as to satisfy the demands of a growing population and increasing capacity use in import-substituting industries.

Manufacturing industries in Malaysia registered impressive overall gains over the 1975-85 period, in terms of output and employment. Manufactured exports as a percentage of total gross commodity exports rose from $6,269.8 million in 1980 (22 per cent) to about $12,229.0 million in 1985 (32 per cent), representing an average annual growth rate of about 14.3 per cent per annum (Malaysia 1986: 48-9). The share of the manufacturing sector in GDP rose from about 16.4 per cent in 1975 to about 20 per cent in 1980 ($8,932 million) but dropped to 19 per cent in 1985 ($11,357 million). This relatively poor showing was the result of slower annual growth rates following the world recession of the 1980s, and also the deterioration in the competitiveness of Malaysian manufactured exports.

Table 5.1 shows that four states were pre-eminent in their manufacturing sector's contribution to the GDP - Selangor, Pulau Pinang, Johor and Kuala Lumpur in either 1980 or 1985. Another feature was that, apart from Selangor and Pulau Pinang, the manufacturing sector was relatively important to the economies of Negri Sembilan and Melaka. This may be explained by the location of oil refineries in the former and agro-industries in the latter. Except for the states mentioned above, manufacturing was relatively insignificant in all other states. It is expected, however, that the establishment by the Heavy Industries Corporation of Malaysia Berhad (HICOM) may contribute to the growth of manufacturing in other states, for example the cement plant in Kedah, a steel billet plant in Terengganu, a methanol and hot briquette iron plant in Sabah, and a liquified natural gas and fertilizer plant in Sarawak (Malaysia 1986: 335-7).

Manufacturing provided 72,900 new jobs between 1981 and 1985, as compared with the planned target of 125,800 jobs. The shortfall was reflected in the slow growth of employment in manufacturing at 1.9 per cent per annum (1981-85) which was below the target of 3.2 per cent. Most of the new jobs were found in textiles and clothing, electrical machinery, including electronics, plastic products, printing and publishing, basic metal, and other non-metallic products (Malaysia 1986: 137, 345). In the *Fifth Malaysia Plan* the government has set a target growth rate of 2.6 per cent per annum. Employment in manufacturing was projected to account for 17.5 per cent of the total number of new jobs during the plan and this was to be provided by metal products, non-metallic mineral products, non-electrical machinery, and transport equipment (Malaysia 1986: 143-6). Table 5.2 suggests that such growth

Table 5.1. Malaysia: Manufacturing contributions to GDP, 1980 and
1985

State	1980			1985		
	$ m.	*% of total*	*% of state*	*$ m.*	*% of total*	*% of state*
Johor	1,109	12.4	23.7	1,379	12.1	22.6
Kedah	192	2.1	8.4	235	2.1	8.3
Kelantan	86	0.9	6.6	137	1.2	7.7
Melaka	255	2.9	24.3	331	2.9	24.5
Negri Sembilan	638	7.1	33.0	705	6.2	28.6
Pahang	323	3.6	13.0	387	3.4	11.2
Perak	723	8.1	14.3	918	8.1	15.0
Perlis	43	0.5	13.1	45	0.4	10.6
Pulau Pinang	1,399	15.7	40.1	1,666	14.7	38.9
Sabah	110	1.2	3.6	203	1.8	4.6
Sarawak	257	2.9	8.6	441	3.9	9.5
Selangor	2,570	28.9	37.5	3,310	29.1	37.0
Terengganu	125	1.4	6.4	179	1.6	6.0
Wilayah Persekutuan/						
Kuala Lumpur	1,102	12.3	18.1	1,421	12.5	16.0
Malaysia	*8,932*	*19.9*	*-*	*11,357*	*19.1*	*-*

Source: Malaysia (1986: 172-5).

Table 5.2. Malaysia: Projects granted approval, by industry, 1981-85

Industry	Number of approvals 1981-85		Total proposed capital investment 1981-85	
		(%)	($ m.)	(%)
Food	241	8.5	1,406.1	6.5
Beverages and tobacco	39	1.4	247.8	1.1
Textile and textile products	246	8.7	449.8	2.1
Leather and leather products	11	0.4	16.2	0.1
Wood and wood products	217	7.7	883.6	4.1
Furniture and fixtures	55	1.9	101.9	0.5
Paper, printing, and publishing	134	4.7	2,347.8	10.9
Chemicals and chemical products	210	7.4	3,711.3	17.2
Petroleum and coal	58	2.0	703.1	3.3
Rubber products	139	4.9	477.5	2.2
Plastic products	170	6.0	381.8	1.8
Non-metallic products	272	9.6	3,436.0	15.9
Base metal products	118	4.2	2,672.3	12.3
Fabricated metal products	237	8.4	696.3	3.2
Machinery	149	5.3	833.2	3.8
Electrical and electronic products	278	9.8	1,321.4	6.1
Transport equipment	169	6.0	1,693.7	7.8
Science measuring equipment	19	0.7	39.8	0.2
Miscellaneous	68	2.4	201.0	0.9
Total	*2,830*	*100.0*	*21,620.6*	*100.0*

Source: Malaysia (1986: 339).

targets are not unrealistic when the number of approvals for projects in various industries are matched against whether they are capital- or labour-intensive. The largest number of approvals were in non-metallic products, electrical and electronic products, and textile and textile products. The dichotomy between labour-intensive and capital-intensive industries is evident from the grouping in terms of the largest number of approvals as against total investments. It would appear, however, that despite these overall trends and aggregate performance rates, manufacturing will continue to be heavily concentrated in a few export-oriented industries such as textiles, clothing, and electronic assembly.

With the passing of favourable market conditions, the changing economic environment calls for a more systematic and consistent approach towards an industrial sector that is more outward-oriented than before. The key elements in this will include improving the incentive system, expanding exports, upgrading and modernizing small-scale industries, developing research, and strengthening the institutions responsible for fostering the growth of the manufacturing sector. These programmes are contained in the *Industrial Master Plan 1986-1995* and in the Malaysian Industrial Policies Study[3] (Malaysia 1986: 356-60). In general, the private sector is expected to play the major role in industrial development.

The IMP emphasizes the development of resource-based industries such as rubber, palm oil, food, timber, and metals. These industries will play an important role in the manufacturing sector as a whole. The IMP was critical of the various weaknesses of past industrialization policies, particularly the over-dependence on foreign investments and over-concentration on the electronics and textiles industries. Moreover, the protection of domestic industry over long periods resulted in less efficiency and a decline in the motivation to upgrade products, technology, and management systems. As a consequence, domestic manufacturing was more costly to consumers and the economy as a whole. Inter-industry linkages were extremely weak and did little to reinforce the industrial base of the economy. The IMP was critical also of the lack of an overall perspective for heavy industries For example, it questioned the need for three iron and steel mills when one would have sufficed.

As for the IMP itself, the growth target of 6.4 per cent over the next ten years appears over-optimistic given the decline in commodity prices. Moreover, the plan is directed towards export-orientated industries. The consequence of this orientation is that the world market may dictate the country's fortunes. For example, protectionism, technological competitiveness, and bilateral trading regimes in the world market pose immediate hurdles to Malaysian manufacturers. Rather than commit the industrialization programme towards an export market totally, the programme should also direct efforts at producing high quality products for domestic consumption. This two-pronged approach could provide the basis for future industrial strategies. However, before discussing future industrial patterns, it is necessary to evaluate some of the characteristics of industrialization in Malaysia. We will begin with its spatial distribution, followed by a discussion of its inherent dualism and public sector activities.

THE LOCATION OF INDUSTRIES

In 1971 industrial development was geographically concentrated in four states which together accounted for 75 per cent of all employment and output in manufacturing (Hoffman and Tan 1980: 21). The pattern for the 1980s was remains unchanged. In 1965 Selangor produced 180 per cent more than the next ranked state, with Pahang, Terengganu, and Kelantan together accounting for 8.3 per cent of total establishments and 3.7 per cent of the total gross value of output. Similar data for 1972 showed that Selangor had grown much larger than its next rival, Johor, with 250 per cent more output. The primacy of Selangor is attributable to economies of scale, market concentration, accessibility, and rapid early development which all added considerably to the industrial position of the state. Selangor has become the nation's premier industrial region and, not surprisingly, a majority of foreign-controlled companies are found in the Kelang Valley of Selangor.

In 1965 Selangor was the only state that had progressed beyond the processing or manufacture of goods based on local material. Johor was the second most important state in terms of manufacturing, specializing in textiles and the processing of raw materials based on primary produce - pineapples, oil palm, rubber, copra, and timber. No doubt the close proximity of Johor Bahru to Singapore provided the impetus to industrial development as the latter was a major consuming and export market. The third important manufacturing centre was the state of Perak, with the Kinta Valley and Krian districts providing the lead. Here most industries were linked to and supported the tin mining industry in terms of either the processing of tin or the manufacture of equipment for use in tin mining. There were also industries related to agro-processing but by and large these were of less importance. Among them were rubber processing, timber milling, and the production of light consumer goods for the local market.

Negri Sembilan was drawn into the heavy industrial sector with the establishment of petroleum refineries at Port Dickson, other ancillary industries related to petroleum refining, and to service and other consumer industries located principally in Seremban. In terms of heavy industry the iron and steel works at Prai Industrial Estate as well as the older, more established industrial estate at Mak Mandin provided Pulau Pinang with an industrial base. Again the activities in these industrial estates concentrated on tin smelting, rice milling, the production of industrial grade Standard Malaysian Rubber and consumer and industrial goods for domestic use.

Thus industries were heavily concentrated in a few areas, and incentives were needed to induce a spread of development throughout the country. In Malaysia locational incentives have been given in designated development areas in less developed states to encourage private investment. The question of whether this investment has produced the expected multiplier effects is difficult to measure. But it is true to say that industrial agglomerations with their resulting economic and social infrastructure will create external economies which may attract other firms. Without policy direction, expansion would probably occur in the heavily concentrated complexes of the Kelang Valley and Pulau Pinang area. While no clear guidelines have been given concerning the gazetting of locational incentive areas under the 1971 Investment Incentives Act, it may be inferred that such areas are located in less developed states, namely Johor Tenggara, Kedah (excluding Kuala Muda district), Perlis, Pahang (excluding Kuantan), Terengganu, Kelantan, Sabah, and Sarawak. During the period of the *Second Malaysia Plan*, there were over 1,200 projects located within these locational incentive areas.

Between 1976 and 1978 about 1,253 industrial projects were approved; 731 of these were located outside the industrially developed areas. Kedah, Perlis, Kelantan, Terengganu, Pahang, Sabah, and Sarawak together received 27 per cent of the approved projects while 32 per cent went to less developed areas in Johor, Melaka, Negri Sembilan, Pulau Pinang, Perak, and Selangor. Agro-based industries such as food, rubber, and wood products as well as chemicals and electrical products comprised the majority of the new firms (Malaysia 1979: 150).

The objective of industrial dispersal was to redistribute manufacturing output and employment. As outlined above, fiscal incentives were accompanied by the development of industrial estates and ready-built factories together with the development of infrastructure (Malaysia 1976: 212). The location of industrial estates has been co-ordinated with overall growth strategy. By 1979 there were ten fully or partially occupied industrial estates and a further 15 had been proposed. However, the pattern of investment has not sustained expectations in terms of the dispersal policy. Only seven of the fully or partially occupied estates were located in Kedah, Perlis, Kelantan, and Terengganu, while seven were located in Selangor and eight in Pulau Pinang (Malaysia 1979: 88). The marginal results of attempts at industrial dispersal have been recognized in the *Fifth Malaysia Plan* where 'other than Kulim and Sungei Petani the industrial estates in Kedah and Perlis showed low occupancy rates' (Malaysia 1986: 176).

Nevertheless, a total of 8,744 hectares of land had been developed as industrial estates by mid-1985, as compared with 6,500 hectares in 1980, an increase of 28 per cent. Of the 21 new estates, half were located in Kedah, Kelantan, Pahang, Perlis, Sabah, Sarawak, and Terengganu - states which enjoyed tax relief under the locational incentive scheme. When the data are disaggregated by income status of states, the high- and middle-income states continued to receive more of the most viable projects. For example, in terms of capital investment, projects in Selangor and Kuala Lumpur accounted for about 37.8 per cent of the national total. By contrast, in low-income states such as Kedah and Kelantan the proposed capital investment was $1,427 million, about 6.6 per cent of the national total (Malaysia 1986: 340).

Another method of promoting industrial exports and attracting foreign investment was the establishment of FTZs and licensed manufacturing warehouses (LMWs). In these FTZs or EPZs (export processing zones) various incentives operate. For example, under the Free Trade Zone Act of 1971 firms enjoyed duty-free imports of raw materials and capital equipment since, for the purposes of the act, these zones were considered to be 'outside' Malaysia. Imports to and exports from FTZs also involve fewer customs documentation requirements. The infrastructure provided in these FTZs was similar to those in industrial estates. In addition, there were also company tax incentives. Instead of the company income tax of 45 per cent and an additional excess profit tax of 5 per cent where taxable company income exceeds 25 per cent of shareholder funds or $200,000, relief from taxes has been made available.

The incentives found in LMWs are similar to those described for FTZs except that the subsidized development of infrastructural facilities is not available. Provision for duty-free imports of raw materials and components, streamlined customs formalities, and the company income tax incentive measures are also available at LMWs. The difference between FTZs and LMWs is therefore one of jurisdiction.

The concept of FTZs began as a state initiative in the early 1970s. Pulau Pinang was the first to adopt the FTZ in its efforts to rescue its flagging economy as a consequence of the withdrawal of its 'free port' status. Subsequent to the establishment of the Bayan Lepas FTZ in 1971 (and later at Pulau Jejerak) in Pulau Pinang, two other states - Selangor (at Sungai Way, Ulu Kelang, and Telok Panglima Garang) and Melaka (at Batu Berendam and Tanjung Keling) - developed their own FTZs.

Under the Customs Act, 1967, exporters were entitled to a 'drawback' of import duties where imported goods were subsequently re-exported. Because of delays and difficulties in getting these refunds the LMW system was introduced in 1975 to allow the manufacture of goods under customs bond. Firms using the LMWs have tended to be smaller, more labour-intensive than in FTZs, and engaged principally in the manufacture of garments. LMWs also accrued locational incentive benefits if they were located in development areas.[4]

The total exports from the FTZs in 1982 amounted to $3.93 billion (14 per cent) of $27.97 billion total Malaysian merchandise exports. Firms in FTZs contributed 51 per cent of total exports of manufactured goods from Malaysia of $7.72 billion (Malaysia 1983). Total employment in the FTZs was approximately 70,000 in 1982, which was 8.8 per cent of total manufacturing employment in Malaysia (Warr 1986: 189). FTZs were wholly export-oriented, with the electronics industry predominant in terms of output and employment (85 per cent of total FTZ exports in 1982 and 76 per cent total FTZ employment in 1982).

Total exports from LMWs amounted to $770 million in 1982, constituting 2.8 per cent of total merchandise exports from Malaysia and 10 per cent of total exports of manufactured goods. In terms of employment, LMW firms provided 27,800 jobs in 1982, 3.5 per cent of total manufacturing employment in Malaysia. Local raw materials were used more extensively among LMWs than in FTZs (10.5 per cent as against 3.6 per cent) and 26 per cent purchased capital equipment from local sources as compared with 8 per cent among firms in FTZs (Warr 1986: 194).

According to an economic cost-benefit study of FTZs and LMWs in Malaysia, by the end of 1982 the net benefits to the country already exceeded the net costs incurred in establishing these zones (Warr 1986). Because of generous tax incentives, which were partly responsible for the success of the programme, the revenues raised from taxes have been negligible. But to use these FTZs to raise revenue would probably cause an exodus of firms from the zones. Tax holidays for some firms in these zones are beginning to run out and the government will have to finalize a policy with respect to company tax to entice firms to remain rather than relocate in another country.

Since individual states have jurisdiction over the administration of the FTZs, the programme for the country is uncoordinated. There may be a deterioration of the situation when states hand over to local councils the functions of running FTZs. Sales of products from FTZs to the domestic market as imported goods should be relaxed so long as the appropriate duties are paid. Customs delays and procedural difficulties have continued to hamper the operational efficiency of FTZs. The degree of linkage between FTZ firms and the domestic economy through the purchase of domestically produced raw materials and capital equipment has been disappointing. This is probably because of the difficulty of obtaining the types of raw materials required by FTZ firms. A further reason may be that since most of these firms are MNCs they would obtain most of their backward linkages from within the company or from other MNCs. Whatever the explanation, local industries will need to be developed to provide greater linkages with firms in FTZs.

The LMW programme could also be expanded as it is more closely integrated with the domestic economy in terms of either the use of local raw materials or in purchasing domestically produced capital equipment. The main obstacle seems to be an administrative one, making co-ordination with local firms cumbersome, time-consuming, and costly to LMW firms.

From a broader perspective it is arguable that FTZs and LMWs are caught up in a technology spiral in which the rate of industrial development in one country is tied to the rate of planned obsolescence in developed countries - the theory of the product cycle. Major industrial countries that have control over research and development pass on to developing countries those industries that are either obsolete or no longer competitive. Later these intermediate nations in turn pass these industries on to less developed countries so that in time the technology spiral will run itself down and bring little or no benefit to the adopting country. An important implication is that the degree of technology transfer is not great, especially for a more successful economy like Malaysia. Evidence of the technology spiral operating in the Malaysian context is not readily available, however.

FTZs are relatively easy to set up and are physically separate from the local economy. All that may be required is a suitable site with basic power and water supplies, some investment incentives, and the promise of cheap labour. While very lucrative to foreign firms as an investment opportunity, the isolated nature of these zones reduces their national economic impact *vis-à-vis* 'downstream linkages'. The supply of necessary raw materials and local inputs, and the 'narrowness' of industries within the zones where only limited types of goods are produced, have meant very localized impacts. A good example is the manufacture and assembly of electronic components and machines where raw materials and finished products can virtually be flown in and flown out of FTZs.

It is also doubtful whether at the end of the incentive period the industries in FTZs will add to the deepening of industrialization within the country. Either the productive capital will be at the end of its economic life or, worse still, they will produce goods that are obsolete and no longer needed. This, of course, presumes that the capital equipment has not been repatriated or shifted to yet another country's EPZ.

Malaysia's export-oriented industrial enclaves - FTZs and LMWs - have contributed to the country's economic welfare mainly through their absorption of unskilled and semi-skilled labour. However, a most important recent change is the growing protectionist sentiment of major industrialized countries. This may cast doubt on the long-run value of FTZs and LMWs as a viable industrialization strategy. This has been foreshadowed in the *Fifth Malaysia Plan*, which has abandoned the policy of industrial decentralization advocated in the early 1970s for one aligned to notions of neoclassical location theory. In this reorientation, greater importance is accorded to the aggregate economy. The plan asserts that

> [i]ndustrial [*sic*] type and market orientation, will, therefore, determine where specific industries will be located. Industries earmarked for the export market, using highly skilled labour and imported inputs, are expected to be located in areas enjoying agglomeration economies. Industries of an import substitution nature, and footloose industries will be encouraged to be located in smaller towns so that over time, the intervening areas between established urban growth centres will be developed. Heavy industries are expected to be located in areas convenient to the supply of their inputs and ports, if they are export-oriented.

(Malaysia 1986: 354)

The government concedes that in the past the location of many industrial estates in lagging regions placed them in a less competitive position and at a disadvantage relative to the more established industrial centres along the west coast of peninsular Malaysia. Thus the industrial corridors of the Kelang Valley, Kinta Valley, Georgetown-Butterworth, and Johor Bahru will be allowed to grow to enable these locations to compete successfully with other industrial centres overseas (Malaysia 1986: 26). This spatial reorientation has been dictated by market forces and efficiency criteria in the light of the economic recession, structural adjustments to the economy, and the necessity for financial prudence. The approach is radically different from previous ones since maximum use will be made of existing infrastructure and resources so as to avoid thinly distributing industrial estates to areas which have been unable to sustain their pace of growth. For example, two industrial estates in Sabah and one in Kedah have ceased to function. Thus the location of industries will be largely determined by market orientation. Export-oriented industries will be encouraged to locate in order to tap agglomeration economies while industries producing for the domestic market will be encouraged to relocate in smaller towns.

THE 'DUALISM' IN INDUSTRIALIZATION

As already noted there appears to be an export-domestic dualism in the industrial sector. This dualism is characterized on the one hand by a relatively efficient use of plant and capital in an EPZ catering wholly for foreign markets. On the other hand, there is a domestic import-substituting industrial sector that is either working behind high tariff barriers or has evolved from small-scale family enterprises with the common characteristics of low efficiency and low capital use. Terms such as 'footloose industries' (as compared with 'traditional' industries that suffer from locational and structural inertia) are characteristic of this dichotomy. A spatial dualism also exists where the *laissez-faire* approach to industrialization within a pioneer industry framework may have contributed to a widening of disparities between regions and among socio-economic groups. Thus export enclaves emerged in large urban centres and in developed parts of the country. The majority of the less industrially progressive states were left to grapple with industries that produced goods for the domestic market. An examination is therefore required to ascertain whether some policy instrument to promote a balanced growth of traditional and modern industries may be required.

In chronological terms it may be said that industrialization in Malaysia prior to 1970 was at an evolutionary stage. Factories were mainly traditional industrial units that had been established to respond to local market demand. Such units used methods not much more advanced than cottage-type industries. A lack of capital, isolation from mainstream developments in technology in that particular industry, and a lack of entrepreneurial skill meant that these industries were stagnant in terms of techniques and efficiency. These characteristics provide some of the criteria in distinguishing traditional from modern sectors. The differentiation between backyard type industries and modern capital-intensive industries may be easily identifiable. Where there is a use of intermediate technology, the distinction between traditional and modern can be more difficult.

The *Second Malaysia Plan* provides guidelines for such a classification. The traditional urban sector is comprised of those parts of manufacturing in which work is done with little benefit from modern equipment or techniques; the modern urban sector consists of technically advanced manufacturing (Malaysia 1971: 37). Thus the modern sector is more organized, uses more capital, and is associated with more highly specialized and productive areas. This distinction, however, is a general one because there are as yet no universally accepted criteria for classifying industries as traditional or modern (Kelley *et al.* 1972).

To illustrate the differences between the two sectors and to provide some 'order of magnitude' estimations, it is necessary to report on data obtained from a sample survey. Cheong *et al.* (1979: Ch. 7) conducted a survey of 82 firms in south Johor and classified them into one or the other sector on the basis of variables such as the age of machinery in use, the degree of automation, the location of the firm, and the background and relevant experience of the chief executives.

About half of the traditional firms were involved in repair and service activities and about a third in metal products. Only about a quarter of modern firms in the survey were concerned with metal products. Activities in the metal product industry included a wide range of operations from simple drilling, boring, and welding to more complex ones such as metal forming, casting, and forging. Thus it is not uncommon to find both the modern and traditional sectors involved in this line of activity. As there are no substantial economies to be gained in repair and service activities, the metal product industry has remained the domain of the traditional sector. The traditional sector was also involved in other activities such as plastic products, printing, and paper where the needs for labour were relatively greater. In contrast, modern sector activities were more diffuse, with firms engaged in food, plastics, chemical, rubber, and oil processing - activities requiring relatively more capital investment.

To study the labour absorptive capacity of firms, a capital-intensity coefficient was used. This measured the ratio of fixed assets to labour. About two-thirds of traditional firms in south Johor and half of modern units have a capital-intensity ratio of $5,000 per person or less. The average value of fixed assets per employee in Malaysia was about $11,800. A comparison of both figures suggests that industrial establishments in south Johor were labour-intensive. When data for modern firms are disaggregated it was shown that 32 per cent have a fixed asset/labour ratio of more than $20,000 per person, reflecting a fairly high level of capital intensity and use of sophisticated manufacturing techniques.

Finally, in terms of information sources, about 45 per cent of traditional firms had no particular source but depended on past experience for innovations and improvements. On the other hand, 40 per cent of modern firms used journals, books, and other sources of technological information; nearly a fifth sent their chief executive abroad to keep in touch with new developments. Clearly, from an examination of the three factors above, the differences between the two sectors are marked and highly differentiated. What is critical, however, is not that the differentiation is there but that it has locational and policy implications.

In a locational sense, any policy of managed industrialization should aim at promoting economic equity, especially for the poor regions where most traditional industrial firms are found. The pattern of development expenditure, at least since the Third Malaysia Plan, has shown a growth and perpetuation of the dual economy characterized by a dynamic enclave sector linked to foreign markets and a large underdeveloped traditional industrial sector serving the domestic market. In many ways this may be undesirable. For example, planned expenditure to finance industrialization on west coast states that are reliant on foreign investment will do little to eliminate the inherent bias and dualism. Traditional industrial firms will be inhibited in their growth and inevitably will be prevented from contributing to poverty eradication programmes. The potential labour-absorptive capacity of such firms and its contribution to developing small-scale Malay industrialists may thus remain untapped.

Industrial dualism also has important implications for economic efficiency. A highly efficient, mobile export sector located mostly in FTZs and a somewhat inefficient domestic market sector operating in a protected environment can exacerbate dualistic trends. Shepherd (1980: 189) gives an example of dualism in the textile industry in Malaysia. A textile company in a FTZ exports fabrics identical to those produced locally, with the latter produced at prices about 25 per cent higher. Much of this inefficiency could be remedied since many producers for the domestic market for textiles and clothing could lower their prices. However, it is contended that in motor vehicle assembly, even with reduced profits and increased technical efficiency, economic efficiency would be unlikely because of fragmented and small-scale production.

A further effect of dualism may be generated within the export processing zone itself. Many of the firms in the FTZs are branch plant operations of MNCs producing for world markets. Most employ unskilled, low-paid female workers in conjunction with highly automated techniques of production, for example, the electronics assembly industry.

Apart from low wages (due to a lack of skills), the lack of career prospects results in a high rate of turnover. These branch plant industries tend to move about to areas where factor costs such as labour and land are cheapest. Such industries have not resulted in the transfer of skills or achieved high output per worker because of the high capital investment per unit of labour.

Mehmet (1983) has characterized the development of these cheap-labour manufacturing industries in FTZs as promoting the growth of a secondary labour market. Low-status jobs are typically held by transitory and marginal workers while career-oriented positions requiring high levels of skill and training are in short supply. The phenomenon of the secondary labour market may be linked to the problem of the 'working poor'. This occurs where the earnings of workers are so low that in some cases they actually fall below the official poverty line income; in others they are not significantly higher. The growth of the secondary labour market may be counter productive on both social and economic grounds. A careful reappraisal of public policies is highly desirable, especially in conjunction with programmes that encourage industrial growth based on cheap labour. If foreign investment is to be encouraged, the emphasis should be on the transfer of skills and technology and on promoting the growth of human capital. In tandem with this reappraisal there is also the need to evaluate the dispersal of industries as a viable strategy for transferring the advantages so far enjoyed by modern sector industries to the traditional sector.

PUBLIC ENTERPRISES AND INDUSTRIAL GROWTH

The government provided the necessary management structure initially in the decentralization of industries and later in influencing the locational decisions of locally based foreign-owned firms. However, the government has also gone a step further by participating in industrial development through state-owned enterprises. Such intervention has been brought about because under the NEP a *Bumiputera* industrial and commercial class is being encouraged at the managerial and artisan levels. It was hoped that government intervention would hasten the pace of *Bumiputera* equity participation in various industries and thereby fulfil the objectives set out in the *Outline Plan* by 1990. From a theoretical point of view Wheelwright (1965) has suggested that there can be advantages in using public enterprises to counter the destructive effects of the 'logic of development through free enterprise'. The effects referred to include uneven development, monopolies, and the increasing income gap between the 'haves' and 'have-nots'.

Active state participation in the economy has been a feature in Malaysia since the 1970s. State enterprises virtually form a separate sector of the economy and come under the Ministry of Public Enterprises. For the purposes of planning and monitoring public expenditure only large non-financial public enterprises (NFPEs)[5] with a government equity ownership exceeding 50 per cent and an annual revenue exceeding $5 million are included within the operational definition of the public sector. There are about 35 NFPEs, including PETRONAS, PERNAS, all public utilities (telecommunications, gas, electricity), all public transport authorities, corporations, and systems, HICOM, all cement manufacturing, FELDA, RISDA, FELCRA, MARDEC, Sabah Forest Industries, and FIMA (Malaysia 1986: Table 7.1).

Financing of the NFPEs' expenditure depends on funds from the federal government as well as external borrowing. Although the operating surplus of NFPEs doubled from $2,826 million in 1981 to $5,955 million in 1985, a substantial proportion was contributed by PETRONAS. Excluding the earnings of PETRONAS, the operating surplus of NFPEs amounted to $606 million in 1981 and $155 million in 1985. However, when development expenditure is taken into account there was an overall deficit of $1,850 million in 1981, rising to $3,219 million in 1985 (Malaysia 1986: 237-9).

As will be observed, in the commercial and industrial area, NFPEs have been designated to facilitate and regulate the process of managed industrialization. Public holding companies and joint ventures are used exclusively as devices for increasing Malay equity in commercial and industrial assets, in accordance with the *Outline Plan* target of a 30:40:30 share by ethnic distribution[6] of equity ownership of fixed assets in the corporate sector by 1990. Nevertheless, it must be recognized that it is an indirect and artificial strategy because the assets are held 'in trust' for the Malay and *Bumiputera* community by public agencies, banks, and financial institutions. How and when this redistribution of assets will take place depends on how quickly individual members of the community are able to accumulate financial assets to buy into the equity of these enterprises.

From a broader perspective, public enterprises can serve advantageously as a basic instrument of economic planning. Where the market is small, and to prevent wasteful competition among a multiplicity of firms, such enterprises may be granted a statutory monopoly. The case of cement manufacturing is an eminent example in which prices are controlled, and the industry may also affect the pace of downstream activities in the construction industry. Moreover, in a developing market, subsidies granted judiciously could encourage the development of competition. This would avoid the provision of indirect tariff benefits or direct subsidies to private groups. In addition, the volume and quality of the output of public enterprises are more amenable to control and supervision. Finally, once public enterprises have pioneered industrial development, they may be sold off to private enterprise as a means of divestiture.

Matched against these advantages are countervailing factors that may impinge upon the efficacy of the NFPE strategy. First, with state involvement there is a tendency for the enterprise to be insulated from the competitive market, thereby reducing the operational efficiency of the endeavour. While this may be absolutely necessary to achieve other social goals that in the short term may be incompatible with economic goals, there still needs to be some time frame after which the protection from competition is removed. This is to avoid the problem of an inefficient state-owned business becoming a drain on the economy, dependent on increasing amounts of *de facto* subsidies and financial aid.

Second, it has been asserted that profitable state enterprises such as national petroleum and gas enterprises have a habit of 'empire-building', preferring to reinvest their surplus revenue in their own expansion (Mehmet 1983: 46). For example, the Petroleum Development Act of 1974 gave PETRONAS exclusive rights to explore and exploit Malaysia's onshore and offshore petroleum reserves. Under the Malaysian Constitution, mining is a state matter. Thus when the Negri Sembilan SEDC began developing the petrochemical complex at Port Dickson, PETRONAS cited the 1974 Act to remind the state that it required a licence from PETRONAS to develop the project. It also seems that PETRONAS has been determined not to share its monopoly. In 1975, after the official signing of an agreement giving PETRONAS exclusive rights in Perak, the *Mentri Besar* (Chief Minister) could only express the hope that PETRONAS would consider joint ventures with the state government in future (Gale 1981: 1133).

Finally, the unintended development of a substantial public sector may generate resource misallocation and thereby decelerate aggregate growth rates. The stock of skilled and highly trained managerial and technical staff to run public enterprises properly is limited at best. Draining the civil service of such staff may be counterproductive, since an efficient bureaucracy is equally important. An even more worrying problem of which warning has already been given is that 'corrupt practices, nepotism and favouritism may well replace the rules of operational efficiency, [and] ultimately [lead] to economic mismanagement' (Mehmet 1983: 46).

Thus, in terms of the *Outline Plan* and restructuring the industrial employment pattern, three levels may be considered: increasing the share of Malays in employment in the modern sector; increasing the Malay share in corporate ownership; and increasing the number of Malay entrepreneurs and the degree of Malay managerial control.

Ownership gives Malays the ability to enjoy the fruits of wealth. Entrepreneurial and managerial talents give them the ability to create wealth

(Shepherd 1980: 199)

The Malay share of wage income in manufacturing has been less than that of the general workforce for locational and historical reasons. Most Malays live in rural areas and this has had a tendency not only to lower their wages but also to reduce their participation in higher-wage modern activities located in urban areas and in the industrially more advanced states. In structural terms, the employment of Malays has been concentrated in the lower-paid unskilled and semi-skilled occupations. Government policy was therefore directed at the dispersal of industries to regional locations and to changing the structure of Malay participation in industrial employment. The Industrial Co-ordination Act, 1975, has been used as much as the informal but powerful administrative pressures such as the granting of licences, loans, and the government's own procurement policies.

In sum, the crucial question that remains is how appropriate the NFPEs have been as a means of helping the government achieve its objectives of corporate ownership by *Bumiputera*. It is felt that this enquiry can only be satisfied on the basis of a very long-term longitudinal study. For the present, greater effort is required in bringing about some coherent planning and co-ordination between enterprises, the private sector, and the bureaucracy so that all participants become aware of the objectives and their common endeavours.

FUTURE INDUSTRIAL PATTERNS

The continuation of rapid industrial growth, particularly of labour-intensive manufacturing, is essential to attaining the objectives of the NEP. Without the contribution from the industrial sector the 'redistribution through growth' of the national economic cake may be impossible. A shift from import substitution to export-led manufacturing growth will be crucial as more obvious areas of import substitution become exhausted. Moreover, manufacturing growth will be from a much larger base, and increasing protectionism in other countries may force Malaysian manufacturers to adopt more aggressive export strategies.

The Malaysian economy has been characterized as one that is attractive to foreign and domestic investors. Most significantly, its political stability within a free enterprise environment has been a major factor in instilling such confidence in the country. A well-disciplined bureaucracy structured along the lines of the British civil service, coupled with the necessary physical and socio-economic infrastructure for rapid economic development, gives the country a decided edge over the rest of the developing world. An abundance of natural and human resources provides ample opportunities for investment in many types of processing activities. Investors can expect high rates of returns. Reddaway (1967), for instance, cites a rate of return of 26.9 per cent per annum for investments in Malaysia, as compared with 8.9 per cent per annum for British investments world-wide. While the data are dated, the conclusion reflects the tendency to undertake investments in developing countries only where there are good prospects of high rates of return.

Shepherd (1980: 208-10) has reported that there is significant evidence to show a deterioration in the rate of investment in the manufacturing sector since 1974. The downturn in investment in manufacturing could be the result of a combination of factors. The economic recession of 1975-85, the disquiet expressed over the Industrial Co-ordination Act, 1975, following on the heels of the peak year for private investment in Malaysia, and the possibility that manufacturing industry in Malaysia may have lost some of its competitive edge have been identified as the main factors behind the drop in investment. Moreover, it is still unclear whether there are cyclical or structural factors at work: if cyclical factors are identified as the cause, the fall in investment may be beyond the country's control. The flexible implementation of policies to restructure employment and the offer of financial incentives will sustain Malaysia's competitiveness in attracting investments and in capturing markets abroad. A thorough analysis of market demand and market penetration is required to design policies that will facilitate the exploitation of opportunities as and when these arise.

Shifts in the corporate strategies of MNCs, such as the relocation of offshore processing plants from Malaysian FTZs to other countries, would place Malaysia in an unenviable position. Malaysia may have to grasp what it can, rather than plan a measured, deliberate 'hard-nosed' strategy of pursuing only those types of MNCs and industries that fit the long-term planning framework. At least in the semiconductor industry, the reverse seems to be happening as there appears to be a recentralization of production in selected geographical locations in Malaysia (McGee 1986). However, Salih and Young (1986) caution that over-reliance on MNCs exposes the economy even more severely to global downturns. It will also spell the loss of autonomy, especially since the country may be unable to adapt the level of technology to local requirements.

To determine long-term requirements for growth a forecasting model has been used by Young (1980b) to project and assess the goals of the *Outline Plan*. Inputs into this seven-sector macro-model included the rate of growth of private and public investment in the relevant sectors. Using different scenarios, three alternatives were offered: 'moderate', 'rapid', and 'accelerated' growth. Results from the simulation suggest that only the accelerated growth model would achieve all the growth and most of the restructuring targets set under the *Outline Plan*. Manufacturing was identified as the key sector in providing the necessary growth rates. To achieve the target of 13 per cent per annum in manufacturing output growth, the model projected a growth requirement of 17 per cent per annum for the whole period of manufacturing investment. According to the *Fifth Malaysia Plan*, between 1982 and 1985 the manufacturing sector recorded an annual growth rate of 5 per cent - well below the target set. In fact, only electrical machinery, the subsector with the highest growth rate (12.8 per cent per annum between 1982 and 1985) approached anywhere near the planned target. Negative growth rates have been recorded for beverages and tobacco (-0.5 per cent per annum) and for non-ferrous metal based industries (-3.2 per cent per annum). That the *Outline Plan* has set overly ambitious targets in 1970 is self-evident. What was perceived to be the general trend of growth given the 1970-75 economic environment has become vastly different as the expiry date of 1990 approaches. But then too it is arguable that in any event such forecasts provide only a perspective and an outline for future action.

The first policy conclusion is that there are already a number of manufacturing industries that have shown an ability to compete in the international market place. Such industries have so far been on a relatively small scale. The implication is that in a bid to maintain an efficient allocation of resources, incentives must also be provided to export-oriented industries of the same magnitude as those to import-substituting industries. Second, there may be some advantages in establishing small-scale manufacturing industries[7] that make intensive use of unskilled labour. Not only would these industries form useful linkages as suppliers to larger industries, they would also have a favourable impact on income distribution in terms of employment (Chee 1979: 138). Thus a policy for small industry needs to be formulated so as to promote industries that are modern, self-supporting, and economically viable. Then, a comprehensive plan for the promotion of this sector is required so that problems of capital shortage, outmoded methods of production, ineffective marketing, poor product quality, and inefficient management may be eliminated (Chee 1979: 150). Without such a plan there is the danger of the proliferation of a large number of small industries of various types, each vying for government assistance. This has been characterized as the 'peasantization' of local industries, which by its very nature is anti-developmental. The encouragement of small-scale industries does not in any way detract from the fostering of industries requiring moderate levels of skilled labour and capital since these can be profitable from the point of view of investment.

Finally, there is a need to reduce the element of subjective risk in industrial development by at least guaranteeing investment incentives and demonstrating that Malaysia is a suitable location for foreign manufacturing subsidiaries serving the South East Asian region. The uncertain investment climate of Hong Kong with its return to the People's Republic of China in 1997, the volatility of the Philippines' socio-political climate and the fledgeling industrial characteristics of some near neighbours all combine to place Malaysia in a strong position. It is therefore desirable that present incentives policy to encourage foreign investment in manufacturing be continued. At the same time new incentives should be devised to make it an even more attractive place for foreign investment.

6

PERSPECTIVES ON PROBLEMS, POLICIES, AND PROSPECTS

This chapter examines Malaysia's socio-political economy in the 1980s. Malaysia's relative attractiveness to foreign investment is first described in order to evaluate such investment as a source of continued growth. The second section evaluates the complexities that derive from the cultural, ethnic, and religious diversity of Malaysia. The Malays, United Malay National Organization (UMNO), and Islam prompt special attention as these form the linchpin of an understanding of the policies and prospects for economic growth. The third section discusses the rights, privileges, and powers of the hereditary rulers and the friction with the executive arm of the government. The special position of Sabah and Sarawak is said to have inhibited rapid development. These claims are examined in the fourth section while the final section assesses new directions and new dilemmas. An evaluation of Malaysian efforts in the privatization of public enterprises is undertaken in the context of failures, financial scandals, and corruption.

Malaysia's future prospects are inextricably linked with the maintenance of an attractive investment climate. In this process, long-term political stability is vital. It is argued here that where political stability and communal unrest surface, the economic cost may be in terms of slow growth, the loss of overseas investment, and unemployment.

A MALAYSIAN BIAS

When Malaysia turned 21 in 1978, a special feature in *Time* magazine painted a bright picture of the country's economy, attributable to a steady economic growth of 7-8 per cent per annum, largely as a result of world demand for its rubber, tin, and other primary commodities.[1] The optimistic outlook then was that the nation's economic prospects were sufficiently encouraging for all to share in peace and prosperity. How and why was this so? According to observers, neighbouring Thailand and the Philippines were considered too unstable, Singapore too structured, and Indonesia too unpractical to merit the same optimism. According to the same view, Malaysia was just about the best investment in South East Asia (*Time*, July 27, 1981, p. 48). While the same may be said of the rest of ASEAN, in Malaysia English is widely spoken even though *Bahasa Malaysia* is the national language; the productivity of labour is high and wage rates are competitive. Tariff rates are among the lowest in the developing world, with liberal policies on the repatriation of profits. There are tax incentives as well as tax holidays for designated 'pioneer industries', and as in many transactions in Asia, one can even haggle for a reduction of corporate and excess profits taxes.

At the beginning of Malaysia's development as an independent resource-rich nation, its economy was 'outer-directed'. The transition from colonialism was relatively painless as is attested by the continuation of private foreign investment, even though this could be interpreted as a form of economic neocolonialism. Capital and technical assistance were forthcoming from abroad as the inherited political, economic and social institutions progressed to adjust to an independent existence. Apart from the suspension of parliamentary democracy for a brief period of 21 months between May 19, 1969, and February 20, 1971, there has been relatively little to upset economic growth and progress (Rogers 1972). Inheriting the structure of the British civil service as a role model has meant that in theory there was no 'spoils system'. Civil servants were supposed to be apolitical, with the expectation that they would loyally carry out the policies of whatever party was in government (Chik 1978).

However, in the 1980s this happy state of affairs has turned sombre and less bright. Archaic social structures and debilitating communal disputes have threatened to undermine much of the potential of the country. The observation has been made that friction between communities has tended to rise when the economy is doing badly. However, the more perceptive view is that overemphasis on the redistribution and rectification of economic imbalances in favour of the Malays had a negative impact on local and foreign investment, and this has flowed on to the political arena. The curtailment of civil liberties and wide-ranging government participation in business, commerce, and industry with the aim of raising the living standards of the *Bumiputera* have been divisive. It seems the distribution of the fruits of the New Economic Policy was either not quick enough or not widespread enough, so that only a privileged few and those best equipped to take advantage of the opportunites have benefited. The potential instability has made many foreign investors very wary (Bass 1970: 155).

One commentator has gone so far as to say that the state appears to play the central role in generating disequalizing tendencies, especially through its policies affecting land, agricultural, and industrial development (Tan 1981: 232). It has been said that the last five years have seen the politicization of commerce and the commercialization of politics (Pinwill 1987).

Yet despite these negative observations, Malaysia has survived, developed, and prospered. According to the *Economist* (January 31, 1987, p. 4) the auguries are gloomy. The market for rubber and palm oil is poor, while the market for tin has collapsed and the market for oil is weak. Pepper remains the sole export that is doing well. Thus the context of change in Malaysia will be one in which policies are directed at facilitating rapid economic growth while retaining the features of an open capitalist economy. The goal is modernization and growth. Anything less will mean that the desired objectives of a restructured society will not be attained by 1990. This is an unenviable task since the very openness of the Malaysian economy itself makes it highly vulnerable to external forces, which at times work against national interests. But at the same time, the economy needs to produce enough to satisfy the social contract of the NEP. In some ways the openness of the economy exerts such pressures as to make it anti-developmental, for example, as a disincentive to both domestic and foreign private investment, and in encouraging capital flight, uncertainty, and instability.

To appreciate investment activity in Malaysia, for example, a study of the data for the 1980s suggests the level of confidence in the economy. Data showing investments abroad and in Malaysia for 1980-87 are shown on Table 6.1. Net direct investment abroad increased steadily between 1981 and 1983 and fell dramatically between 1983 and 1984 but picked up again between 1984 and 1985. There are, however, no particular reasons to explain these fluctuations although it is believed that a tight credit squeeze domestically and a recession in the local economy may have played a significant role. In fact, if a comparison is made with direct investments in Malaysia, the picture is less bright. Apart from the increase in investments in 1980-81, there has been a steady decrease in investments in Malaysia which only abated in the 1986-87 period. Again no explanations are readily available. It may be noted, however, that up to 1984, the Malaysian *ringgit* enjoyed a favourable conversion rate to special drawing rights (SDRs) as computed by the International Monetary Fund (IMF 1988). But the rate has become more unfavourable in relative terms since 1985.

Table 6.1. Malaysia: Direct investments abroad and within the country, 1981-87 ($ million)

	1980	1981	1982	1983	1984	1985	1986	1987
Direct net investment abroad	-	1,065	1,897	2,732	682	1,002	-	-
Direct investments in Malaysia*	2,035	2,800	3,139	2,886	1,849	1,823	1,506	1,574
Conversion rates: *ringgit* per SDR+	2.835	2.610	2.561	2.448	2.377	2.665	3.180	3.536

Source: IMF (1988: 415-21).

Notes: * Data for direct investments in Malaysia are derived from annual financial surveys of limited companies. Entries include the reinvestment of undistributed earnings.
 + SDR - special drawing rights - are provisions by which governments belonging to the IMF are permitted to draw upon it for gold or foreign currencies to settle the balance of international payments.

Change in the 1990s may witness a reversion to cautiousness verging on conservatism, rewards for efficiency, and the elimination of corruption, however defined. Furthermore, an articulate consumer movement and the conservationists' concern for the environment give two indications that Malaysian society has progressed from merely satisfying basic needs. It is now concerned also with the quality of life. But pitfalls exist; for example, the suddenness of the development of the petroleum industry and the dimensions of the wealth it produces have affected the priorities of development (Voon and Khoo 1986: 46). This probably describes the affliction known as the 'Dutch disease'[2] in which an export boom in one part of the economy sets up complex effects that actually retard growth in other parts of the economy (Roemer 1985: 236).

There are several ways in which objective perceptions about the Malaysian economy have been measured. One is the use of an index that purports to gauge the business environment risk (BERI). Investors are asked to give scores of between one and ten on the basis of 11 criteria.[3] In a press report an average score of 82 out of a total score of 110 was given by executives in the telecommunications industry, 73 by Rotarians in Kuala Lumpur, and 76 by a group of British investors (*New Straits Times*, January 26, 1987). While such a score may be useful as a rough indicator of the perceptions of a favourable investment climate it is also useful as a comparative device for indexing different countries on the basis of the same set of criteria. However, as far as may be ascertained such an index has not been used in other ASEAN countries to provide comparative data. Moreover, the index is superficial in that particular aspects of the business environment, for example, returns to capital, are not measured.

Another method of getting at the key issues confronting a country's economy may be to analyse the contents of the daily press. A basic assumption of this method is that only newsworthy items and questions of economic growth or non-growth are reported and the magnitude of its importance is roughly proportional to the amount of space devoted to it. This method of analysing content[4] allows the coding and hence quantification of written material and shows what appears to be topical at any one point in time.

Following an analysis of data obtained from three daily newspapers and three news journals, content analysis provided the basis for conclusions on key issues facing the Malaysian economy.[5] In the newspapers examined, stock market prices, investment, and trade were given prominent coverage in the economics section. The next most important item concerned the court case in London involving the activities of Bumiputra Malaysia Finance Ltd. and its alleged conspiracies to defraud. Some space was devoted to the activities of government off-budget agencies (OBAs), land development, and promotion of the Malaysian-made car, the Proton Saga. In terms of political affairs, the prime minister's visit to India was given coverage, as were major political parties in government and on the opposition benches. Various items on aspects of social affairs were reported, including legal aid, housing, Islamic offences, and education. International news items and advertisements took up the remaining space (see Table 6.2).

Table 6.2. Malaysia: Content analysis of three selected local newspapers, February 2, 1987 (%)*

Topic/News item	New Straits Times Feb. 2, 1987	Star Feb. 2, 1987	Malay Mail Feb. 2, 1987
Economy			
Financial	73.6	35.5	-
Investments / trade	59.1	2.9 pages	-
Shares / commodity market	2.0 pages	3.1 pages	-
Off-budget agencies	56.8	-	-
Land development	8.1	-	-
Transport / Road Act	9.3	41.6	-
Malaysian car	3.4	3.5	19.4
Politics			
Prime Minister	43.5	45.8	-
Politicians	7.3	5.9	-
Political parties UMNO	1.4 pages	20.1	-
MIC	38.4	9.7	52.0
Gerakan	10.8	-	-
DAP	6.9	-	-
PPP	-	-	21.3
Social Affairs			
Perak	-	1.0 pages	-
Sarawak	4.9	84.1	-
Sabah	20.2	28.4	-
National ideology	14.6	-	-
Islamic law offences	44.3	-	-
Social welfare	65.1	76.8	-
Migration overseas	13.8	-	-
Education - teachers	39.9	49.9	1.4 pages
Consumer affairs	2.6	36.0	16.6
Trade unions	7.1	13.6	-
Miscellaneous			
Local news	7.4 pages	13.9 pages	11.7 pages
International news	7.1 pages	4.3 pages	3.7 pages
Sport	6.1 pages	6.1 pages	11.7 pages
Advertisements	22.0 pages	12.4 pages	11.5 pages
Total number of pages	*36.0+*	*44.0*	*32.0*

Sources: *Malay Mail*, February 2, 1987; *New Straits Times*, February 2, 1987; *Star*, February 2, 1987.

Notes: * Data refer to percentage of a standard tabloid page.
+ Standardized as a standard tabloid page measuring 260 mm x 365 mm.

Table 6.3. Malaysia: Content analysis of three selected news journals, 1987

News journal	Coverage
Asiaweek February 1, 1987	
Malaysia. Getting together.	31 % of one page
Deposits: Mismanagement, corruption or both	1 page
People (in Malaysia)	68 % of one page
The Economist January 31, 1987 (Special Report)	*% of report*
Struggle for survival	14.4
Buying a bargain Rolls	9.4
Prices in a jig-saw	19.1
Busy fingers	20.7
Altogether now	8.7
Wobbling Sabah and in Sarawak too	11.5
So what is to be done?	16.2
Far Eastern Economic Review January 29, 1987	
The law: The rewards of crime. A former Bank Bumiputra director is jailed for corruption	1.1 pages
Policies: New Year's resolution. Malaysia wishes to refund some co-op depositor's money	1.2 pages
Stock market: Kuala Lumpur	5 % of one page

Sources: *Asiaweek*, February 1, 1987; *The Economist*, January 31, 1987; and *Far Eastern Economic Review*, January 29, 1987.

Note: A standard page for news journals used here measures 208 mm x 272 mm.

The analysis of the three news journals demonstrated varying degrees of disapproval of Malaysian socio-economic life (Table 6.3). The *Far Eastern Economic Review* devoted more than two pages to corruption among deposit-taking co-operatives, a theme taken up in *Asiaweek*. There was also a report on political alliances between states and space devoted to human interest stories such as drug offences or religious offences. The *Economist* report was an investigation of Malaysian economic well-being and the social consequences of a society divided along ethnic lines.

The content analysis suggests strong messages to the government and foreign investor alike. Any visitor to the country landing at Subang International Airport and reading these journals or newspapers would be bombarded with stories of financial imprudence, mismanagement, and corruption. Added to these are ethnic politics, divisiveness, dissension from the various states, and general uncertainty about the industrialization programmes of the country. If, as the news stories suggest, all these are true, a prudent foreigner might forgo investing in Malaysia. The government on its part has reacted to such adverse publicity in the press with a campaign decrying corruption and fraud, and the setting up of various Commissions of Inquiry. At the same time, the government reorganized the bureaucratic machinery to eliminate any likely source of weakness that might drive foreign investors away. Thus there is a pressing need to address these issues individually and to evaluate each in the light of surrounding circumstances. The following sections attempt these tasks.

A NATION OF MINORITIES

History has shown that ethnic and cultural diversity in Malaysia has not weakened the nation, but allowed it to achieve one of the fastest rates of development in Southeast Asia. These qualities of the nation and the people need to be further strengthened and mobilized if the challenges that lie ahead are to be overcome.

(Malaysia 1976: 92)

The above statement has echoes of the Malaysian coat of arms, which bears the inscription *Bersekutu Bertambah Mutu* (Unity is Strength). But peninsular Malaysia's three-sided society has yet to reach the goal of racial harmony. While there is a veneer of peaceful coexistence and fraternity, linguistic, religious, educational, and class differences crisscross the multi-ethnic fabric so that homogeneity is non-existent, and talk of closer integration is next to impossible. On inspired occasions there is mention of creating a true national Malaysian identity rising above communalism. However, a call for a 'Malaysian Malaysia' by the Gerakan Party, for example, is politically unacceptable since there can be no ethnic equality in all aspects of life in Malaysia.

Journalists are prone to the sensational when discussing inter-ethnic relations in Malaysia. That the country is a 'festering cauldron of inter-racial rivalry and animosity' suggests much bitterness and outright hatred. But to say that the issue of race is underrated and understated is simplistic at most (Loudon 1987). It has also been stated that economic, racial, and religious tensions could all come to the fore as Malaysia becomes a nation more riven by dissension than joined by protestations of unity (Rothwell 1987: 23). The truth perhaps lies closer to the middle view that the dominant Malay and the minority Chinese and Indian communities are going through turmoil and self-analysis and are not quite coming to terms with the generational and attitudinal changes that are taking place among them. Their perceptions have changed over the years and there is a ready willingness to challenge the other communities and articulate their point of view, whatever the consequences (Pillai 1987a). It is here that politicians, engaged in brinkmanship and opportunism, will attempt to score political points off one another. The ever-present danger is that any issue might be seized upon and grow quickly out of hand to become a serious political issue. The spectre of open conflict between various groups of people is one which the government assiduously wishes to avoid.

For example, the unrest in 1987 caused by the Ministry of Education's decision to appoint non-Mandarin speaking headmasters and senior assistants to Chinese primary schools is one such example (editorial, *Sydney Morning Herald*, October 30, 1987). The Chinese claimed that the decision violated a constitutional guarantee that no person should be 'prohibited or prevented' from teaching or learning any language. In truth, the official explanation that there were insufficient applicants willing to move from Pulau Pinang, where most of the qualified teachers were to be found, to other parts of peninsular Malaysia for a $20 per month increase in salary makes a persuasive argument.

Malaysian ethnic problems interlock in such a way as to provide a permanent obstacle course and a test of statesmanship. There is a constant struggle to maintain harmony and tolerance. Any diminution will inevitably impact on economic, political, and security issues. The question is not whether the different ethnic groups can coexist in peace and harmony but whether the country can effectively modernize its political thinking and grow into political maturity in line with its economic gains.

The relationship between Malays and non-Malays has had and will continue to have a profound influence on economic development and growth. Among the Malays, there is a small class of the rich and powerful who control the reins of government, some of whom are also captains of industry. The majority of Malays are poor by national standards and inhabit rural areas. The Chinese and, to a lesser degree, the Indians dominate the cities; some among them participate in the higher levels of commerce, industry, and finance. Where rubber estates and tin mines are not in the hands of foreigners, they are invariably in Chinese hands. It is within this complex blend of communal ingredients balanced by measured proportions of shares of interest groups that any discussion of the NEP will have to take place. In this regard Malaysia has had some success in dealing with its multi-ethnic complexities.

The strategy of rapid economic growth with redistribution has been the centrepiece of every five-year development plan since the *Second Malaysia Plan*. The NEP has brought about important shifts in income distribution. There has been a narrowing of inter-ethnic income disparities, although intra-ethnic income distribution has become more unequal. For example, the *Bumiputera* mean household income increased by about 30 per cent between 1979 and 1984, as compared with 20 per cent for the Chinese and 9 per cent for Indians in the same period (Malaysia 1986: 99). Comparisons over time also suggest a decline. The *Mid-term Review of the Third Malaysia Plan* (Malaysia 1979) reported that the ratio of Chinese to Malay median monthly household income for the period 1970-76 at constant 1970 prices had declined from 2.23 to 2.10. The same pattern was repeated for Indian to Malay and 'all groups' to Malay differentials. The suggestion was that the Malays had been catching up with other groups during this period. Data from the *Fifth Malaysia Plan* show a further decline in the disparity of incomes. At constant 1970 prices, the ratio of Chinese to *Bumiputera* median monthly household income for the period 1979-84 declined from 1.89 to 1.76 and similarly for Indian-*Bumiputera* and 'all groups'-*Bumiputera* ratios. Part of the decline was attributable to a much faster growth rate among the *Bumiputera* compared to the other groups.

However, urban-rural income differentials have increased, suggesting clearly that only the urban residents gained. At constant 1970 prices the ratio of median income between urban and rural groups for 1979 and 1984 was 1.62 and 1.72 respectively. Within specific ethnic groups there has been an increase in inequality, with the richer households gaining relative to the lower-income families. However, on the basis of the Gini coefficient[6] between 1970 and 1984 the ratio has narrowed from 0.51 to 0.48, indicating an improvement in overall income inequality (Malaysia 1986: 100).

Despite these gains, there remain problems of adjustment and perception. A paternal Malay leadership could quite easily misjudge the mood of the Malays, failing to see the problems being created for them and those left untouched by the NEP. This lapse could come about as a result of misconceptions as to what the NEP is really designed to achieve.

The strategy of redistribution with growth works well where there are new additions to wealth for sharing. Thus, the observation that ethnic harmony is dependent upon a buoyant economy can be rationalized in the following way. Depressed economic conditions tend to heighten ethnic animosity and rivalry arising from conflicts over the distribution of more limited resources. The government has given priority to stimulating the growth of all sectors of the economy in its diversification and industrialization programmes in the hope that a temporary shortfall in one sector would be offset by a gain in another sector. For this to work successfully, ethnicity can have no place. Success in the market place requires a recognition that there is diversity in the world. Such a recognition demands tolerance and openness, thus pushing inter-ethnic differences further into the background. But ethnic pluralism is becoming a social and political problem. The rise of a middle class with special interests is predicted at least in the urban areas. In the rural areas, on the other hand, problems of adjustment have yet to be solved, including those of grappling with Muslim fundamentalism, 'deviationism',[7] migration, and a transition to modernization while retaining traditional Malay values.

MALAYS, UMNO, AND MUSLIMS

A common misconception of the NEP is that it is a programme for transferring wealth to Malays in urban and rural areas. It is not and was never intended to be (Leigh 1983: 23). Rather, the twin aims of the policy were to reduce poverty and to restructure society. The NEP rejects market forces as a means of achieving distributive justice since it was believed that the 'invisible hand' tended to make the division of wealth more unequal. Government intervention in the economy was required to eradicate poverty and restructure the ownership of wealth within an avowedly capitalist economy. This task of social engineering has had its detractors. There have been assessments to the effect that the economic stagnation of the economy in the 1980s was attributable to the NEP and the Malay-first emphasis. For example, the advancement of under-qualified and low achieving Malays into positions of responsibility in government and public enterprise was sometimes associated with a decline in efficiency and productivity (Suzuki and Cummings 1985: 505). The explanation may lie in the rapidity of the promotion and replacement by Malays, rather than in an innate inability to do the job. However, that point of view is also debatable since this inability to cope may be the price to be paid for the rapidity of change and growth. It is suggested that such problems might sort themselves out through a form of meritocracy in which those with ability and skills are given promotion.

Another discernible feature is the impact of government policies on Malays and non-Malays alike. Initially the policies were heavily weighted in favour of Malay interests, but in time, with the reality of implementation and political expediency, there was a diminution of the initial impression. This has been termed the 'fixed pie mentality' whereby after introducing a policy dramatically in order to impress the Malays, its implementation was slowed in an effort to placate non-Malays (Scott 1968). However, such practices, if followed too often, may have the opposite effect in that while Malay expectations are raised unrealistically, non-Malays are antagonized unnecessarily (Bass 1970: 159). The government has been able to tread this narrow path by appeals to the traditional Malay preference for indirection and compromise.

> Traditional Malay politics ... [is] the art of papering over cracks and strains of coalition; rallies [are] masterpieces of tact and graceful allusion.
>
> (Rothwell 1987: 23)

It is often asserted that any system will remain viable so long as individual economic needs are met and there is a pragmatic political organization able to absorb and unite divergent interests. A change in either variable, such as prolonged material hardship, a dysfunctional use of force or coercion, or a shift to doctrinal authoritarianism can endanger the stability of the system (Indorf 1978: 193). Whether UMNO fills a role in providing that pragmatic political organization has become a moot point. The fact that most Malays are associated with UMNO and the truism that UMNO is a Malay party means that it speaks for about half of the population of the country, at least before February 1988.[8] Added to this is UMNO's dominant role in the coalition party *Barisan Nasional* (BN) which gives it a standing equivalent to a *primus inter pares* (first among equals). When this primacy has been shaken or questioned, the consequences have reverberated throughout the system.

Much has been written about the May 13, 1969, incident and its causes (Reid 1969). It appears that the Alliance government in general and the UMNO party in particular had lost much of their popular mandate and there was disenchantment in the ranks. Clearer still was the message that a united UMNO could and would lead to a stable nation. The expulsion in 1970 from UMNO's Executive Council of Dr Mahathir Mohamed for circulating a letter critical of *Tunku* Abdul Rahman, and the sacking of UMNO's Secretary General, *Datuk* Musa Hitam, for disloyalty are manifestations of intra-party politics. It is also an inter-generational conflict between the older and the younger (Bass 1970: 156). But by the mid-1970s UMNO had begun to restabilize, with new-found confidence emanating from renewed mass Malay support, and emerged as sole arbiter of political, economic, and cultural development (Chee 1973: 154). Despite personal and factional intrigue within UMNO by the beginning of the 1980s, the triumph of the moderates over more extreme views 'presages an era of calmness for UMNO politics' (*Haji* Ahmad 1981: 203). The prevailing view therefore was that stability in Malaysia has always depended on the Malays feeling secure. 'Whenever UMNO, as the unchallenged repository of Malay confidence, looks weak, or whenever its leadership looks weak, the Malays show signs of insecurity and they turn on non-Malays' (Loudon 1987: 25).

Recent challenges to the UMNO leadership, agitation among other member parties within the coalition for a greater voice in policy-making, and constructive criticisms of established government policy have all been interpreted as signs of weaknesses within UMNO. The racial tensions in 1987, followed by arrests under the Internal Security Act, 1960, have been perceived to be the result of a schism within UMNO itself. The view is that much of Malaysia's political stability depends upon a united UMNO (Pillai 1987b: 26). If this hypothesis is correct, there would be much to be gained by buttressing this position.

Islamic fundamentalism is a further topic of discussion in political circles, whether it concerns the White Dakwah (a radical Muslim fundamentalist group) or simply a Muslim revivalism that rejects western attributes of modernization and its decadent features of moral laxity, corruption, and usury. A less extreme view is one that sees the neglect of the positive values of Islam - justice, honesty, and equality - although by its nature Islam is an exclusivist religion. This very feature keeps Malay culture and traditions separated from the other groups in Malaysia. The idea of an Islamic state has been tried out unsuccessfully.

For example, Parti Islam, a fringe political party, had aspirations of turning Malaysia into an Islamic state. In the 1986 general elections the message of this party was that in an Islamic state only male Muslims could vote. Further, the idea of simple living, self-sufficiency, and making the country less dependent on foreigners had widespread appeal even among the Chinese. The selling point was that Islam did not discriminate on the basis of race, creed, colour, or region of origin. The Chinese would be better off living in an Islamic state because of the elimination of any discrimination against them and because they would be free to pursue any education they wanted. Most alluringly, a Chinese Muslim could even become head of state (*Economist*, January 31, 1987). While Parti Islam did not obtain the electoral mandate it sought, the party is hopeful of more success in the next general elections.

There are possibly two factors that hinder the Malaysian government's stance against advocating Muslim values for the wider population. First, the government is fearful of being unable to control radical extreme Islamic groups and the turmoil that would follow. Lessons from the Iranian revolution have not been lost among politicians in this regard. Instead, the position of the more moderate group as the legitimate proponent of Islam has been advanced to counter the extremists and radicals. Second, Malaysian society is multi-religious and although Islam is a state religion there are constitutional guarantees[9] for other forms of religions to be practised. Thus if the government were to insist, for example, on diligence based on Muslim values, non-Muslim groups would take offence. These factors may therefore preclude the foisting of Islam, not only as a religion but also as a way of life, on the majority of the Malaysian population.

It is to be noted also that the notion of military intervention has never been entertained at any time since the country's independence. The closest the armed forces have come to direct intervention was during the 1969 inter-ethnic troubles when the Alliance government's popularity was at a low ebb. In general, the legitimacy of the government has always been assured through the electoral process and only when this avenue was closed would military intervention be a possibility. There are no easy explanations for the lack of 'activism' from the armed forces. It can only be presumed that the close-knit relationships among the various royal houses and the top echelons of the armed forces, the strong sense of loyalty towards the Sultanates and the symbolic rank which Sultans traditionally have as commanders-in-chief of the armed forces may provide some of the reasons for a lack of direct involvement in government. This situation is very unlike regimes in various parts of South East Asia in which political legitimacy has been obtained on the basis of strong military backing. The examples of military governments at various times in this century in Burma, Thailand, Indonesia, and the Philippines may be cited.

The victory of the BN at the April 1982 general elections[10] heralded the advent of a new era in political leadership in Malaysia. For the first time, neither the prime minister nor his deputy had come from the ruling elite or the 'princely' class of leaders.[11] Instead, they had come from within the *rakyat* (people) and had much grass-roots support from the rank and file of UMNO. Another factor to note was the complete political rehabilitation of both leaders, since they had previously been expelled from the Supreme Council of UMNO after the May 1969 incident. The government of the '2Ms' (Dr Mahathir and *Datuk* Musa Hitam) aimed to provide a state that was clean, efficient, and trustworthy. However, it was probably the zeal of the prime minister and his deputy for efficiency that brought them into open conflict with the rulers, sparking off the so-called 'constitutional crisis' of 1983.

RIGHTS AND PRIVILEGES OF THE RULERS

The Malay Sultanate[12] plays an important dual role in the socio-political life of the country. It is a symbol of political organization and constitutionality and it denotes the primacy of the Malays. At the same time the Sultanate represents the rule of law and the arbiter of proper procedures in political participation for both Malays and non-Malays alike. The roles and prerogatives of the monarchy[13] under the Malaysian Constitution are given protection from legislative action so that the prior consent of the rulers is required for any legislation that touches on the 'rights, privileges and powers of the rulers'.[14] The constitutional crisis of 1983 was precipitated by attempt of the executive to modify some of the entrenched provisions relating to the monarchy in the Constitution.

In August 1983 a Constitutional (Amendment) Bill, 1983 (hereafter the 1983 Bill), was tabled in Parliament which proposed three main changes. First, royal assent was 'deemed' after a lapse of 15 days from the day of presentation to the *Yang di Pertuan Agong*. Second, the 1983 Bill proposed to provide for the issuance of a proclamation by the *Yang di Pertuan Agong* if the prime minister was satisfied that a grave emergency existed in which the security, economy, or public order of the Federation or any of its parts was threatened. The third change sought to amend the provisions for royal assent to State Bills. The central issue was whether the king was constitutionally bound to assent to the 1983 Bill. Here we are reminded that 'in modern constitutional monarchies, the King reigns but does not rule; authority derives from popular consent through elections, parties and legislatures' (Huntington 1968: 177). An analytical chronology of the Malaysian crisis is provided by Lowe (1984); and a legal analysis is given by Lee (1986).

One issue that has been raised was whether the king must automatically assent to legislation passed by both Houses of Parliament. While there have been no precedents concerning this issue, considered legal and academic arguments suggest that the king can never withhold assent. This is the conclusion of Trindade (1978: 103) and *Raja Tun Azlan Shah* (1982: 1). If these conclusions are correct then it is submitted that the issue in the Malaysian constitutional context is settled.

The 1983 constitutional crisis was not resolved until a compromise formula was agreed and the amendments in the 1983 Bill were revoked. The final act of revocation came about on January 9, 1984, with the passing of the Constitutional (Amendment) Act, 1984. Under a new Article 66 (4B) a Bill presented to the *Yang di Pertuan Agong* shall be assented to within 30 days of its submission. A non-financial Bill may be returned by the king to the House for reconsideration giving a statement of reasons for the objections. Where the king neither approves nor returns the Bill within the specified 30 days, the Bill becomes law at the expiration of that period, as if he had assented to the Bill. From a socio-political point of view this was perhaps the first occasion on which parliamentary democracy as a political system had gained precedence over one of the chief symbols of Malay primacy. It also implied that 'since Malay dominance in the parliamentary process is so complete, the Sultanate is no longer needed as an ideological rationale for Malay supremacy' (Lowe 1984: 12). The crisis also probably signified the last time the granting or withholding of assent could be used by the rulers to gain or to maintain rights and privileges.

Another feature of this crisis was that while it captured the attention of all Malaysians, the manner through which they became informed left many to wonder whether it was the Supreme Council of UMNO who governed the country or the multi-party coalition BN.

The crisis also marked a transition in the leadership of Malay society from the rulers, representing tradition, duties, and obligations, to those representing political power, modernity, rights, and responsibilities. Attempts at amendments to the Constitution thus almost literally fell between two stools. It is only an ironic twist of fate that the newly elected *Timbalan Yang di Pertuan Agong* (deputy king), Sultan Azlan Shah of Perak, had previously held the post of Lord President of the Supreme Court, the highest judicial office in Malaysia, and had previously heard a case involving the king (Pathmanathan 1985: 214).

It is to be noted that the role of the rulers in Malaysia, thus far dormant, can yet have a potentially divisive role in domestic affairs. The displeasure of the royal house and the elected representatives has also surfaced in some states.[15]

The rulers are becoming more involved in affairs of state and are shedding their merely symbolic image of head of state. But conflicts have arisen with the elected representatives. How these differences will be resolved and what the relationship between the executive and the monarchy will be is very important not only to the Malays but also the non-Malays. In an oblique way the latter will be the most affected community in any change. The question of constitutional guarantees affecting those living in Sabah and Sarawak deserves attention. This 'special position', as enshrined in the federal Constitution, has arguably been a barrier to the rapid progress and closer integration of these two states with peninsular Malaysia.

THE SPECIAL POSITION OF SABAH AND SARAWAK

Sabah

Among Sabahans there is a general apprehension of 'peninsular influence' in their domestic affairs. The question of the exploitation of its timber and mineral resources, in addition to economic policies which originate from Kuala Lumpur, has produced uneasiness in Sabah. But, more than these, Sabahan politics has played a leading role in dictating the types of relationships which have emerged. Since the formation of Malaysia, for example, Sabah has been anxious to assert its independence. This anxiety is manifested in claims that its people were 'partners' in the formation of Malaysia, and by implication they did not 'join' the Federation. The distinction is very subtle but no less important since it is a further assertion of Sabah's special position within Malaysia. Among Sabahans there is therefore a sense of wanting to belong and at the same time wanting to be treated differently. The geographical separation of Sabah and Sarawak in part contributes to this conundrum. Parochial regionalism apart, national integration must surely require major areas of policy in which there is a commonality of vision. For this to be so, the problems of growth and development will need to be viewed as objectively and as dispassionately as possible in the interest of the common good. In the case of Sabah and Sarawak, the importance of their special position needs to be de-emphasized so that rapid development can proceed.

On September 12, 1962, the Legislative Council of North Borneo (Sabah after independence) approved and welcomed the decision in principle to establish the Federation of Malaysia subject to safeguards for the special interests of the peoples of Sabah. A similar motion was passed a fortnight later in the neighbouring state of Sarawak. According to the Commission, chaired by Lord Cobbold, to ascertain the views of the people of Sabah and Sarawak, the Federation was to be 'an association of partners'. The constitutional arrangements of this partnership of states were to be worked out by an inter-governmental committee (IGC) under Lord Landsdowne - the Minister of State for the Colonies in the Harold Macmillan government in the United Kingdom - with *Tun* Abdul Razak as deputy chairman and three nominees of the Legislative Assembly of Sabah.[16]

The Borneo Declaration, more commonly known as the 'Twenty Points'[17] and representing a joint memorandum prepared by five political parties, contained conditions and safeguards which they wanted before joining Malaysia.[18] These were presented to the IGC for consideration. Among the major requests was to have education remain a state matter. While Malay was to be the national language, English was also to be the official language for Sabah for all state or federal purposes without any time limitations. But as will become apparent, the Twenty Points were neither entrenched nor attached to the legislative acts giving birth to the new nation. The recommendations of the IGC were incorporated in the Malaysia Act of 1963 and later found their way into the Federal Constitution of Malaysia (Fung 1986: 93-8).

Sabah has its own state legislature with a cabinet system of government. Unlike peninsular Malaysian states, it has exclusive legislative powers over matters specified in the 'State List' such as land, agriculture and forestry, and local government.[19]

The federal Constitution spelt out the financial arrangements under which Sabah derived its revenues. The reservation of positions in the civil service to natives of Sabah is enshrined in the Constitution. A 'native' in relation to Sabah means a person who is a citizen, child, or grandchild of an indigenous person of Sabah and was born either in Sabah or to a father domiciled in Sabah at the time of birth. However, the passing of the Constitution (Amendment) Act, 1971, ended the exclusive and special position of the natives in relation to positions in public service, and to the grant of permits in the state.

It appears that in striving for the equality of all partners in the Federation and to further integrate the east Malaysian states, amendments to the Constitution have been necessary.[20] Conceivably, the culmination of this process could be that the tribal peoples of the Borneo states ultimately become 'Malays'[21] and so by default relinquish their special position within Malaysia.

But nomenclature alone is not as clear-cut as is suggested above. The issue in the Sabah context that natives may or may not be Muslim makes the problem even more intractable. For example, the term *Kadazan* was used originally to describe indigenous people living in the Penampang district near Kota Kinabalu. Many *Kadazans* were educated in Catholic mission schools and obtained jobs in the colonial civil service. In the 1950s, through the efforts of Donald Stephens (later known as *Tun* Fuad Stephens), the term *Kadazan* applied to all non-Muslim indigenous peoples in the state. Other groups in the interior, however, have not adopted this name, preferring instead the more generic term *Dusun* and in most cases their tribal or traditional names such as the Muruts of the southern highlands of the interior and the Rungus in the northwest. While retaining their autochthonous identity, these groups may be neither Muslim nor Christian and in all probability are animists. The contrast is provided by the coastal indigenes of Malayo-Muslim origin such as the Malays, Bajaus, and Illanums who are invariably Muslim. This group has far greater potential for assimilation and eventually emerging as Malays under the Constitution.

The issue of secession for Sabah first surfaced when it was revealed by the *Yang di Pertua Negeri Tun* Fuad Stephens in July 1975 that the Chief Minister, *Tun* Mustapha, intended to form his own Muslim state of Sulu-Mindanao-Sabah. *Tun* Fuad had on that occasion resigned to become the president of Berjaya - *Bersatu Rakyat Jelata Sabah* (Sabah People's United Front), the newly formed political party.[22] Misuse of power, corruption, and mismanagement were cited as reasons for the challenge to *Tun* Mustapha's government but the key issue was undoubtedly that of secession. There was a general belief that the formation of Berjaya had the full knowledge and blessing of Prime Minister *Tun* Abdul Razak, who had had reservations about *Tun* Mustapha's actions and power within Sabah. Evidence of the Federal government's feeling of disquiet includes the unsuccessful enticement of *Tun* Mustapha with the offer of the Defence portfolio (third in the federal list of seniority). The feeling then was that this office would remove *Tun* Mustapha from Sabah and at the same time place him under close scrutiny in Kuala Lumpur. For his part, *Tun* Mustapha was unhappy about being unable to negotiate loan funds from overseas on his own without Federal government supervision.[23] This prompted *Tun* Mustapha to circulate a memorandum, entitled 'The future position of Sabah in Malaysia', among members of his political party, United Sabah National Organization (USNO). The memorandum outlined Federal undermining of Sabah's autonomy and the potential sharing of the state's enormous resource wealth with the Federal government (*Far Eastern Economic Review*,

August 8, 1975). *Tun* Mustapha was deprived of his detention powers under the Internal Security Act (ISA) and the prime minister also ordered the release of all political prisoners held in Sabah. A new Commissioner of Police was installed in Sabah to ensure the political neutrality of the state's police force.

In the Sabah state elections of April 15, 1976, Berjaya won 28 of the 48 seats and thus formed the new state government. USNO won the other 20 seats and the 13-year reign of *Tun* Mustapha came to an end. The Berjaya victory had been impressive in view of early setbacks at two by-elections and of having to fight the well-organized and well-funded political machinery of USNO. Sin (1979: 379-89) provides a useful analysis of this constitutional *coup d'état*. In a speech made at Kota Kinabalu in December 1981, a senior federal minister (later deputy prime minister), *Datuk* Musa Hitam (*Star*, December 8, 1981), said that Sabah could no longer be considered unique as it had been in the Federation for 18 years. He stressed the need for Sabahans to integrate into the mainstream polity and to develop a Malaysian attitude. To bring this about, East Malaysians would no longer need passports to enter peninsular Malaysia, and the country was to adopt East Malaysian time from January 1, 1982, to place the whole of Malaysia on a single time zone (Selvaratnam 1982: 254). Peninsular Malaysians, however, were still required to produce their passports or work permits when entering Sabah or Sarawak. A further initiative to integrate Sabah into the Federal sphere was the declaration of the island of Labuan a Federal Territory on April 16, 1984. The intention of the Federal government was to strengthen the role of Labuan as a free port and *entrepôt* for ASEAN (Malaysia 1984: 16).

In the state elections of April 20-1, 1985, Parti Bersatu Sabah (PBS), led by *Datuk* Joseph Pairin Kitigan, won 25 out of 48 seats in the state assembly. The ruling party Berjaya, which had ruled Sabah since 1976, and a member of BN could manage only six seats while its near rival, the resurgent party USNO of *Tun* Mustapha, captured 16 seats. Pasok's President Ignatius Malanjum captured the remaining seat. Pasok later joined PBS in government. The Chief Minister and President of Berjaya, *Datuk* Harris Salleh, was defeated in Tenom by a PBS candidate (*Malaysian Digest*, April 30, 1985). *Tun* Mustapha tried to pre-empt *Datuk* Pairin by inducing the *Yang di Pertua Negeri Datuk* Adnan Robert to swear in an USNO-Berjaya coalition government before dawn on April 22, 1985. Even though the chief justice of the Sabah High Court and the Attorney General had maintained that the action was unconstitutional, the swearing-in of *Tun* Mustapha was carried out under duress because the *Yang di Pertua Negeri* and his family had felt threatened by *Tun*

Mustapha's party of supporters. However, as it turned out, *Datuk* Pairin was sworn in at 8.00 p.m. that same day. Thus began the High Court challenge of *Tun* Mustapha and Sabah's constitutional crisis of 1985.

Following the election victory, PBS was admitted to BN as was USNO (which had previously been expelled from the coalition on April 15, 1984). Federal-state relations have the appearance of being on the mend, although occasionally there are calls for greater autonomy or independence on state matters or where national interests conflict with state's rights and policies. A case in point concerns the ceding of Labuan, in which at a PBS Congress on August 22, 1986, a referendum was canvassed to seek its return to the state. This issue was equally disturbing and embarrassing to the Federal and state governments since closer integration had always been in the forefront of Federal thinking and, politically, PBS was part of BN.[24]

It has been observed that 'any assessment of [the] future must take into account the fact that genuine multiracial parties have not been able to survive long in Malaysian politics' (Gale 1984: 46). The political demise of Berjaya attests to that observation. The history of USNO under *Tun* Mustapha and Berjaya under *Datuk* Harris Salleh has shown 'that parties which had at first appeared to have policies highly attractive to the Federal government would not necessarily retain them' (Gale 1984: 35). Thus while it may be difficult to predict the future of Sabah, it may be concluded that it was indeed 'special' within the context of federal-state relations and politics and, second, that the people of Sabah were 'equal [to] but different' from mainstream Malaysians.

Sarawak

At the formation of Malaysia, Sarawak, the largest state in the Federation and almost equal in area to all the states on the peninsula, was just emerging politically from the era of the 'White Rajahs'. Physically and economically, it was underdeveloped. It contained various ethnic communities based either on riverine basins or highland affiliations for their identity, sustenance, and 'nationhood'. The fear therefore was that the land would be exploited and the people supplanted by more modern, progressive, and educated peninsular Malaysians (and Singaporeans). This fear prompted the need to entrench the 'special' position of this state, like that of Sabah, in some form of constitutional guarantee. In line with the report of the IGC, special interests covered such matters as religion, immigration, education, citizenship, the distribution of legislative power, land, the special position of the indigenous groups, financial provisions, the judiciary, the national language, the civil service, and emergency powers. These were items in the so-called 'State List'.25 As in the case of Sabah, these safeguards have been embodied in the Constitution of Malaysia.

Sarawak, like Sabah, has legislative competence under the Federal Constitution to pass laws to incorporate statutory authorities and bodies other than municipal and local government authorities without limitations or restrictions. The Federal government was precluded from extending its executive authority to bodies set up by or under a state law, so that a body such as the Sarawak Economic Development Corporation can, if it wishes, operate contrary to Federal government guidelines and policy. But the Federal government has some measure of control in terms of the allocation of grants and in guaranteeing loans on behalf of these bodies.

As a result of the great contrast in economic development and fiscal capacity of the Borneo states at the time of federation, steps were taken to ensure that no state was disadvantaged while at the same time the special needs of particular states were given priority. Thus conflicting claims, such as those arising from the wealthier states in contrast to poor states seeking assistance on the basis of need, have had to be rationalized.

For example, the question of revenues from petroleum was not discussed in the report of the IGC; liquified natural gas had not been discovered then. Thus the ownership of petroleum found in the state both on land and on the continental shelf contiguous to the coast had not been negotiated. Under the state constitution, the state has control and jurisdiction over minerals and other natural resources, including those areas over the continental shelf contiguous to the territorial waters. However, with the promulgation of the Petroleum Development Act, 1974, and the setting up of PETRONAS, and apparently as a compromise between Federal and state governments, the corporation was vested with all rights of ownership and exploration for oil and gas. In return, states were to be given 'such cash payment as may be agreed between the parties concerned'.26 Thus while the state's claim to ownership of petroleum resources has been recognized, financial controls have become centralized.

An aborigine is defined in Article 160 of the Constitution to mean an aborigine of the Malay Peninsula. However, aborigines in Sarawak, as distinct from those groups included under 'natives' in Article 161A(6), are left out in both definitions of 'aborigine' and 'natives'. The natives of Sarawak are given a special position under Article 161A of the Constitution and their position is equivalent to that of the Malays in peninsular Malaysia. Thus the aborigines in Sarawak are left in a constitutional no-man's-land - an oversight that requires rectification.

Such a discussion is all the more cogent given the amount of controversy and resentment that can arise with the use of inappropriate ethnographic nomenclature. It is submitted that instead of differentiating between the indigenous groups, the retention of their traditional names in addition to a generalized term such as *Pribumi* would be appropriate since the number, subgroups, and linguistic origins of groups in Sarawak are much less diverse than in neighbouring Sabah.

Some general comments are needed in examining Sarawak's tenure in Malaysia. The existence of two separate High Courts and the continued use of English in Sarawak may be symbols of divisiveness that inhibit national unity. As the *Yang di Pertua Negara* could be appointed, he may not necessarily profess the Islamic faith. Article 3 of the Constitution proclaims that Islam is the religion of the Federation, but Sarawak has so far not declared Islam as the official religion of the state. The matter is viewed with much concern among Muslims in the state. Nevertheless, relative economic prosperity and the sheer necessity of interdependence and co-operation among various ethnic groups have meant that Sarawak has not been forced to put to the test some of the constitutional guarantees discussed above.

A constitutional crisis of a sort occurred in 1966 when the chief minister lost the confidence of the majority of the members of the legislative assembly. Article 7(1) of the state constitution required his resignation. Instead the chief minister chose to request the *Yang di Pertua Negara* to dissolve the state assembly under Article 10(2). However, the latter refused to dissolve the assembly as he had absolute discretion to withhold consent. A constitutional stalemate ensued and the Federal government had to choose either to invoke its emergency powers under Article 150 and rule the state directly from Kuala Lumpur or enact Federal legislation to empower the *Yang di Pertua Negara* to dismiss the recalcitrant chief minister. Thus, under the Emergency (Federal Constitution and Constitution of Sarawak) Act, 1966, the chief minister was removed from office. While such an enactment could be censured when done in bad faith, no such motive was apparent in this case. Nevertheless, there were many who felt strongly that such power should not be used (Serjan 1986).

Summary

The physical separation of both Sabah and Sarawak has meant that the Federal government has been unable to monitor closely the socio-political developments in these states, as compared to those in the peninsula. Thus closer integration with the Bornean states has had to be achieved through other means. The proclamation of Labuan as a Federal Territory and similar negotiations for such a territory in Sarawak will at least put a physical Federal presence in these states. Other ideas that have surfaced include the setting up of an inexpensive ferry service between the peninsula and Sarawak and Sabah to encourage greater travel, tourism, and, most importantly, contact between the peoples of all states. It appears that in diversity there might be unity where the differences between groups of people are capitalized and combined for the benefit of the Federation - the very essence of the federal system.

A further idea for which feasibility studies have been completed is that of transmitting electricity from hydro-electric power sources in Sarawak to peninsular Malaysia by an underground cable. When this project is implemented Sarawak will be seen to be contributing to the development of peninsular Malaysia and this would remove the stigma of merely being a recipient of development aid from Federal sources. The issue of integration is more real in the case of Sabah with the growing number of international refugees and illegal immigrants from the southern Philippines and Indonesia. Unemployment, unrest and general instability may need to be tackled and these problems could perhaps be overcome with strong Federal government support and assistance. There are also incipient problems related to the exploitation of other resources, for example, timber and copper, which has led to a conflict of interests between the state and federal government. In any event, both Sabah and Sarawak will still have and enjoy their 'special' status, whether for better or for worse, for some time to come.

NEW DIRECTIONS, NEW DILEMMAS, AND A NEW DEAL

The NEP has been the linchpin of public sector allocations in development plans since the *Second Malaysia Plan*. The eradication of poverty and the restructuring of society is directed mainly at *Bumiputera*, although the *Third Malaysia Plan*, almost as an afterthought, included the phrase 'irrespective of race'. These objectives have both a quantitative target and a temporal endpoint. In charting the course to achieve those targets and endpoints, various strategies have been adopted in terms not only of how best to do so but also how quickly. Invariably, there will be contradictions, for example, the 'best' solutions may be achievable but only in the long run. This may conflict with the relatively short time-span of 20 years given in the *Outline Plan* (1970-90) to achieve any particular target. It is in this kind of planning environment that there is a need for compromise, adjustments, and the rethinking of programmes. Ultimately it is expected that most of the targets can be achieved with as few compromises as possible - a sort of Pareto-optimal solution to economic planning and growth.

New Directions

In the mid-1980s the vision of the planners has focused on two areas that will potentially bring about the fulfilment of the targets set under the NEP. There is a greater degree of state participation in the economy through various 'business' arms of the government concurrent with the rearrangement of the private ownership and control of industrial and corporate wealth.

Industrial policy, for example, has been revised to include an increasing commitment to capital-intensive heavy industry rather than to light industry such as textiles, electrical, and electronic equipment. Thus the setting up of the Heavy Industries Corporation would help 'initiate, implement and manage capital intensive industries' (Malaysia 1981). Already HICOM has been involved in cement production (Kedah Cement), sponge iron and steel billets (Perwaja Terengganu), and the Proton Saga car. By implication, therefore, the view has been rejected that the way forward for Malaysia is 'a competitive move up-market, into scientific, technical and information processing skills typical of the advanced economies of the West'.[27] The rejection of such a path derives from past experience, especially in free trade zones, licensed manufacturing warehouses, and industrial estates where there is very little evidence that genuine transfer of new technology has taken place. Most of the industries have been no more than assembly-line operations. Moreover, even where there has been the growth of employment opportunities, by and large these were at an unskilled level. A further lesson has been that the gains from such high-tech industries were rather more volatile, especially in the electrical, electronic, machinery, and appliance subsectors whose growth and decline were dictated from outside the national economy. The role of MNCs may partly explain this observation.

The Treasury has put the view that the selective development of heavy industry would provide linkages and spin-off effects for domestic industry, particularly the small- and medium-scale firms, as well as promote the development of management skills and technology.[28] However, there has not been overenthusiastic support for such a scheme since some believe that there should be equal consideration of the 'second wave' of import substitution. The rationale for this argument is that the population base became much larger in the 1980s and the purchasing power of this group of people expanded. There was also the need to accompany this second wave with vigorous export-oriented industrialization of the capital-intensive kind. The promotion of small- and medium-scale industries would provide a base for entrepreneurial and managerial development and training. Examples of such industries include textiles and clothing, confectionery, furniture, leather footwear, machine tools, and industrial machinery components.

As mentioned, the local application of foreign-developed technology does not necessarily lead to the transfer of that technology, as for example, in the case of micro-chips in FTZs. However, there is a further consideration identified by James (1986: 214), namely that heavy industry is a high-cost and high-risk investment; profits are by no means assured. The example provided by the Proton Saga car is a case in point. HICOM has a 70 per cent equity holding in conjunction with the Mitsubishi Corporation of Japan. Production of the 1.3 litre and 1.5 litre cars began in mid-1985, with full production projected in 1988 of 120,000 units per year.[29] With duty exemption of up to 40 per cent, the imported components arrived in completely knocked down form. Together with a high level of local content, the cars have been sold at a price of between 12-17 per cent below that of equivalent rivals. The estimated project cost was about $560 million.[30]

According to James (1986: 213), a more aggressive pricing policy, vigorous marketing, and the imposition of high tariffs on competitors so as to support the Proton Saga car project could result in the closure of existing motor vehicle assembly plants, thus increasing rather than decreasing unemployment. Moreover, Mitsubishi's role as the main supplier of technology would put it in a position where it could exert more influence than might be beneficial for the Malaysian national interest. However, the national car project might stimulate ancillary car component manufacture and servicing industries. The skills acquired may also be useful for other new heavy industry that will come on stream in the 1990s and beyond. To date, however, it has been demonstrated that simple car assembly was cost-inefficient, and failed to generate local linkage industries to any significant extent. The car project was aimed at redressing these specific shortcomings.

There was also a push by the government towards the private sector, which has been viewed as the engine of economic growth. Thus, in contrast to the 1970s, there is now a concerted move away from public enterprises towards a free enterprise system. To this end fiscal incentives have been used to attract increased private sector participation. A liberal foreign exchange control regime has been put in place.[31]

A review of the Industrial Co-ordination Act has seen the relaxation of controls on foreign equity participation. The new arrangements allow 100 per cent foreign ownership of companies manufacturing products not produced locally. Subject to certain conditions, companies set up between October 1986 and December 1990 will be forever exempted from the need to restructure their equity. The conditions include the stipulations that at least 50 per cent of output must be sold to firms in FTZs or LMWs and that the company must employ at least 350 full-time Malaysian workers in proportions that reflect the ethnic composition of the country (Ariff 1987: 214).

There is another view that in order to achieve the twin targets of the NEP

> the State must come in more strongly and pervasively to guide the competitive market operations with the sets of short-term targets, as specified in the *Second Malaysia Plan* and the *Third Malaysia Plan* and the long-term objectives contained in the Outline Perspective Plan 1970-1990.
>
> (Tan 1981: 206)

The reasons behind such a view are not obscure and have been neatly put in their historical perspective by Corner (1983). According to her, the May 13, 1969, incident marked a watershed in Malaysian development policy. Prior to that date development planning was largely indirect, macro-scale, and based on the assumption that whatever gains accrued in the development process would permeate the economic system and benefit disadvantaged groups of Malaysian society. However, this 'trickle-down' of development pulses did not take place as anticipated. Dilution of development benefits and the slow-paced delivery through sectors that were dominated by non-*Bumiputera* presaged the demise of such a strategy in favour of one that was more positive and direct. Thus, the *Second* through to the *Fifth Malaysia Plans* have included specific policies that enforced positive discrimination in favour of *Bumiputera* interests in education, employment, and in the economy generally. In so doing there seems to be a tacit recognition that Darwinian approaches (that is, the survival of those best equipped to cope with change) have no place in socio-economic development planning on either ethical or efficiency grounds.

An alternative view is that there are many dangers and shortcomings in state involvement in the economy. First, it is felt that increasing state involvement will affect private investment because of uncertainty, fear, the possible displacement of non-Malay interests (Lim 1983: 12), and unfair competition as the state invariably occupies an advantaged position. The *Mid-term Review Third Malaysia Plan* acknowledged that the fall in private investment in the late 1970s was partly attributable to the Industrial Co-ordination Act, 1975, and the uncertainty generated by the Petroleum Development (Amendment) Act, 1975. Second, the concentration of economic power in the hands of a small group of bureaucrats can be economically inefficient: politicians and civil servants do not necessarily make good business managers and neither are they immune to the temptations of self-aggrandisement.

New Dilemmas

In the quest for a 30 per cent *Bumiputera* control of the corporate sector by 1990, a small class of Malay capital managers have been entrusted with the task of handling enormous funds on behalf of the entire *Bumiputera* community to invest and to make capital gains. However, as recent events have shown, there have been enormous problems of financial mismanagement and misuse of these funds. This rise of an incipient Malay capitalism has given birth to a new Malay Dilemma. In moving in new directions, the nation is confronted with challenging new problems; corruption and financial mismanagement have become supreme examples of this malaise.

As noted by Leigh (1983: 18),

[t]here remains a fine line between what are legitimate and what are corrupt practices, given the power of this group to dispense commercial favours that are a prerequisite for many private businesses to flourish.

However, Rothwell (1987: 24) is more forthright in saying that the issue of corruption was only a symbol of Malaysia's present dilemma. Yet Malaysia has not always been this way; indeed, there was little evidence of previous corruption in Malaysia. Five reasons for the generally good record in this regard have been given by Milne and Mauzy (1978: 275) and they are very persuasive.

First, the comparatively high level of civil service pay as a legacy of expatriate British civil servants ensured a high level of satisfaction which precluded the need to seek other covert income sources. Second, the smooth transition from colonial to independent rule left behind a fairly strong and honest bureaucratic framework. Third, the Westminster model of government had become the adopted Malaysian tradition so that the pride, status, and esteem of the bureaucracy militated against its members being seen to be less than honest when dealing with the public, especially in financial matters. Fourthly, a well-educated and large middle class, a relatively free press, and an independent judiciary with a strong common law background of English jurisprudence served as checks and balances in the system of government. Finally, Malaysia has had a political opposition that has acted as the watchdog of government business. It is thus widely held that the level of corruption was lower than elsewhere in South East Asia (Marican 1979: 597).

In this context the term 'corruption' generally includes any activity conducted in return for consideration, by which a person does or neglects to do an act in contravention of his or her public duties. In *Bahasa Malaysia* this is likened to *pagar makan padi* (fence consuming the rice crop) where the weeds and grass by the fence have overtaken the rice crop. The misuse of the economic power of public enterprises for political patronage is one example of undue influence.

The Malaysian Bar Council *Newsletter* in April 1987 called for a Royal Commission into the 'manifold problems facing all sectors of the economy'. The Council cited 11 instances of alleged fraud or mismanagement involving the government or some minister. The following illustrate the lack of financial discipline and fiscal prudence which have been the subject of much discussion.

The attempt to establish a cartel in the world's tin market was partly responsible for the suspension of trading on the London Metal Exchange in October 1985. A year later it was revealed that a Malaysian government-sponsored company was involved and had lost about $600 million in that attempt which resulted in a slump in the price of tin. Rumours of a net loss of $1 billion are, however, unconfirmed (Ariff 1987: 204).

Loans to the Hong Kong-based Carrian group of companies by Bank Bumiputra Malaysia Berhad's subsidiary Bumiputra Malaysia Finance resulted in a $2.5 billion loss to the banks. The 1986 government White Paper, while not implicating top government officials, was of the view that fraud, lack of control, and general mismanagement had raised serious doubts as to the competence and managerial ability of Malay entrepreneurs.

The collapse of a public company, though incorporated in Singapore, led to the unprecedented closure of both the Singapore and Kuala Lumpur Stock Exchanges in December 1985 for three days. The central figure in that collapse was the president of the Malaysian Chinese Association

(MCA), who was sent to gaol for two years in August 1986 and fined heavily. The MCA's chief investment arm, Multi Purpose Holdings (MPH) also incurred huge losses in other investments. The financial losses of deposit-taking co-operatives have been estimated at $1.5 billion so that fund members could expect only 30 per cent of their investments to be returned (Ariff 1987: 204).

The implications of these illustrations are many. Apart from the financial repercussions, the plunge in the price of tin adversely affected many small tin producers. A press report that 314 of the country's 488 tin mines had closed and about 8,760 mine workers had been laid off in 1985 (*New Straits Times*, January 20, 1985) arguably could be ascribed to what had taken place on the LME.

Uncertainties in the monetary sector have affected confidence in the financial system. The closure in June 1985 by the Hong Kong authorities of the Malaysian-owned Overseas Trust Bank sparked off panic selling on the Kuala Lumpur Stock Exchange. Investigations by Bank Negara of two public banks led to speculation which was only dispelled by statements by the governor of Bank Negara (James 1986: 210).

An examination of Federal government finance for the period 1980-86 shows that the activities of public enterprises (NFPEs and OBAs) have had a significant negative impact on the economy. They may have led to problems with the balance of payments and debt servicing. For example, in 1975 the overall deficit was $1.891 billion, but by 1980 this deficit had risen to $7,022 billion and in 1985 it was estimated at $6,746 billion. The deficit is further compounded by the amount that has been reserved for development expenditure. The expenditure by OBAs in 1981 was about $2,334 billion; this figure had risen to $6,547 billion two years later, and was estimated at $8,012 billion in 1985 (Malaysia 1985). Thus a combination of over-indulgent spending and financial losses had led to substantial trade and budget deficits. The unexpected world-wide recession in the mid-1980s did not help. The result was that the government has had to curtail public expenditure during the *Fifth Malaysia Plan*. These cutbacks are seen as genuine attempts to redress trade and budget deficits (James 1986: 216-7).

A New Deal

It is only speculative to suggest that perhaps the press is no longer as 'free' as it was previously and that the political opposition is not as strong. There is also, coincidentally, a rise in the incidence of fraud and corruption in the country. However, in the light of the events reported above, the government has attempted to transform public enterprises into private entities. In that way it was hoped that better management and more competitive attitudes would be encouraged. The concepts of privatization, 'Malaysia Incorporated', and 'Look East' have been touted as the vehicles by which private investment and hence economic growth may be sustained in the 1990s. The moves in these directions may be seen as an escape clause in the event that the attainment of targeted economic growth rates under existing strategies of development do not achieve the desired degree of restructuring in employment and corporate wealth. The cycle that has been set in motion is that shortfalls in targets further increase the role of the state in the economy. This has the effect of depressing private investment, thus necessitating further government intervention and producing further shortfalls, and so on. To reverse this cycle, it is hoped that the sale of public enterprises will be the start of a cycle leading to economic growth.

Privatization or the divestment of public enterprises may be achieved in one of three ways. First, there can be a formal (or informal) liquidation. Next, there may be privatization of ownership through the sale of assets to the private sector, and finally, privatization of management under leases and management contracts. The obstacles to privatization hinge on profitability, socio-political considerations, and financial realities. Frequently, the least profitable public enterprises may be put on the market for sale. These are invariably enterprises which private investors are unwilling to buy at prices acceptable to the government. Employees feel insecure when they no longer come under the umbrella of the public sector - a point that will not be lost on opposition parties who predict a loss of jobs and increasing unemployment. The public, on the other hand, fear that the productive assets of the country are either going into the hands of foreigners or the rich elites of a particular ethnic group. Finally, in developing nations such as Malaysia, the capital market may be undeveloped so that individual buyers (ostensibly, the group of people which the government wishes to benefit) may have difficulty in financing large purchases of stock. With an emphasis on profitability, privatization offers an alluring alternative towards improving economic efficiency and dynamism in the economy (Malaysia 1986: 218).

The Prime Minister, *Dato Seri* Mahathir (1984: 3), mindful of the obstacles and potential problems of privatization, has reiterated that privatization would not negate the objectives of the NEP. He stated that there could be no divestment where there were losses to employees and that the government was more in favour of partnerships between *Bumiputera* and non-*Bumiputera* than among exclusive groups.

The response of academics, bureaucrats, and business managers has so far been mixed. According to Chan (1984: 42), 'the privatisation policy is somewhat overdue. This is because the intrusive role of the state has begun to overburden society and is crowding out the private sector.' Furthermore, the effect of privatization would be overall economic liberalism because it would help introduce more foreign capital, enterprise, and technology, leading to a democratization of ownership and management. It was thought that there could only be more, not fewer, opportunities for big and small investors and businesses. In the alternative view, the policy has

> been viewed as government 'decrees' that were ill-defined and vague. There was no clear statement as to which of the public sector activities were to be privatized, the manner in which such privatization was to be achieved and the time frame to implement these policy initiatives.

> (Rachagan 1987: 222)

Mohamad (1984: 71) predicted that, with privatization, the days when workers could negotiate minimum output for a long and secure career in public service were over: 'A new workers' meritocracy will replace it.' However, Mohamed (1984: 11) was more cautious and laid down several key issues to be addressed when considering privatization. These issues include the criteria for selecting the activities to be privatized, the financial performance of the enterprise, the structure of the industry, and the extent of duplication and co-ordination between agencies and the law with respect to privatization. In view of these complexities, it may be observed that the government has been very cautious and pragmatic in implementing this policy instrument.[32]

The Privatization Master Plan 1988 sets the blueprint for Malaysia's privatization programme (*Malaysian Digest*, October 1987, p. 4). In tandem with this policy of privatization is the idea of 'Malaysia Incorporated'. This concept does not include government equity participation but rather requires the private and public sectors to see themselves as part of the same 'corporation'. Thus, while the private sector serves as the commercial and economic arm, the government sector constitutes the service arm. It means that there should be close and mutually supportive co-operation between the private and public sectors (Mohamad 1984: 2). Thus in August 1985 Parliament approved two Bills providing for the takeover of the Telecommunications Department and Malaysian Airlines System (MAS) by private companies. MAS successfully floated 30 per cent of its share equity for public purchase and was listed on the Kuala Lumpur Stock Exchange. It can be surmised that a faster paced privatization programme will hinge on the success of these two instruments as private companies.

The country's 'Look East' policy is of much older vintage than either of the two policies discussed above. The prime minister announced the policy in 1982 with the following words:

> [S]o in order for Malaysia to progress, we have to learn from the better example and the better example is the Japanese example. That is why we want to look East -- thus not 'Look West' but 'Look East.[33]

The policy was aimed at introducing Japanese work ethics and managerial systems to improve economic performance and productivity in Malaysia.[34] However, as Lim (1984: 231) points out, the policy is unrealistic in that there are culturally-based differences that may seriously impair the successful implementation of the policy. While Malaysia is a heterogeneous society, Japanese society is more homogeneous. There are cultural differences that impinge on social and religious values and differences in historical background. Moreover, to be successful, learning from Japan would be a painstaking task, requiring the formulation and implementation of plans that might take years to develop.

Other critics of the policy have suggested that it was either a way of expressing government pique towards the United Kingdom for its discriminatory policies towards Malaysia in recent times or a ploy to flatter the Japanese and Koreans into expanding their level of investment in the country. Deeper analysis suggests that the critiques fail to take account of the fact that in the 1980s investment from western sources had been levelling off and economic growth was stagnating in Malaysia. Thus, there is a broader and more compelling range of factors behind this policy (Suzuki and Cummings 1985: 509).

Privatization, Malaysia Incorporated, and Look East policies constitute guides for action that tend to resemble slogans or even moral injunctions. As Milne (1986: 1379) observes, they are designed to alter people's way of thinking, rather than to effect physical changes.

Foreign Relations

National economic development strategies need to be complemented by a foreign policy that maximizes power and resources for national development (Chong 1981: 299). A stable and pragmatic foreign relations policy can do much to foster confidence in the direction and impetus of growth in the domestic economy. The declared order of priorities of the Malaysian government is as follows: ASEAN, the Islamic Conference Organization, the Non-aligned Movement, and the (British) Commonwealth.[35] The order of this hierarchy is traceable to the 1971 subscription by the members of ASEAN to a Zone of Peace, Freedom, and Neutrality. It also provided the basis for the promotion of self-reliant regionalism.

Rather than discuss foreign policy *per se*, it will be sufficient to note that Anglo-Malaysian relations have weakened while those with Singapore have strengthened (Chin 1982). The imposition of full fees for all students, including those from Malaysia, in Britain in 1980 sparked the weakening process. Appeals for a waiver had been unsuccessful, apart from a small scholarship fund set up in 1982 to assist students already in the country who were experiencing financial difficulties as a result of the fees (Chew 1982: 351). The manoeuver by Perbadanan Nasional Berhad (PNB)[36] in 1981 to gain a controlling interest in Guthrie Corporation, a British-based plantation group that owned assets in Malaysia, in a dawn raid on the London Stock Exchange prompted the UK Council of the Securities Industry to amend its takeover rules. This move was interpreted as being directed at the Malaysian government.

A further area of friction was the view that British companies had not complied with or assisted in the objectives of the NEP by enlarging the equity participation of *Bumiputera*. The selling-off of British-owned companies to non-*Bumiputera* has been interpreted as non-compliance with government objectives. That the sales were profit-motivated and transacted on the open market did not feature in the interpretation. Thus MPH acquired part of Dunlop by offering the highest price for its shares just as PNB was able to do in the case of Barlows, a British-owned plantation group. In 1981 Guthrie Corporation sold 73 per cent of its industrial and trading divisions to MPH (Chew 1982: 352).

Furthermore, the Malaysian government issued a directive that all trade relations with Britain must be vetted by the Prime Minister's Department. These events together outline the mood of the Malaysian government's dealing with Britain. However, by the mid-1980s Anglo-Malaysian relations had improved.

A less dramatic yet equally important international relationship is that between Malaysia and Singapore. There seemed to be very real efforts in the 1980s to mend the scars of separation and to begin anew. The meeting of the two prime ministers in Singapore in December 1981 signalled the beginnings of a new relationship. It is significant to note that Singapore chose to follow Malaysian time with the introduction of a common regional time for peninsular Malaysia, Sabah, and Sarawak (*Far Eastern Economic Review*, December 25, 1981, pp. 13-14).

Apart from the reciprocal return of lands used by the railways, the military and naval bases, and an agreement on a common boundary, the setting up of the Inter-governmental Committee (IGC) in 1980 helped to streamline closer relationships. The relations between Malaysia and Singapore are reflected most significantly in trade. Exports to Singapore increased from $5,385 million in 1980 to $6,772 million in 1985, the latter figure being approximately 19 per cent of total Malaysian trade. Imports from Singapore increased also from $2,753 million to $4,776 million for the same period, the latter representing about 16 per cent of total Malaysian trade (Malaysia 1986: 367). Singapore, it is to be noted, is still an *entrepôt* port in that it imports crude petroleum, palm and palm kernel oil, and sawn timber from Malaysia and then re-exports them in processed form to third countries.

7
POSTSCRIPT

The development challenge for Malaysia in the decade of the 1990s and beyond may yet prove to be demanding and difficult. In the finely balanced societal milieu of *Bumiputera* and non-*Bumiputera* peoples, any government intervention on behalf of one section might carry with it unsavoury interpretations that subtend the autonomy, legitimacy, and democratic ideals of a modern capitalist society. But the government cannot afford to be neutral because such a stance would not guarantee its political viability. There is no escaping the fact that national aspirations are by and large *Bumiputera* aspirations. This then is the dilemma of any Malaysian government, since political legitimacy is defined by the *Bumiputera*.

Although this is generally accepted by (and acceptable to) a majority of Malaysians, there are divisive elements at work. There are, for instance, radicals in the entrepreneurial classes of both the *Bumiputera* as well as the Chinese who eye one another warily since the promotion of one is interpreted as being to the detriment of the other. This situation can engender an environment of distrust and resentment. Thus, in both politics and business, there appears to be a sort of a zero-sum game being played out with new situations matched by changing rules of the game. In the end this may not be good for the country as a whole since no one wins but everybody loses.

There is a saying that one gets what one deserves. It would be nice if the rewards were fair and just for effort and past endeavours. However, it will be another story if these rewards are curbs on political liberty through the installation of an authoritarian regime. It is as if the masses let the elite get their way and because of implied consent deserve what they get. This is a harsh interpretation but it may yet be shown to contain some truth.

Recent political analysis suggests that mass attitudes are supportive of the growing trend towards authoritarian rule in Malaysia. The general attitude among Malaysians seems to be that the diminution of freedom is a small price to pay for enhanced security. Another reason is the fear that unfettered discussion will provoke communal violence - an ever-present danger. Even more persuasive is the government's emphasis on economic development on the one hand, matched by the 'administrative back-ground' of leading political figures on the other. This combination of government objectives and the personal background of the leaders provides the hierarchical structure to political organization that lends itself easily to an authoritarian-type regime. The argument that equates opposition with disloyalty, however, has found less support in Malaysian democratic politics (Bass 1970).

However, the above may be an over-simplification of the nation's problems. There is some debate, discussion, and publication of alternative views, albeit within the narrow guidelines laid down by the legislature such as the Official Secrets Act, 1972, (OSA) and a 'catch-all' Internal Security Act, 1960, (ISA). But there would still be no guarantees in a different political and social climate because the debate might still spiral away from, rather than towards, solutions.

Thirty or so years as an independent nation have only brought about adjustments and some integration, for example in education, but no assimilation. Generally, communalism is fostered by ethnic-based parties that have forced the development of a coalition style of government. It seems that there is a 'consociational' political system in which, because society is divided along ethnic lines, the leaders of each of the communities co-operate with one another in the government.

While the fight against communism persists, there is also a difficult battle against traditionalism and regionalism which may prevent a more rapid growth of the economy. Thus, while Malaysia has built a very strong political and economic foundation the predictions that communalism will be anti-developmental may yet prove to be groundless. However, it is true that political objectives, development goals, educational and economic policies, and even attitude formation in foreign relations are inevitably influenced by communal considerations. The future of Malaysia is inextricably intertwined with its societal milieu (Indorf 1979: 115).

One major issue that has occupied the minds of economists, planners, and citizens alike is the fate of the NEP after its expiry date. Because of the possibility that the quantitative objectives and restructuring aims of the NEP realistically cannot be achieved, the likely course of action would be that these objectives would have to be extended beyond 1990, probably in a different form. Semi-official pronouncements appear to have taken this line. For example, the Finance Minister, *Datuk* Daim Zainuddin, has conceded that the NEP might have to be continued beyond 1990 (*Malaysian Digest*, April 30, 1985). The Deputy Finance Minister, *Datuk* Sabaruddin Chik, mentioned the likelihood of a National Economic Policy after 1990 that will incorporate the basic features of the NEP but with possibly fewer benefits than at present given to *Bumiputera* (*Star*, August 9, 1985; *Straits Times* (Singapore), August 19, 1985) although the dissenting view by *Datuk* Abdullah Ahmad seems to be that the continuance of the NEP is to ensure Malay political dominance (Seward 1986: 77). Whatever form the 'new' or 'national' economic policy takes, it must be premissed on growth, exactly as it was when first enunciated. Figure 7.1 shows the relative shares of three groups of people in the Malaysian economy in 1971, 1985 and projections for 1990 in relation to an expanding national 'cake' measured in terms of gross national product or gross domestic product. The indications are that the objectives of the *Outline Plan* may be difficult to achieve.

Given this precondition of growth-based redistribution, any new policy must stimulate foreign investment, which has been recognized as the main generator of growth, while encouraging local investment, especially from non-*Bumiputera*. To achieve the latter there need to be some modifications in the *modus operandi* as well as a restatement of the policy to appeal to all communities and to placate fears of a bias towards any particular community. Emotional overtones surrounding economic policy need to be removed. Given the right kinds of fiscal and economic incentives, the new policy could tap the resources of the private sector for its public development programmes. Whether or not such a proposal can convince the masses will be a moot point. For instance, it is not clear whether material wealth will bring the communities closer together, given the cultural divide that exists in language, religion, and culture. Another view is that '[t]he New Economic Policy's objectives could not be achieved without economic interpenetration of traditional ethnic preserves' (Chee 1973: 155). Such an observation, however, gives rise to fears among the non-*Bumiputera* that the achievement of a 30 per cent share ownership by *Bumiputera* in all stockholding companies might be at their expense, rather than at the expense of foreign holdings.

A further issue concerns whether, assuming the achievement of an equitable *Bumiputera* share of the economy, the non-*Bumiputera* can rightfully claim an equal share of political power with its attendant benefits. These sorts of issues ultimately give momentum to the vicious cycle of ethnic compartmentalization and alienation to the extent that a more egalitarian and universal political and economic system is prevented from evolving. While *amok* is a Malay word, there is no need for

Figure 7.1. Malaysia: Shares in the economy by GNP and GDP, 1971, 1985 and projections for 1990

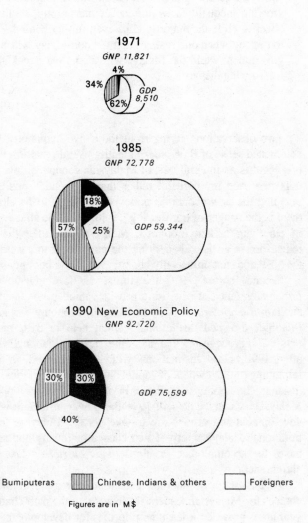

1971
GNP 11,821

GNP 11,821
4%
34%
62%
GDP 8,510

1985
GNP 72,778

18%
57%
25%
GDP 59,344

1990 New Economic Policy
GNP 92,720

30%
30%
40%
GDP 75,599

■ Bumiputeras   ▥ Chinese, Indians & others   □ Foreigners

Figures are in M$

Source: Malaysia (1971: 41; 1976: 86; 1986: 9, 62).

Malaysians to go berserk under the stress of genuine economic restructuring. However, it has been observed that

> [i]t is ironic that policies based on ethnic prejudices should lead to growing inequalities *within* each ethnic group, so that a small elite benefits while the majority slips even further behind. The irony turns to tragedy when one realizes that the non-Malay will blame a 'Malay' government while the Malays will blame the non-Malay bourgeoisie for growing disparities

> (Wilmott 1982: 66)

Two observations spring from the above quotation. First, there is a heightened sense of *Bumiputera* identity. While it is accepted that 'Malay privilege' is an integral part of Malaysian economic development, where it is perverted for political rather than economic ends, the wisdom of pursuing the new economic policy would need to be challenged. Thus there is the danger of transferring wealth from one elite to another, that is, of enriching certain individual Malay elites rather than realizing the redistributive goals of benefiting the masses. If this were to be the case, the NEP does not universally benefit the Malays but only some Malays.

Second, before 1970 the thrust of development and trade was principally aimed at benefiting private capital in the hands of foreigners and non-*Bumiputera*. Under the NEP, the economy was geared to benefit *Bumiputera*-owned institutional capital held in trust on behalf of the masses. It is suggested that under the 'new' or 'national' economic policy after 1990, class distinctions will be introduced in all discussions impinging on the owners of capital and their beneficiaries. There will, for instance, be more *Bumiputera* in the middle and upper echelons of Malaysian society who will have the power to dictate where and when development and growth are to take place. It may be foreseen that the traditional Malay society of two classes of royalty and commoners may have to accommodate a third *nouveau-riche* class of successful entrepreneurs.

At this stage of national economic development there are limited choices for Malaysian leaders. It seems that the path charted by the five-year plans provides at least the priorities for development. While income inequalities will persist and probably enlarge, the preoccupation with poverty-line income should be switched to address the very roots of disparities in income at all levels of society. The planning at this stage should involve all parties and needs to be decentralized and comprehensive. In this way the country could work towards a just and self-reliant economy devoid of ethnic allegiances or class distinctions, or of rich and poor people. Were that to be the case, Malaysian society could truly be described as just, equal, and free.

NOTES

1 Malaysia: The socio-economic background

1 However, the term 'Malaysia' has been in use since the nineteenth century. See Wang (1964: 15-22).

2 A good account of the historical geography of the Malay peninsula for the period before AD 1500 is given by Wheatley (1966). For a modern account of Malaysian history see Tregonning (1964; 1965) and Andaya and Andaya (1982).

3 For a detailed discussion of ASEAN economies see Wong (1979).

4 See Chin (1982), for a discussion of a new assertiveness in Malaysian foreign policy.

5 This term *Pribumi* appears to have been used for the first time in an official government publication. It is used here in the same sense as *Bumiputera* (sons of the soil), the more commonly used term. The terms may have been used interchangeably in the Indo-Malay world. See an interesting discussion by Siddique and Suryadinata (1981-82) on this topic.

6 These issues are discussed in Alatas (1977) and Ross-Larson (1977).

7 Major target groups include rubber smallholders, padi farmers, estate workers, fishermen, coconut smallholders, and the urban poor. The incidence of poverty for 1970 was based on a per capita poverty line income while in 1976 and 1984 it was based on the respective gross poverty line incomes.

8   There is, however, a warning by Chia and MacAndrews (1982) that development strategies should not be unrealistic in their declared aims of trying to reduce general poverty levels or spread widely the benefits of development.

9   See Higgins (1981: 22-3) for a discussion of these various approaches.

10 See Lo, Salih, and Douglass (1981) for an in-depth discussion of this model.

2   Planning Development (1950-90)

1   Known locally as the racial riots of May 13. According to official reports 196 people lost their lives. A good balanced account of this incident is given by Reid (1969).

2   Warp refers to lengthwise threads stretched in a loom to be crossed by the weft. Here taken in the sense of providing the 'backcloth' to the criss-crossing of government policy.

3   The term 'gerrymander' is used to describe any method of arranging electoral districts in such a way that one political party can elect more representatives than they could if the district boundaries were fairly drawn. The term derives from Governor Elbridge Gerry of Massachusetts who established in 1812 a curiously bow-shaped electoral district north of Boston, which resembled a salamander, in order to favour his own party.

4   The origin of this appellation is uncertain. Perhaps because the document was bound in yellow - the traditional royal colour in the Malay States.

5   The Federation of Malaya Loan Ordinance of 1949 passed by the Legislative Council authorized the raising of a loan of M$100 million (of which M$69 million was to be floated in London and the remainder locally). The Federation of Malaya Security Loan Ordinance, 1952, enabled the government to find M$100 million in loans locally (Malaya 1950: 2)

6   For an interesting description of this so-called 'Ops Room

Technique', see Moynihan (1964: 391-414).

7 Lim (1975: 8) uses the language of the satisficer model to describe how these objectives may be achieved.

8 Employment-output elasticity was used by Malaysian planners to forecast the number of jobs to be created over a plan period. As different methods of estimation will produce different results, the projected employment levels will necessarily depend on the method used (Lim 1975: 218).

9 The *Colombo Plan* is an arrangement for discussing economic development plans and facilitating technical and financial assistance for development projects in South and South East Asia. It was established at Colombo, Sri Lanka (Ceylon) in 1951 as a result of discussions by the governments of India, Pakistan, Sri Lanka, Australia, New Zealand, and Britain. The United States, Japan, and a number of South East Asian countries also joined later *(The New Encyclopaedia Britannica* (1979), vol. 3, p. 15, Chicago: Encyclopaedia Britannica).

10 For example, in March 1950 the price of the best grade of sheet rubber (Ribbed Smoked Sheet no. 1 RSS1) in London was $1.28 per kilogram. This price rose steadily to peak at $5.41 per kilogram in February 1951, representing a jump of about 323 per cent in one year. However, the boom from the Korean War lasted for only two years. Prices in London declined to $1.97 per kilogram at the end of 1954 (Barlow 1978: 80-1).

11 In 1970, foreigners owned 62 per cent of share capital, Chinese 23 per cent, Malays 1.5 per cent, and Indians 0.9 per cent (Malaysia 1971: 40).

12 Sacerdoti and Wilson (1978); Ong (1984: 206); Pathmanathan (1985: 230-2).

13 See Lim's (1986) prognosis for this state of affairs.

14 This is unmistakably due to the influence of *Dato* Hussein Onn who throughout his career was a keen supporter of Malaysian unity - following the footsteps of his father, *Dato* Onn Jaafar who nearly 30

years ago formed UMNO and fought for independence for all Malaysians.

3 Rural content of regional planning

1   The urban-based 'capital-intensive approach' to development in Malaysia has little foundation, as the examination of development expenditures in the previous chapter has shown (Selvaratnam and Dissanayake 1979: 33).

2   The Jengka Triangle in Pahang, started in 1966, is such an example. There, the concept of regional development was made compatible with the national policy of reducing inequality and promoting export commodities such as rubber and oil palm.

3   The Muda irrigation project of the Kedah-Perlis plains comes under the supervision of MADA (Muda Agricultural Development Authority) while in Kemubu the authority responsible is KADA (Kemubu Agricultural Development Authority).

4   It has been estimated that almost two-fifths of all manufacturing output in Malaysia is produced in Selangor (29 per cent) and Kuala Lumpur (12 per cent) (Malaysia 1986: 172-3).

5   A development board has been set up for this region known as PERDA - Lembaga Kemajuan Pulau Pinang, or the Pulau Pinang Development Board.

6   Mosher's (1969) agricultural locality concept is similar but more limited. The locality is an area in which a farmer 'can with the means of transport available to him, go from his home to market centre where the off-farm facilities he needs are available and return home certainly within the same day' (Mosher 1969: 3).

7   It will be interesting to explore why this political or ideological framework of 'top-down' planning is preferred in the Malaysian context and what some of its consequences are.

8   Similar notions have also been expressed by de Koninck and McTaggart (1987: 341).

9 For a comprehensive history of FELDA and its achievements see Bahrin *et al.* (1977; 1979).

10 Since 1974 the passing of the Environmental Quality Act has spawned further legislation and regulations to control pollution and to protect the natural environment. These include the Environmental Quality (Crude Palm Oil) Regulations, 1977; Environmental Quality (Prescribed Premises, Natural Rubber) Regulations, 1978; Environmental Quality (Sewage and Industrial Effluents) Regulations, 1978; Clean Air Regulations and Motor Vehicles (Control of Smoke and Gas Emission) Rules, 1977.

11 Chan (1979) has reported on the new wave of out-migration from land schemes, particularly amongst those who have received a higher level of education and who have developed an inclination for urban living.

12 This debate, however, has been largely superseded. See Stöhr and Taylor (1981) and Gore (1984).

13 The Memali incident is one example of the distress arising from unemployment and landlessness which manifested itself in open conflict with the authorities. The clash between about 400 villagers and 200 policemen at Memali near Baling, Kedah on November 19, 1985, left 18 people dead and scores injured. See *Asiaweek*, January 19, 1986, pp. 8-9; *FEER*, January 16, 1986, p. 14; and *Aliran*, vol. 6, no. 4 (April 1986: 18).

14 The ratios for the other enterprises were: KEJORA (5) 1.17; DARA (5) 0.37; KETENGAH (3) 0.82; FIMA (3) 0.03; and SEDCs (10) 0.23.

15 'Escape spending' is a term used in retail geography whereby people in small towns spend money in a larger centre or town. The income which the smaller town would have earned has thus 'escaped'.

16 For example, the operation of the SLDB has been contracted out to Sime Darby, a well-known plantation agency, to manage its oil palm and rubber schemes in Sabah (*New Straits Times*, July 21, 1981).

17 Other categories of land include mixed-zone land, reserved land, and interior area land.

18 *Berdirikari* - an abbreviated form of the Bahasa Malaysia phrase *berdiri atas kaki sendiri* - means 'to stand on one's own feet'.

19 Directed development refers to that which is initiated by forces outside the social system. Change agents are deliberately introduced to direct the development.

4 Cities at the crossroads

1 That is, it is 'visible' in so far as urban characteristics have an impact on the ground and in spatial terms, while the term 'apparent' refers to urbanization on the basis of a statistical criterion in which for administrative convenience two or more non-contiguous areas are amalgamated as an 'urban area', for example, Kelang-Port Kelang and Ipoh-Pasir Pinji-Guntong.

2 These include the giant land development schemes of the JENGKA triangle, DARA, KEJORA, KESEDAR, and KETENGAH. See details given in Chapter 3.

3 Georgetown, Kelang, Melaka, and Seremban fell in rank while Ipoh, Petaling Jaya, Kuala Terengganu, Kota Baharu, Taiping, and Kuantan improved their rank positions.

4 The opposite condition is the primate pattern in which one city dominates the urban system in both absolute and relative terms; see Berry (1961).

5 This is modified from Subramaniam (1971: 15), which computes the ratio of the proportion of population in localities of 20,000 and over, to the proportion in localities of 100,000 and over.

6 The corresponding correlation coefficient between urban population and mining, manufacturing, construction, and utilities was 0.19 (not significant) and that between urban population and services was 0.68 (significant at the 95 per cent level).

7 However, note that the scattergrams that accompany the text in Lee's article have been labelled incorrectly. The conventional method is to have the x-axis along the horizontal and the y-axis along the vertical;

see Lee (1977: 230).

8 The chi-squared values computed from Table 4.8 were as follows: Malaysia 198.84, peninsular Malaysia 194.58, and Sabah 4.95. These were significant at the 95 per cent level for one degree of freedom. The value for Sarawak was 0.043 and this was not significant at the 95 per cent level.

9 The chi-squared values computed from Table 4.9 were as follows: Malays and other indigenous groups 88.65, Chinese 34.01, and Indians 25.73. These are significant at the 95 per cent level for one degree of freedom. The chi-squared value for 'others' was 1.33 and this was not significant at the 95 per cent level.

10 The 1980 Population Census defines an employed person as one 'who, at any time during the reference week worked for pay, profit or family gain'. Also considered as employed were persons who did not work during the reference week because of illness, injury, disability, bad weather, vacation, labour dispute, or social or religious reasons but had a job to return to. The unemployed are persons who were not seeking work because they believed no suitable job was available; were prevented from seeking work because of bad weather, illness, confinement; were waiting for a new job; were waiting for replies to job applications or had looked for work prior to the reference week; or considered themselves as having no qualifications (Khoo 1983: viii-xix).

11 Pahang had an average annual rate of urban growth of 7.7 per cent between 1970 and 1980; see Table 4.3 above.

12 Kuala Terengganu recorded a growth of 12.6 per cent per annum between 1970 and 1980 whereas Kota Baharu recorded 11.3 per cent. Note that Kuantan had a growth rate of 11.6 per cent in the same period; see Table 4.4 above.

13 Data elsewhere in the 1980 census report (Khoo 1983) show that in every age group, in both urban and rural Malaysia, the female unemployment rate was higher than that for males. The sex differentials are less pronounced in the middle-age groups of 25-49 years than for the younger and older age groups.

14 See Mazumdar (1981: Ch. 14) for the situation in 1970.

5 Promoting Industrial Growth

1   One definition of a multinational corporation is 'an organization that extends its business operations under one guiding direction in two or more countries' (Galbraith 1978: 3), but there are many others.

2   Here the present concern is with 'manufacturing multinationals' and ignores discussion of tin-based multinationals, rubber-based multinationals, agency houses, and trading multinationals. For a discussion of the origins of MNCs in Malaysia, see Singh and Chi (1981).

3   Unfortunately this plan and study are not readily accessible. Thus only a sketch of the broad outline is provided here. These have been gleaned from press reports; see *The Economist*, September 17, 1985, p. 17.

4   There were no LMW firms located outside peninsular Malaysia in 1983.

5   Previously these enterprises were known as 'off-budget agencies' and were engaged in socio-economic, commercial, industrial, and public utility activities.

6   This is in terms of a 30 per cent share for Malays and other *Bumiputera*, a 40 per cent share for other Malaysians, and 30 per cent for foreign investors.

7   This is defined as that group of establishments which employ between five and 44 paid full-time workers and whose activities may be classified as manufacturing activities.

6 Perspectives on problems, policies, and prospects

1   'Malaysia at 21. Uneasy Coming of Age', *Time* magazine, September 18, 1978.

2   So termed because of the observed impact of North Sea gas production on the Dutch economy.

3   The 11 criteria used in the BERI include: attitudes towards foreign

investors and nationalization tendencies; monetary inflation; currency convertibility; balance of payments; economic growth; bureaucratic delays; enforceability of contracts and professional service contracts; labour productivity; communications and transport; local management; short-term and long-term financing, political risk, and transfer risk.

4 A general introduction to content analysis is given by Goode, W., and Hart, P. (1952: Ch. 19); and Robert C. North *et al.* (1963).

5 The newspapers are *The New Straits Times* (NST), *Star*, and *Malay Mail* (MM); all English language dailies published in Malaysia. The sample data are from the February 2, 1987 issue. The news journals used in the study are *Asiaweek* (February 1, 1987), *The Economist* (January 31, 1987) and *Far Eastern Economic Review* (FEER) (January 29, 1987).

6 The Gini coefficient measures the extent of equality. It ranges between 0 and 1 with 0 representing perfect equality and 1 perfect inequality.

7 A label for Malays who do not follow the teachings of Islam.

8 The legitimacy of UMNO has been challenged in the courts. The High Court in Kuala Lumpur ruled in February 1988 that UMNO is 'illegal' as a political party. The implications of this ruling may be wide-ranging.

9 Article 3 of the Constitution of Malaysia.

10 The coalition BN won 132 of the 154 parliamentary seats.

11 The first three prime ministers of Malaysia have had very similar backgrounds. *Tunku* Abdul Rahman was a member of a royal family, the late *Tun* Abdul Razak and *Tun* Hussein Onn were from established aristocratic backgrounds.

12 In the Federation of 13 states there are hereditary Sultans in nine, and appointed *Yang di Pertua Negeri*s in the remaining four. In the hereditary Sultanates all rulers are the Sultans except the *Raja* of Perlis and the *Yang di Pertuan Besar* of Negri Sembilan. Melaka, Pulau Pinang, Sabah, and Sarawak have appointed heads of state.

13 Hereditary Sultans at a Conference of Rulers elect a king - the *Yang di Pertuan Agong* - and a deputy king based on an election list drawn up on the basis of their respective dates of accession to their thrones. A king is elected for five years. The last election was in 1984.

14 Article 38(4) of the Constitution of Malaysia.

15 For example, the division between Sultan Mahmood Iskandar Shah of Johor and his *Mentri Besar Tan Sri* Othman Saat forced the latter to resign following the state and national elections in 1982. Pahang also saw changes arising from differences of opinion between the Sultan and the *Mentri Besar Haji* Abdul Rahim Abu Bakar (see Selvaratnam 1982: 249-55). In the state of Perak the Sultan's decree on the date of *Hari Raya Puasa* (the end of the fasting month of Ramadhan) was one day ahead of the rest of the country in 1982. This was seen as a challenge to the prerogative which had long resided in the *Yang di Pertuan Agong*. The claim by the Sultan of Perak to some border territory is a further example of such 'activism'.

16 The nominees included Mr Donald Stephens (later known as *Tun* Fuad Stephens), *Datu* Mustapha *Datu* Harun (later elevated to *Tun*), and Mr Khoo Siak Chiew.

17 See Sabah (1963: 24-6) for textual details of this twenty-point agreement.

18 The five parties involved were later to form the Sabah Alliance. The parties included USNO (United Sabah National Organization), UNKO (United National Kadazan Organization), PM (United Pasok Momogun) People of the Country National Party, SCA (Sabah Chinese Association), and SIC (Sabah Indian Congress).

19 However, these exclusive powers are not protected under Articles 95D and 95E of the Federal Constitution.

20 The specific amendments include Article 161A and the later repeal of Article 161C (Muslim education in the Borneo states) and Article 161D (freedom of religion in the Borneo states) by the Constitutional (Amendment) Act, 1976.

21 A 'Malay' is defined in the Federal Constitution as a 'person who

professes the Muslim religion, habitually speaks the Malay language and conforms to Malay customs' (Art. 153, Federal Constitution).

22 The party was formed on July 15, 1975, by *Datuk* Harris Salleh, former Minister of Finance, and other cabinet ministers and assemblymen of the ruling USNO party.

23 The negotiations for a large petro-dollar loan through the Sabah Development Corporation, with the state of Sabah as guarantor, were one such example (see Ross-Larson 1976: 155).

24 The island of Labuan was ceded without the usual compensation. Selangor was paid more than $3 billion for surrendering Kuala Lumpur to the federal government. Pahang is negotiating for similar payment for federalizing Bukit Tinggi near Kuala Lumpur, and Sarawak has requested $6.4 billion in compensation for the federalization of part of its state (Kalimutu 1986: 820).

25 A fuller discussion of these items is found in *Datuk Haji* Serjan (1986: 114-34). The following discussion is based largely on this article.

26 Section 4 of the Petroleum Development Act, 1974.

27 *The Economist*, January 31, 1987, p. 12.

28 Malaysia, The Treasury (1985: 20).

29 FEER, October 3, 1985. This target is probably over optimistic since there has been a slump in the passenger car market in 1986. More realistically, production should reach about 60,000 cars.

30 By 1985 HICOM had already invested $405.4 million (Barraclough 1986: 190).

31 Investors must observe four rules of exchange control in Malaysia:

   1. Export receipts must be brought back and sold to any bank in Malaysia but can just as quickly be taken out again if so wished
   2. Borrowings abroad require prior permission but such permission is readily given as a matter of course where it is used to either generate or save foreign exchange

3. Non-residents who borrow in Malaysia require prior approval to ensure that foreign investors bring with them technology and some cash to show their commitment to the country.

4. On payments abroad, both residents and non-residents are allowed to do whatever they like with their own money. Borrowing domestically to finance remittances is discouraged.

See statement by the Governor of Bank Negara, *Tan Sri* Jaafar Hussein, *Malaysian Digest*, October 1987, p. 1.

32 It has been announced that the government will launch its Privatization Master Plan (PMP) in 1988. This will set the blueprint for the country's privatization programme (*Malaysian Digest*, October 1987, p. 4).

33 'Mahathir's Restoration', *FEER*, June 11, 1982, p. 38.

34 Such methods include 'one at a time', or dealing with one problem at a time to minimize risks and losses; 'lowest cost production' in procurement, distribution, and production; 'shifting battlefields', where ways are found to shift from the established strongholds of competitors; and 'just in time' methods that involve zero-based production and zero-based design to reduce stockpiling and incorporate change over time (see Ohame 1984).

35 A useful analysis of Malaysian foreign policy is summarized in Chin (1982).

36 This is the National Equity Corporation, set up in 1979 to accelerate the restructuring objectives of the NEP.

REFERENCES

Abdullah, Abdul Hamid and Mohamad, Sulong. (1982) 'Regional development planning in peninsular Malaysia: A critique of and an alternative to current approach [*sic*]', in Ismail Ahmad and Jamaluddin Md. Jahi. (eds), *Geography and the Third World*, Kuala Lumpur: Penerbit Universiti Kebangsaan, pp. 1-30.

Haji Ahmad, Zakaria. (1981) 'Malaysia in 1980: A year of political consolidation and economic development', in *Southeast Asian Affairs 1981*, Singapore: Institute of Southeast Asian Studies, pp. 201-16.

Aiken, S. R. and Leigh, C.H. (1975) 'Malaysia's emerging conurbation', *Annals, Association of American Geographers* 65: 546-63.

Alatas, *Syed* Hussein. (1977) *The Myth of the Lazy Native*, London: Frank Cass.

Ali, *Syed* Husin. (1975) *Malay Peasant Society and Leadership*, Kuala Lumpur: Oxford University Press.

------. (1978) *Kemiskinan dan kelaparan tanah di Kelantan: Satu penyelidikan socio-ekonomi Kelantan*, Petaling Jaya: Karangkraf.

------. (1983) *Poverty and Landlessness in Kelantan, Malaysia*, Bielefeld Studies on the Sociology of Development, no. 20, Saarbrucken: Verlag Breitenbach Publishers.

Alias, *Raja* Muhammad. (1975) 'Pioneering into the interior: The Malaysian experience', (October) Kuala Lumpur: FELDA, mimeograph.

Aliran, Penang. Published bimonthly by Aliran Kesedaran Negara (National Conscience).

Anand, Sudhir. (1983) *Inequality and Poverty in Malaysia. Measurement and Decomposition*, New York: Oxford University Press for The World Bank.

Andaya, B.W. and Andaya, L.Y. (1982) *A History of Malaysia*, London: Macmillan Press.

Anderson, James A. (1982) 'Philippines: Rapid rural "development". Performance and consequences in the Philippines', in MacAndrews, Colin and Chia, Lin Sen. (eds) *Too Rapid Development. Perceptions and Perspectives from Southeast Asia*, Athens, Ohio: Ohio University Press, pp. 122-71.

Ariff, Mohamed. (1987) 'Malaysia in a recessionary setting: An overview', in *Southeast Asian Affairs 1987*, Singapore: Institute of Southeast Asian Studies, pp. 197-216.

Armstrong, W.R. and McGee, T.G. (1968) 'Revolutionary change and the Third World city: A theory of urban involution', *Civilisation* 18: 353-78.

Arudsothy, Ponniah. (1975) 'Malaysia', in Ichimura, S. (ed), *The Economic Development of the East and Southeast Asia*, Honolulu: The University Press of Hawaii, pp. 81-128.

------. (1985) 'Government policies, planning strategies and development performance in Malaysia', *Kabar Seberang* 15: 25-35.

Asian Development Bank. (1971) *Southeast Asia's Economy in the 1970s*, London: Longman.

Asiaweek, Hong Kong. Published weekly by Asiaweek Ltd.

Aznam, Suhaimi. (1985) 'The Sabah stablemate', *Far Eastern Economic Review*, November 21, pp. 16-17.

Bahrin, *Tunku* Shamsul. (1979) 'Development planning: Land settlement policies and practices in Southeast Asia', in Pryor, Robin. (ed) *Migration and Development in Southeast Asia*, Kuala Lumpur: Oxford University Press, pp. 295-303.

------. (1981) 'Review and evaluation of attempts to direct migrants to frontier areas through land colonization schemes', in United Nations, *Population Redistribution Policies in Development Planning*, papers of UN/UNFPA Workshop, Bangkok, 4-13 September.

Bahrin, *Tunku* Shamsul and Perera, P.D.A. (1977) *FELDA. Twenty-one Years of Land Development*, Kuala Lumpur: FELDA.

Bahrin, *Tunku* Shamsul, Perera, P.D.A., and Lim, H.K. (1979) *Land Development and Resettlement in Malaysia*, Kuala Lumpur: University of Malaya.

Barlow, Colin. (1978) *The Natural Rubber Industry. Its Development, Technology and*

Economy in Malaysia, Kuala Lumpur: Oxford University Press.

Barraclough, Simon. (1986) 'Malaysia in 1985: A question of management', in *Southeast Asian Affairs 1986,* Singapore: Institute of Southeast Asian Studies, pp. 185-207.

Bass, Jerome R. (1970) 'Malaysia: Continuity or change?', *Asian Survey* 10 (February): 152-60.

Berry, B.J.L. (1961) 'City size distributions and economic development', *Economic Development and Cultural Change* (July): 573-88.

------. (1972) 'Hierarchical diffusion: The basis of development filtering and spread in a system of growth centres', in Hansen, N.M. (ed) *Growth Centres in Regional Economic Development*, Chicago: Free Press, pp. 108-38.

Blair, J.A.S. and Noor, Nache M. (1980) *Changing Rural Lifestyles*, Trolak: FELDA.

------. (1983) 'Migration and land development in Malaysia', *Development Forum,* (Malaysian Centre for Development Studies), 13: 23-55.

Blaug, M. (1964) 'A case of emperor's clothes: Perroux's theories of economic domination', *Kyklos* 17: 551-64.

Brown, M. (1985) 'Tin men open can of worms', *The Weekend Australian*, November 9-10, p. 20.

Burrough, Boenish J. and Jamin, Alik. (1972) 'Traditional methods of Dusun rice cultivation', *Sabah Society Journal* 4: 352-64.

Business Times. (1981) 'Fourth Malaysia Plan submitted to Parliament', March 28, pp. 1-11.

Carter, R.D. (1969) 'The effect of a capital development project on the national income of a developing country: Malaysia', Ph.D. thesis, Ohio State University, Cincinnati, Ohio.

Chan, P.T.H. (1979) 'Preliminary findings of a survey of out-migration in West Johore region', Faculty of Economics and Administration, University of Malaya, mimeograph.

Chan, Paul. (1981) 'Migration related policies in peninsular Malaysia: An evaluation', in Jones, G.W. and Richter, H.V. (eds) *Population Mobility and Development: Southeast Asia and the Pacific*, Development Studies Centre Monograph no. 27, Canberra: Australian National University, pp. 407-30

------. (1983) 'The political economy of urban squatters in Metropolitan Kuala Lumpur', *Contemporary Southeast Asia* 4 (March): 486-508.

------. (1984) 'The impact of Malaysia Incorporated and privatisation', in Mohd. Nor Abdul Ghani *et al.* (eds) *Malaysia Incorporated and Privatisation: Towards National Unity*, Petaling Jaya: Pelanduk Publications for Institute of Management Consultants and Prime Minister's Department, pp. 37-44.

Chan, Paul and Lim, Lin Lean. (1981) *Case Study of Migrant Settlers in Three Land Development Schemes in peninsular Malaysia*, Kuala Lumpur: Faculty of Economics and Administration, University of Malaya.

Chan, Paul and Richter, Hazel. (1982) 'Land settlement, income and population redistribution in peninsular Malaysia', in Jones, G.W. and Richter, H.V. (eds) *Population Resettlement Programmes in Southeast Asia*, Development Studies Centre Monograph no. 30., Canberra: Australian National University, pp. 73-92.

Chee, Peng Lim. (1979) 'Small industry - Its role in Malaysian industrial development', in Cheong, Kee Cheok, Khoo, Siew Mun, and Thillainathan R. (eds) *Malaysia: Some Contemporary Issues in Socioeconomic Development*, Kuala Lumpur: Persatuan Ekonomi Malaysia, pp. 129-54.

------. (1985) 'Regulating the transfer of technology: An analysis of Malaysia's experience', *Contemporary Southeast Asia* 7 (June): 13-33.

Chee, Stephen. (1973) 'Malaysia and Singapore: Separate identities, different priorities', *Asian Survey* 13 (February): 151-61.

Cheong, Kee Cheok *et al.* (1979) 'Regional development in Malaysia', in Institute of Developing Economies, Regional Development Research Unit, *Regional Development in Southeast Asian Countries*, Tokyo: Institute of Developing Economies, pp. 155-260.

Chew, Huat Hock. (1982) 'Changing directions in foreign policy trends: A comparative analysis of Malaysia's bilateral relations with Britain and Singapore in 1981', *Contemporary Southeast Asia* 5 (December): 346-68.

Chew, T.A. and Shand, R.T. (1984) *The Off-farm Labour Supply of Padi Farmers in Kelantan, Malaysia*, Development Studies Centre Working Paper no. 38, Canberra: Australian National University.

Chia, Lin Sen and MacAndrews, Colin. (1982) 'Problems of rapid development', in MacAndrews, Colin and Chia, Lin Sen. (eds) *Too Rapid Development. Perceptions and*

Perspectives from Southeast Asia, Athens, Ohio: Ohio University Press, pp. 1-13.

Chik, Sabaruddin. (1978) *National Ideology and Bureaucracy in Malaysia*, Occasional Paper no. 5, Kuala Lumpur: Pusat Pengajian Pembangunan Malaysia (Malaysian Centre for Development Studies).

Chin, Kim Wah. (1982) 'A new assertiveness in Malaysian foreign policy', in *Southeast Asian Affairs 1982*, Institute of Southeast Asian Studies, Singapore: Heinemann Asia, pp. 273-82.

Chong, Li Choy. (1981) 'The power theory of development: A short presentation', *Contemporary Southeast Asia* 3 (December): 286-399.

Cline, W.R. (1975) 'Distribution and development: A survey of literature', *Journal of Development Economics* 1: 359-400.

Comer, L. (1981) 'Linkages, reciprocity and remittances. The impact of rural outmigration on Malaysian rice villages', in Jones, G.W. and Richter, H.V. (eds) *Population Mobility and Development: Southeast Asia and the Pacific*, Development Studies Centre Monograph no. 27, Canberra: Australian National University, pp. 117-36.

------. (1983) 'The persistence of poverty: Rural development policy in Malaysia', *Kajian Malaysia* 1 (June): 38-61.

Courtenay, P.P. (1983) *Nearly at the Crossroads? A Review of Some Issues Raised in Recent Work on the Malaysian Padi Sector*, Development Studies Centre Occasional Paper no. 33, Canberra: Australian National University.

Davis, K. (1971) 'The role of urbanization in the developing countries', paper presented at the Rehovot Conference, Tel Aviv, mimeograph.

Dayal, E. and Shanmugam, B. (1987) 'Bank branching and regional development in Malaysia', *Australian Geographer* 18 (May): 44-50.

de Koninck, R. and McTaggart, W.D. (1987) 'Land settlement processes in Southeast Asia: Historical foundations, discontinuities and problems', *Asian Profile* 15 (August): 341-56.

Dobby, E.H.G. (1952) 'Resettlement transforms Malaya', *Economic Development and Cultural Change* 1: 163-89.

Dwyer, D.J. (1972a) 'Urbanization as a factor in the political development of Southeast Asia', *Journal of Oriental Studies* 10: 23-32.

------. (1972b) 'Future (urban) shock', *Insight* (May): 49-52.

The Economist, London. Published weekly by The Economist Ltd.

Emmerij, L. (1981) 'Basic needs and employment oriented strategies reconsidered', in Misra, R.P. and Honjo, M. (eds) *Changing Perception of Development Problems*, Vol. 1, United Nations Centre for Regional Development, Singapore: Maruzen Asia, pp. 177-93.

Enloe, Cynthia H. (1973) *Ethnic Conflict and Political Development*, Boston: Little, Brown and Co.

Esman, M.J. (1972) *Administration and Development in Malaysia*, Ithaca, N.Y.: Cornell University Press.

Far Eastern Economic Review (FEER), Hong Kong. Published weekly by Far Eastern Economic Review Ltd.

Faridad, A. (1981) 'The nature and scope of regional planning and development', in Prantilla, E.B. (ed) *National Development and Regional Policy*, Vol. 3, United Nations Centre for Regional Development, Singapore: Maruzen Asia, pp. 85-99.

Federal Land Development Authority (FELDA). (1963) *Annual Report and Accounts to 30th June 1962*, Kuala Lumpur: FELDA.

Finck, A. (1973) 'The fertility of tropical soils under the influence of agricultural use', *Applied Science and Development* 1: 7-31.

Fisk, E.K. and Osman-Rani, H. (eds) (1982) *The Political Economy of Malaysia*, Kuala Lumpur: Oxford University Press.

Food and Agriculture Organisation (FAO) and International Bank for Reconstruction and Development (IBRD). (1975) *Problems of Rural Poverty in Malaysia*, unpublished report, mimeograph.

Friedmann, J. (1961) 'Cities in social transformation', *Comparative Studies in Society and History* 4 (November): 86-103.

------. (1973) *Urbanization, Planning and National Development*, Beverly Hills, Calif.: Sage Publications.

Friedmann, J. and Douglass, M. (1975) 'Agropolitan development: Towards a new strategy for regional planning in Asia', Seminar paper for UNCRD, Nagoya, November 3-4, 1975.

Friedmann, John and Wulff, Robert. (1976) *The Urban Transition. Comparative Studies of Newly Industrializing Societies*, London: Edward Arnold.

Friedmann, J. and Weaver, C. (1979) *Territory and Function: The Evolution of Regional Planning*, London: Edward Arnold.

Datuk Fung, Ngit Chung Nicholas. (1986) 'The constitutional position of Sabah', in Trindade, F.A. and Lee, H.P. (eds) *The Constitution of Malaysia*, Singapore: Oxford University Press, pp. 92-113.

Galbraith, J.K. (1978) 'In defence of multinationals', *Horizon* 30: 12-15.

Gale, B. (1981) 'PETRONAS: Malaysia's national oil corporation', *Asian Survey* 21 (November): 1129-44.

------. (1984) 'Politics at the periphery: A study of the 1981 and 1982 election campaigns in Sabah', *Contemporary Southeast Asia* 6 (June): 26-49.

Geertz, C. (1963) *Peddlers and Princes: Social Change and Economic Modernization in Two Indonesian Towns*, Chicago: University of Chicago Press.

Ghani, Mohamed Nor Abdul. (1981) 'Malaysia's development experience: Past strategies and alternatives', in Osman Rani, H., Jomo, K.S., and Shari, Ishak. (eds) *Development in the Eighties with Special Emphasis on Malaysia*, a special double issue of *Jurnal Ekonomi Malaysia* 3 and 4: 285-97.

Ghani, Mohamed Nor Abdul *et al.* (1984) *Malaysia Incorporated and Privatisation: Towards National Unity*, Petaling Jaya: Pelanduk Publications for Institute of Management Consultants and Prime Minister's Department.

Gibbons, David S. (1984) *Paddy, Poverty and Public Policy. A Preliminary Report on Poverty in the Muda Irrigation Scheme Area, 1972 and 1982* Monograph Series No. 7, Centre for Policy Research, Universiti Sains Malaysia, Penang.

Gibbons, David S., de Koninck, R., and Hasan, Ibrahim. (1980) *Agricultural Modernisation: The Distributional Impact of the Green Revolution in Regions of Malaysia and Indonesia*, Farnborough: Saxon House.

Gilbert, A. (1985) *An Unequal World: The Links Between Rich and Poor Nations*, London: Macmillan Education.

Gillis, M., Perkins, D.H., Roemer, M., and Snodgrass, D.R. (1983), *Economics of Development*, New York: Norton and Co.

Goh, Kim Chuan. (1982) 'Environmental impact of economic development in peninsular Malaysia: A review', *Applied Geography* 2: 3-16.

Goode, W. and Hart, P. (1952) *Methods in Social Research*, New York: McGraw Hill.

Gore, Charles. (1984) *Regions in Question*, London: Methuen.

Grijpstra, B.G. (1976) *Common Efforts in the Development of Rural Sarawak, Malaysia*, Assen: van Gorcum.

Gudgeon, P.S. (1981) 'Economic development in Sabah, 1881-1981', in Sullivan, Anwar, and Leong, C. (eds) *Commemorative History of Sabah, 1881-1981*, Kota Kinabalu: Sabah State Government Centenary Publications Committee, pp. 183-360.

Haggett, Peter. (1975) *Geography: A Modern Synthesis* (2nd edn), New York: Harper and Row.

Hainsworth, G.B. (1979) 'Economic growth and poverty in Southeast Asia: Malaysia, Indonesia and the Philippines', *Pacific Affairs* 52 (Spring): 5-41.

Hashim, Alladin. (1979) 'Land development under FELDA: Some socio-economic aspects', in Abdul Rahim Mokhzani, (ed) *Rural Development in Southeast Asia*, New Delhi: Vikas Publishing House, pp. 63-79.

------. (1981) 'Development and planned population distribution', *Land Development Digest* 3: 1-30.

Hashim, *Tun* Mohamed Suffian. (1976) *An Introduction to the Constitution of Malaysia* (2nd edn), Kuala Lumpur: Government Printer.

Hettne, B. and Wallensteen, P. (1978) *Emerging Trends in Development Theory*, Workshop, August 8-12 (1977), Stockholm: Swedish Agency for Research Cooperation with Developing Countries.

Higgins, Benjamin. (1981) 'National development and regional policy', in Prantilla, E.B. (ed) *National Development and Regional Policy*, vol. 3, United Nations Centre for Regional Development, Singapore: Maruzen Asia, pp. 15-55.

------. (1982) 'Development Planning', in Fisk, E.K. and Osman Rani, H. (eds) *The Political*

Economy of Malaysia, Kuala Lumpur: Oxford University Press, pp. 148-83.

Hill, R.D. and Bray, J.M. (eds) (1978) *Geography and the Environment in Southeast Asia*, Proceedings of the Department of Geography and Geology, Jubilee Symposium, University of Hong Kong, 21-25 June, 1976, Hong Kong: University of Hong Kong Press.

Hirschman, Albert O. (1958) *The Strategy of Economic Development*, New Haven: Yale University Press.

Hirschmann, C. (1976) 'Recent urbanization trends in peninsular Malaysia', *Demography* 13: 445-61. Reprinted in Lim, David (ed) (1983) *Further Readings on Malaysian Economic Development*, Kuala Lumpur: Oxford University Press, pp. 111-24.

------. (1987) 'The meaning and measurement of ethnicity in Malaysia: An analysis of census classifications', *Journal of Asian Studies* 46 (August): pp. 555-82.

Ho, Robert. (1965) 'Land settlement projects in Malaya: An assessment of the role of FLDA', *Journal of Tropical Geography* 18: 1-15.

------. (1968) 'Geographical aspects of Malaysian development, 1957-66', in Chatterjee, Shiba Prasad. (ed) *Developing Countries of the World*, 21st International Geographical Congress, Calcutta National Committee for Geography, pp. 273-88.

Hoffman, Lutz and Tan, Siew Ee. (1980) *Review of Industrial Growth, Employment and Foreign Investment in peninsular Malaysia*, Kuala Lumpur: Oxford University Press for the Institut für Weltwirtschaft, Kiel.

Honjo, M. (ed) (1981) *Urbanization and Regional Development*, vol. 6, United Nations Centre for Regional Development, Singapore: Maruzen Asia.

Hoselitz, B.F. (1962) 'The role of urbanization in economic development: Some international comparisons', in Turner, Roy (ed) *India's Urban Future*, Berkeley: University of California Press, pp. 157-81.

Huntington, P. (1968) *Political Order in Changing Societies*, New Haven: Yale University Press.

Haji Husin, Khalid. (1981) 'Rural development and regional planning in Malaysia: The case of Regional Development Authorities', in Dias, Hiran K. *et al.* (eds) *Rural Development and Regional Planning in the '80s: Challenges and Priorities*, Bangkok: Human Settlements Division, Asian Institute of Technology, pp. 251-66.

Ibrahim, Ahmad. (1965) *Islamic Law in Malaya,* Singapore: Malaysian Sociological Research Institute.

Ichimura, Shinichi. (ed) (1975) *The Economic Development of East and Southeast Asia,* Monographs of the Center of Southeast Asian Studies, Kyoto University, Honolulu: The University Press of Hawaii.

Indorf, H.H. (1978) 'Malaysia in 1977: A prelude to premature parliamentary elections', *Asian Survey* 18 (February): pp. 186-93.

------. (1979) 'Malaysia 1978: Communal coalitions continue', *Asian Survey* 19 (February): 115-23.

Institute of Developing Economies, Regional Development Research Unit. (1979) *Regional Development in Southeast Asian Countries,* Tokyo: Institute of Developing Economies.

International Monetary Fund (IMF). (1987) *International Financial Statistics Yearbook 1987* Washington, D.C.: IMF.

------. (1988) *Balance of Payments Statistics Yearbook,* vol. 30, Washington, D.C.: IMF.

Iwasaki, Teruyuki *et al.* (1979) *Regional Development in Southeast Asian Countries: Summary,* Tokyo: Regional Development Research Unit, Institute of Developing Economies.

Jackson, H.M. (1977) 'Contributors' Perspectives' in Birou, A., Henry, P.M., and Schlegel, J.P. (eds) *Towards a Re-definition of Development: Essays and Discussion on the Nature of Development in an International Perspective,* Paris: Pergamon Press for OECD., pp. 13-34.

Jackson, James C. (1963) 'Smallholding cultivation of cash crops', in Wang, Gung-wu (ed) *Malaysia: A Survey,* Melbourne: Cheshire, pp. 246-73.

------. (1968) *Sarawak. A Geographical Survey of a Developing State,* London: University of London Press.

Jacoby, J.H. (1972) 'Effects of the "Green Revolution" in South and South East Asia', *Modern Asian Studies* 6: 63-9.

James, K. (1986) 'The Malaysian economy. The shadow of 1990', in *Southeast Asian Affairs 1986,* Institute of Southeast Asian Studies, Singapore: ISEAS, pp. 208-22.

Johns, B.L. (1973) 'Import substitution and export potential: The case of manufacturing industry in West Malaysia', *Australian Economic Papers* 12 (December): 175-95.

Jones, G. (1975) 'Implications of prospective urbanization for development planning in Southeast Asia', in Kantner, John and McCaffrey, L. (eds) *Population and Development in Southeast Asia*, Lexington, Mass.: D.C. Heath and Co., pp. 99-117.

Jones, G.W. and Richter, H.V. (eds) (1981) *Population Mobility and Development: Southeast Asia and the Pacific*, Development Studies Centre Monograph no. 27, Canberra: Australian National University.

Jones, G.W. and Richter, H.V. (eds) (1982) *Population Resettlement Programs in Southeast Asia*, Development Studies Centre Monograph no. 30, Canberra: Australian National University.

Jones, L.W. (1966) *The Population of Borneo: A Study of the Peoples of Sarawak, Sabah and Brunei*, London: University of London, Athlone Press.

Kalimutu, K. Ramanathan. (1986) 'The Sabah state elections of April 1985', *Asian Survey* 26 (July): 815-37.

Kanapathy, V. (1970) 'Foreign investment in Malaysia: Experience and prospects', *United Malayan Banking Corporation Economic Review* 6.

Katchamat, Suraphol. (1978) 'Analysis and evaluation of the national economic development plans of Thailand, 1961-71 from a comparative regional-urban development perspective', Ph.D. thesis, Michigan State University, Department of Urban Planning.

Kelley, Allen C., Williamson, J.G., and Cheetham, R.J. (1972) *Dualistic Economic Development: Theory and Practice*, Chicago: Chicago University Press.

Keyfitz, Nathan. (1965) 'Political-economic aspects of urbanization in Southeast Asia', in Hauser, P.M. and Schnore, L.F. (eds) *The Study of Urbanization*, New York: Wiley, pp. 265-309.

Khoo, S.H. and Cho, G. (1973) 'The Nabawan Valley scheme: An attempt to change a people', *Ekistics* 213: 89-93.

Khoo, Teik Huat. (1982a) *1980 Population and Housing Census of Malaysia. Local Authority Areas: Population, Households and Living Quarters*, Kuala Lumpur: Department of Statistics Malaysia.

------. (1982b) *1980 Population and Housing Census of Malaysia. Census of Housing, Malaysia 1980. Summary Report*, Kuala Lumpur: Department of Statistics, Malaysia.

------. (1983) *1980 Population and Housing Census of Malaysia. General Report of the Population Census*, vols. 1 and 2, Kuala Lumpur: Department of Statistics, Malaysia.

Kuznets, S. (1955) 'Economic growth and income inequality', *American Economic Review* 45 (March): 1-28.

Kwok, K.K. and Singh, Harbans. (1983) 'Trends and patterns of internal migration in Malaysia: 1970-1980', *Development Forum* (Malaysian Centre for Development Studies) 13 (December): 1-22.

Lai, Ah Hoon. (1975) 'Problems of federal finance in the Malaysian plural society', in Lim, David (ed) *Readings on Malaysian Economic Development*, Kuala Lumpur: Oxford University Press, pp. 399-407.

Lampard, E.E. (1969) 'Historical contours of contemporary urban society: A comparative view', *Journal of Contemporary History* 4 (July): 3-25.

Lee, Boon Thong. (1977) 'Malay urbanization and the ethnic profile of urban centres in peninsular Malaysia', *Journal of Southeast Asian Studies* 8 (September): 224-34.

Lee, H.P. (1986) 'Postscript. The Malaysian Constitutional Crisis: King, Rulers and Royal Assent', in Trindade, F.A. and Lee, H.P. (eds) *The Constitution of Malaysia*, Singapore: Oxford University Press, pp. 237-61.

Lee, Yong Leng. (1965a) *North Borneo (Sabah). A Study in Settlement Geography*, Singapore: Eastern Universities Press.

------. (1965b) 'Agriculture in Sarawak', *Journal of Tropical Geography* 21: 21-9.

Leigh, Michael. (1983) *Malaysia: Charting a New Direction?*, The Parliament of the Commonwealth of Australia, Legislative Research Service Discussion Paper no. 1, Canberra: Department of the Parliamentary Library.

Leinbach, Thomas R. (1971) 'Transportation and Modernization in Malaya', Ph.D. thesis, Philadelphia: Pennsylvania State University.

------. (1973) 'Distance, information flows and modernization: Some observations from West Malaysia', *Professional Geographer* 25 (February): pp. 7-11.

Leong, K.C. (1981) 'Kuala Lumpur: Youngest metropolis of Southeast Asia', in Honjo, M. (ed) *Urbanization and Regional Development*, vol. 6, United Nations Centre for Regional Development, Singapore: Maruzen Asia, pp. 257-80.

Lerner, Daniel. (1963) *Passing of the Traditional Society: Modernizing the Middle East*, New York: Free Press.

Leser, D. (1986) 'Islam on the march: The revolution on our doorstep', *The Weekend Australian*, January 25-26, pp. 1-2.

Lewis, A.W. (1966) *Development Planning: The Essentials of Economic Policy*, New York: Harper and Row.

Lian, F.J.W. (1980) 'Aspects of land development programme in Sarawak', *Geographica* 14: 1-9.

Lieberson, S. (1969) 'Measuring population diversity', *American Sociological Review* 34: 850-62.

Lim, Chong Yah. (1965) 'Malaya', in Onslow, C. (ed), *Asian Economic Development*, London: Weidenfeld and Nicolson, pp. 95-117.

Lim, David. (1973) *Economic Growth and Development in West Malaysia, 1947-1970*, Kuala Lumpur: Oxford University Press.

------. (ed) (1975) *Readings on Malaysian Economic Development*, Kuala Lumpur: Oxford University Press.

------. (1982-83) 'Malaysian development planning', *Pacific Affairs* 55 (Winter): pp. 613-39.

------. (1983) 'The political economy of the New Economic Policy in Malaysia', in Lim, David. (ed) *Further Readings on Malaysian Economic Development*, Kuala Lumpur: Oxford University Press, pp. 3-22.

------. (1986) 'East Malaysia in Malaysian development planning', *Journal of Southeast Asian Studies* 17 (March): 156-70.

Lim, Heng Kow. (1977) *Evolution of the Urban System in Malaysia*, Kuala Lumpur: University of Malaya Press.

Lim, Hua Sing. (1984) 'Japanese perspectives on Malaysia's "Look East" policy', *Southeast Asian Affairs 1984*, Singapore: Institute of Southeast Asian Studies, pp. 231-45.

Lim, L.L. (1974) *The Pattern of Income Distribution in West Malaysia, 1957-1970*, World Employment Programme Research Working Paper, Geneva: ILO.

Lim, Teck Ghee and Ng, Sock Nye. (1979) *Working Towards Meaningful Dialogues: The Malaysian Experience*, Tokyo: The United Nations University.

Ling, Chu Poh. (1977) 'Incentives for potential workers and settlers: A concern for socio-economic research in Trengganu', *Development Forum* (Malaysian Centre for Development Studies, Kuala Lumpur) 7 (June): 17-32.

Lipton, Michael. (1977) *Why the Poor Stay Poor: Urban Bias in World Development*, Cambridge, Mass.: Harvard University Press.

Lo, Fu-chen. (ed) (1981) *Rural-Urban Relations and Regional Development*, vol. 5, United Nations Centre for Regional Development, Singapore: Maruzen Asia.

Lo, Fu-chen, Salih, Kamal, and Douglass, M. (1981) 'Rural-urban transformation in Asia', in Lo, Fu-chen. (ed) *Rural-Urban Relations and Regional Development*, vol. 5, United Nations Centre for Regional Development, Singapore: Maruzen Asia, pp. 7-43.

Lo-Lim, M. (1978) 'Comments on delineating service centre networks in Sarawak, Malaysia', in Misra, R.P., Urs, D.V., and Natraj, V.K. (eds) *Regional Planning and National Development*, New Delhi: Vikas Publishing House, pp. 453-60.

Loudon, B. (1987) 'Malaya: A volcano capped - but only just', *The Weekend Australian*, November 28-29, p. 25.

Lowe, V. (1984) 'Redefining the "constitutionality" of the Monarchy: The 1983 constitutional amendment crisis in Malaysia', *Kajian Malaysia* 2 (December): pp. 1-15.

MacAndrews, Colin. (1977a) *Mobility and Modernisation: The Federal Land Development Authority and Its Role in Modernising the Rural Malay*, Yogyakarta: Gadjah Mada University Press.

------. (1977b) 'The politics of planning: Malaysia and the new Third Malaysia Plan (1976-1980)', *Asian Survey* 17 (March): 293-308.

------. (1982) 'Land settlement policies in Southeast Asia', in Jones, G.W. and Richter, H.V. (eds) *Population Resettlement Programmes in Southeast Asia*, Development Studies Centre Monograph no. 30, Canberra: Australian National University, pp. 9-23.

MacAndrews, Colin and Chia, Lin Sen. (eds) (1982) *Too Rapid Development: Perceptions and Perspectives from Southeast Asia*, Athens, Ohio: Ohio University Press.

MacAndrews, Colin, Fisher, H. Benjamin, and Sibero, Atar. (1982) 'Regional development, planning and implementation in Indonesia. The evolution of a national policy', in MacAndrews, Colin, and Chia, Lin Sen. (eds) *Too Rapid Development: Perception and Perspectives from Southeast Asia*, Athens, Ohio: Ohio University Press, pp. 79-121.

MacFazdean, I. (1947) 'Memorandum on development in Sarawak', Kuching, mimeograph.

McGee, T.G. (1967) *The Southeast Asian City*, London: G. Bell.

------. (1969) 'The urbanization process: Western theory and the Southeast Asian experience', *SEADAG Papers* 59, New York: Asia Society.

------. (1971a) *The Urbanization Process in the Third World: Explorations in Search of a Theory*, London: G. Bell.

------. (1971b) 'Catalysts or cancers? The role of cities in Asian society', in Jakobson, L. and Prakash, V. (eds) *Urbanization and National Development*, Beverly Hills, Calif.: Sage Publications, pp. 157-81.

------. (1976) 'Malay migration to Kuala Lumpur city: Individual adaptation to the city', in Banks, D.J. (ed) *Changing Identities in Modern Southeast Asia*, The Hague: Mouton, pp. 199-236.

------. (1978) 'An invitation to the "Ball": Dress formal or informal?', in Rimmer, P.J., Drakakis-Smith, D.W., and McGee, T.G. (eds) *Food, Shelter and Transport in Southeast Asia and the Pacific*, Research School of Pacific Studies, Department of Human Geography Publication HG/12, Canberra: Australian National University, pp. 3-28.

------. (1981) 'Labour mobility in fragmented labour markets, rural-urban linkages and regional development in Asia', in Lo, Fu-chen. (ed) *Rural-Urban Relations and Regional Development*, vol. 5, United Nations Centre for Regional Development, Singapore: Maruzen Asia, pp. 245-63.

------. (1986) 'Joining the global assembly line: Malaysia's role in the international semiconductor industry', in McGee, T.G. *et al.* (eds) *Industrialisation and Labour Force Processes: A Case Study of peninsular Malaysia*, Research Papers on Development in East Java and West Malaysia, no. 1, Research School of Pacific Studies, Canberra: Australian National University.

McGee, T.G. and Yeung, Yue-man. (1977) *Hawkers in Southeast Asian Cities: Planning for the Bazaar Economy*, Ottawa: International Development Research Centre.

McGee, T.G. *et al.* (eds) (1986) *Industrialisation and Labour Force Processes: A Case Study of peninsular Malaysia*, Research Papers on Development in East Java and West Malaysia no. 1, Research School of Pacific Studies, Canberra: Australian National University, pp. 35-67.

McNamara, R.S. (1973) *Annual Address to the 1973 Annual Meeting of the Board of Governors of the IBRD*, Nairobi, 1973.

McTaggart, W.D. (1972) *Industrialization in West Malaysia, 1968*, Occasional Paper no. 2, Centre for Asian Studies, Tucson, Arizona: Arizona State University.

Mackie, J.A.C. (1974) *Konfrontasi: The Indonesia-Malaysia Dispute, 1963-1966*, New York: Oxford University Press.

The Malay Mail (MM), Kuala Lumpur. Published daily by the New Straits Times Press (Malaysia).

Malaya, Federation of. (1950) *Draft Development Plan 1950-1955* (DDP), Kuala Lumpur: Government Printer.

Malaya, Federation of. (1953) *Progress Report on the Development Plan of the Federation of Malaya 1950-1955*, Kuala Lumpur: Government Printer.

Malaya, Federation of. (1956a) *First Malaya Plan 1956-1960*, Kuala Lumpur: Government Printer.

Malaya, Federation of. (1956b) *Report of the Land Settlement Working Party*, Kuala Lumpur: Government Printer.

Malaya, Federation of. (1957) *Report of the Working Party on the Encouragement of Industrial Development in the Federation of Malaya*, Kuala Lumpur: Government Printer.

Malaya, Federation of. (1961) *Second Malaya Plan 1961-1965*, Kuala Lumpur: Government Printer.

Malaya, Federation of. (1963) *Interim Review of Development in Malaya under the Second Five Year Plan*, Kuala Lumpur: Government Printer.

Malaysia. (1965) *First Malaysia Plan 1966-1970*, Kuala Lumpur: Government Printer.

Malaysia. (1969) *Mid-term Review of Economic Development in Malaysia under the First Malaysia Plan 1966-1970*, Kuala Lumpur: Government Printer.

Malaysia. (1971) *Second Malaysia Plan 1971-1975*, Kuala Lumpur: Government Printer.

Malaysia, Jabatan Perangkaan. (1972) *1970 Population and Housing Census of Malaysia: Community Groups*, Kuala Lumpur: Jabatan Perangkaan Malaysia.

------. (1985a) *Preliminary National Accounts Statistics of Malaysia, 1979-1984*, (September), Kuala Lumpur: Government Printer.

------. (1985b) *Malaysia: Preliminary Figures of External Trade, 1980-1985*, Kuala Lumpur: Government Printer.

Malaysia. (1973) *Mid-term Review of the Second Malaysia Plan 1971-1975*, Kuala Lumpur: Government Printer.

Malaysia. (1976) *Third Malaysia Plan 1976-1980* Kuala Lumpur: Government Printer.

Malaysia. (1979) *Mid-term Review of the Third Malaysia Plan 1976-1980* Kuala Lumpur: Government Printer.

Malaysia. (1981) *Fourth Malaysia Plan 1981-1985* Kuala Lumpur: Government Printer.

Malaysia, The Treasury. (1983) *Economic Report 1983-84*, Kuala Lumpur: Ministry of Finance.

Malaysia. (1984) *Mid-term Review of the Fourth Malaysia Plan 1981-1985* Kuala Lumpur: Government Printer.

Malaysia, Ministry of Information. (1984) *Labuan - A Federal Territory*, Kuala Lumpur: Federal Department of Information.

Malaysia, The Treasury. (1985) *Economic Report 1985-86*, Kuala Lumpur: Ministry of Finance

Malaysia. (1986) *Fifth Malaysia Plan 1986-1990*, Kuala Lumpur: Government Printer.

Malaysian Digest, Kuala Lumpur. Published monthly by the External Division, Ministry of Foreign Affairs, Kuala Lumpur.

Marican, Mansoor. (1979) 'Combatting corruption: The Malaysian experience', *Asian*

Survey 19 (June): 597-610.

Massard, Josiane. (1984) 'De l'économie de subsistence à l'agro-économie: les projets FELDA en Malaisie de l'Ouest', *Archipel* 27: 31-44.

Mat, Johari. (1981) 'Integrated agricultural projects in peninsular Malaysia: Issues of the "Second Stage"', in Dias, Hiran K. *et al.* (eds) *Rural Development and Regional Planning in the '80s: Challenges and Priorities*, Bangkok: Human Settlements Division, Asian Institute of Technology, pp. 231-50.

------. (1983) *Regional Development in West Malaysia: A Comparative Effectiveness Study of JENGKA, DARA, KEJORA, and KETENGAH*, Monograph of the National Institute of Public Administration, Kuala Lumpur: Institut Tadbiran Awam Negara, Malaysia.

Mauzy, Diane K. (1987) 'Malaysia in 1986: the ups and downs of stock market politics', *Asian Survey* 27 (February): 231-41.

Mazumdar, Dipak. (1981) *The Urban Labor Market and Income Distribution: A Study of Malaysia*, New York: Oxford University Press for the World Bank.

Meade, Melinda S. (1976) 'Land development and human health in West Malaysia', *Annals, Association of American Geographers* 66: 428-39.

Means, G.P. (1983) 'Energy resource development and management in Malaysia', *Contemporary Southeast Asia* 5 (December): 330-51.

Mehmet, Ozay. (1971) 'Manpower planning and labour markets in developing countries: A case study of West Malaysia', *Journal of Development Studies* 8 (January): 277-89.

------. (1978) *Economic Planning and Social Justice in Developing Countries*, London: Croom Helm.

------. (1982a) 'Evaluating alternative land schemes in Malaysia: FELDA and FELCRA', *Contemporary Southeast Asia* 3 (March): 340-60.

------. (1982b) 'Malaysian employment restructuring policies: Effectiveness and prospects under the Fourth Malaysia Plan, 1980-1985', *Asian Survey* 22 (October): 978-87.

------. (1983) 'Managed industrialization and poverty redressal policies in Malaysia', in Areif, Sritua and Sundaram, Jomo K. (eds) *The Malaysian Economy and Finance*, East Balmain, NSW : Rosecons, pp. 36-49.

------. (1986) *Development in Malaysia: Poverty, Wealth and Trusteeship*, London: Croom Helm.

Milne, R.S. (1986) 'Malaysia - Beyond the new economic policy', *Asian Survey* 26 (December): 1364-82.

Milne, R.S. and Mauzy, Diane K. (1978) *Politics and Government in Malaysia*, Singapore and Vancouver: Federal Publications and the University of British Columbia Press.

Misra, R.P. (1981a) 'The changing perception of development problems', in Misra, R.P. and Honjo, M. (eds) *Changing Perception of Development Problems*, vol. 1, United Nations Centre for Regional Development, Singapore: Maruzen Asia, pp. 7-37.

------. (1981b) 'Development or disruption: The challenge of culture neutral development planning', in Misra, R.P. and Honjo, M. (eds) *Changing Perception of Development Problems*, vol. 1, United Nations Centre for Regional Development, Singapore: Maruzen Asia, pp. 77-121.

Misra, R.P., Urs, D.V., and Natraj, V.K. (eds) (1978) *Regional Planning and National Development*, New Delhi: Vikas Publishing House.

Misra, R.P. and Honjo, M. (eds) (1981) *Changing Perception of Development Problems*, vol. 1, United Nations Centre for Regional Development, Singapore: Maruzen Asia.

Missen, G. and Logan, M.I. (1977) 'National and local distribution systems and regional development: The case of Kelantan in West Malaysia', *Antipode, A Journal of Radical Geography* 9 (December): 60-73.

Mohamad, *Tan Sri Datuk* Ibrahim. (1984) 'Implementing the privatisation policy', in Mohamed Nor Abdul Ghani *et al.* (eds) *Malaysia Incorporated and Privatisation: Towards National Unity*, Petaling Jaya: Pelanduk Publications for Institute of Management Consultants and Prime Minister's Department, pp. 65-71.

Mohamad, Mahathir bin. (1970) *The Malay Dilemma*, Singapore: Asia Pacific Press.

Mohamad, *Dato Seri* Mahathir. (1984) 'Malaysia Incorporated and privatisation: Its rationale and purpose', in Mohamed Nor Abdul Ghani *et al.* (eds) *Malaysia Incorporated and Privatisation: Towards National Unity*, Petaling Jaya: Pelanduk Publications for Institute of Management Consultants and Prime Minister's Department, pp. 1-7.

Mohamed, *Tan Sri* Sallehuddin. (1984) 'Framework for action', in Mohamed Nor Abdul Ghani *et al.* (eds) *Malaysia Incorporated and Privatisation: Towards National Unity*,

Petaling Jaya: Pelanduk Publications for Institute of Management Studies and Prime Minister's Department, pp. 99-112.

Mokhzani, Abdul Rahim. (ed) (1979) *Rural Development in Southeast Asia*, New Delhi: Vikas Publishing House.

Mosher, A.T. (1969) *Creating a Progressive Rural Structure*, New York: The Agricultural Development Council Inc.

Moynihan, Martin J. (1964) 'Ops Room technique', *Public Administration* 42: 391-414.

Myrdal, G. (1957) *Economic Theory and Underdeveloped Regions*, London: Duckworth.

------. (1968) *Asian Drama: An Enquiry into the Poverty of Nations*, New York: Columbia University Press.

Ness, G.D. (1967) *Bureaucracy and Rural Development in Malaysia*, Berkeley and Los Angeles: University of California Press.

New Straits Times (NST), Kuala Lumpur. Published daily by the New Straits Times Press, Malaysia.

Norris, M.W. (1980) *Local Government in peninsular Malaysia*, Westmead, Hants: Gower Publishing.

North, Robert C. *et al.* (1963) *Content Analysis*, Chicago: Northwestern.

North Borneo. (1948) *Plan for Reconstruction and Development 1948-1955*, Jesselton: Government Printer.

Obregon, A.Q. (1974) 'The marginal role of the economy and the marginalized labour force', *Economy and Society* 3: 393-428.

Ohame, Kenichi. (1984) 'Sharing Experiences', in Mohamed Nor Abdul Ghani *et al.* (eds) *Malaysian Incorporated and Privatisation: Towards National Unity*, Petaling Jaya: Pelanduk Publications for Institute of Management Consultants and Prime Minister's Department, pp. 57-60.

Haji Omar, Afifudin. (1979) 'Implementation of rural development: Institution building in the Muda Region', in Abdul Rahim Mokhzani. (ed) *Rural Development in Southeast Asia*, New Delhi: Vikas Publishing House, pp. 177-200.

Ong, Michael. (1984) 'Malaysia in 1983. On the road to Greater Malaysia', *Southeast Asian Affairs 1984*, Singapore: Institute of Southeast Asian Studies, pp. 197-230.

Ooi, Jin Bee. (1975) 'Urbanization and the urban population in peninsular Malaysia, 1970', *Journal of Tropical Geography* 40 (June): 40-7.

Osborn, J. (1974) 'Area, development policy and the middle city in Malaysia', *The University of Chicago Department of Geography Research Paper* no. 153, Chicago: The University of Chicago.

Oshima, H. (1962) 'The international comparison of size distribution of family incomes, with special reference to Asia', *Review of Economics and Statistics* (November): 439-45.

Palmer, G. (1974) 'The ecology of resettlement schemes', *Human Organisation* 33: 239-50.

Pathmanathan, Murugesu. (1985) 'Malaysia in 1984: A political and economic survey', *Southeast Asian Affairs 1985*, Singapore: Institute of Southeast Asian Studies, pp. 211-34.

Paukert, F., Skolka, J., and Maton, J. (1981) *Income Distribution, Structure of Economy and Employment. The Philippines, Iran, The Republic of Korea and Malaysia: A Comparative Study of Four Asian Countries*, London: Croom Helm.

Pillai, M.G.G. (1986) 'I will return: Sabah leader', *The Australian*, March 22-23.

------. (1987a) 'Point scoring politicians do little to allay Malaysia's fears of racial violence', *The Australian*, October 24-25.

------. (1987b) 'Malaysia to detain leader for two years', *The Weekend Australian*, December 26-27, p. 8.

Pinwill, W. (1987) 'Malaysia on the brink', *Sydney Morning Herald*, May 14, p.17.

Prantilla, E.B. (ed) (1981a) *National Development and Regional Policy*, vol. 3, United Nations Centre for Regional Development, Singapore: Maruzen Asia.

------. (1981b) 'Regional development policy in the context of national development', in Prantilla, E.B. (ed) *National Development and Regional Policy*, vol. 3, United Nations Centre for Regional Development, Singapore: Maruzen Asia, pp. 1-14.

Pryor, Robin J. (1973) 'The changing settlement system in West Malaysia', *Journal of Tropical Geography* 37 (December): 53-67.

------. (1975a) 'Migration trends, population redistribution policies, and development strategies in Malaysia', paper delivered at the 46th Congress of the Australian and New Zealand Association for the Advancement of Science, Canberra, January 21, mimeograph.

------.(1975b) 'Urbanisation in peninsular Malaysia: A factor analytical approach', *Australian Geographical Studies* 13 (April): 13-32.

Puthucheary, M. and Milne, R.S. (1984) 'Joint enterprises in the Malaysian agricultural sector', *Contemporary Southeast Asia* 6 (June): 1-25.

Rachagan, S. Sothi. (1987) 'The 1986 parliamentary elections in peninsular Malaysia', *Southeast Asian Affairs 1987*, Singapore: Institute of Southeast Asian Studies, pp. 217-35.

Rambo, A.T. (1982) '*Orang Asli* adaptive strategies: Implications for Malaysian natural resource development planning', in MacAndrews, Colin and Chia, Lin Sen. (eds) *Too Rapid Development. Perception and Perspectives from Southeast Asia*, Athens, Ohio: Ohio University Press, pp. 251-99.

Rao, Bhanoj V.V. (1980) *Malaysia Development Pattern and Policy 1947-1971*, Singapore: University of Singapore Press.

Razak, *Tun* Abdul. (1969) *New Economic Development Policy in a New Industrial Development Strategy*, Kuala Lumpur: Federal Industrial Development Authority.

Reddaway, W.B. (1967) *Effects of UK Direct Investment Overseas: An Interim Report*, Cambridge: Cambridge University Press.

Reid, Anthony. (1969) 'The Kuala Lumpur riots and the Malaysian political system', *Australian Outlook* 23 (December): 258-78.

Rimmer, Peter J. (1982) 'Urban public transport in smaller Malaysian towns: Threat to the trishaw industry', *Malaysian Journal of Tropical Geography* 5 (June): pp. 54-66.

Rimmer, P.J. and Cho, George C.H. (1981) 'Urbanization of the Malays since independence: Evidence from West Malaysia, 1957 and 1970', *Journal of Southeast Asian Studies* 12 (September): pp. 349-63.

Robertson, A.F. (1975) 'A new kind of Malaysian? A sociological view of the F.L.D.A.', *Journal of Administration Overseas* 14: 30-8.

Roemer, Michael. (1985) 'Dutch disease in developing countries: Swallowing bitter medicine', in Lundahl, Mats. (ed) *The Primary Sector in Economic Development*, London and Sydney: Croom Helm, pp. 234-52.

Rogers, M.L. (1972) 'Malaysia and Singapore: 1971 developments', *Asian Survey* 12 (February): 168-76.

Rondinelli; Denis A. (1983) *Secondary Cities in Developing Countries: Policies for Diffusing Urbanization*, Beverly Hills, Calif.: Sage Publications.

Rondinelli, D.A. and Ruddle, K. (1978) *Urbanization and Rural Development: A Spatial Policy for Equitable Growth*, New York: Praeger.

Ross-Larson, Bruce. (1976) *The Politics of Federalism*, Singapore: Bruce Ross-Larson.

------. (ed) (1977) *Issues in Contemporary Malaysia*, Kuala Lumpur: Heinemann Educational Books (Asia) Ltd.

------. (ed) (1978) *Malaysia 2001: A Preliminary Inquiry*, Kuala Lumpur: Syed Kechik Foundation.

Rothwell, N. (1987) 'The battle for Malaysia', *The Weekend Australian*, June 13-14, pp. 23-4.

Rudner, Martin. (1970) 'The state and peasant innovation in rural development: The case of Malaysian rubber', *Asian and African Studies* 6: 75-96.

------. (1975) 'The Malayan quandary: Rural development policy under the First and Second Five Year Plans', in Lim, David. (ed) *Readings on Malaysian Economic Development*, Kuala Lumpur: Oxford University Press, pp. 80-8.

------. (1977) 'How the structure of Malayan agriculture crystallized: A review of attitudes, interests, policies and goals during the late colonial period', paper delivered at the Asian Studies Association of Australia Colloquium on Malayan Economic History and Development, University of New England, February 12-13, 63 pp.

Sabah. (1959) *Development Plan 1959-1964*, Kota Kinabalu: Government Printer.

Sabah, State Government. (1963) *Sabah Annual Report, 1962*, Kota Kinabalu: Government Printer.

------. (1965) *Sabah State Development Plan, 1965-70*, Kota Kinabalu: Government Printer.

Sabah, Chief Minister's Department. (1977) *State of Sabah Third Malaysia Plan, 1976-1980* Kota Kinabalu: Chief Minister's Department.

Sacerdoti, Guy, and Wilson, Paul. (1978) 'Stock market spoils for sons of the soil', *Far Eastern Economic Review*, October 6: 72-4.

Salih, Kamal. (1981) 'Rural-urban transformation and regional underdevelopment in Malaysia', in Lo, Fu-chen. (ed) *Rural-Urban Relations and Regional Development*, vol. 5, United Nations Centre for Regional Development, Singapore: Maruzen Asia, pp. 109-45.

Salih, Kamal *et al.* (1977) 'Uneven Development in Malaysia. An Interim Report on the Rural-Urban Relations Project', paper delivered at the Colloquium on Rural-Urban Relations and Development Planning in Asia, 7-18 November, Nagoya, Japan, Nagoya: United Nations Centre for Regional Development.

Salih, Kamal and Young, Mei Ling. (1981) 'Malaysia: Urbanization in a multiethnic society. Case of peninsular Malaysia', in Honjo, M. (ed) *Urbanization and Regional Development*, vol. 6, United Nations Centre for Regional Development, Singapore: Maruzen Asia, pp. 117-47.

------. (1986) 'The regional impact of industrialisation. A case study of Penang state', in McGee, T.G. *et al.* (eds) *Industrialisation and Labour Force Processes: A Case Study of peninsular Malaysia*, Research papers on Development in East Java and West Malaysia, no. 1, Research School of Pacific Studies, Canberra: Australian National University, pp. 101-37.

Santos, Milton. (1979) *The Shared Space. The Two Circuits of the Urban Economy in Underdeveloped Countries*, London: Methuen.

Sarawak, State of. (1947) *Development and Welfare Plan 1947-1956*, Kuching: Government Printer.

Sarawak, State of. (1954) *Development Plan 1955-1960*, Kuching: Government Printer.

Sarawak, State of. (1959) *Sarawak Development Plan 1959-1963*, Kuching: Government Printer.

Sarawak, State of. (1963) *Development Plan, 1964-1968*, Kuching: Government Printer.

Saw, Swee Hock. (1972) 'Patterns of urbanization in West Malaysia, 1911-1970', *Malayan Economic Review* 17: 114-20.

------. (1976) 'Urbanization in West Malaysia 1911-1970', in Lim, Teck Ghee and Lowe, Vincent. (eds) *Towards a Modern Asia: Aims, Resources and Strategies*, Kuala Lumpur: Heinemann Books, pp. 59-66.

Scott, James C. (1968) *Political Ideology in Malaysia: Reality and Beliefs of an Elite*, New Haven: Yale University Press.

Seers, Dudley. (1977) 'The new meaning of development', *International Development Review* 19: 2-7.

Selvaratnam, V. (1982) 'Malaysia in 1981: A year of political transition', *Southeast Asian Affairs 1982*, Singapore: Institute of Southeast Asian Studies, pp. 245- 72.

Selvaratnam, V. and Dissanayake, B. W. (1979) 'Migration and development with reference to employment, income and migration in Negri Sembilan Timur', in Abdul Rahim Mokhzani. (ed) *Rural Development in Southeast Asia*, New Delhi: Vikas Publishing House, pp. 15-43.

Sendut, Hamzah. (1962) 'Patterns of urbanization in Malaya', *Journal of Tropical Geography* 16: 114-30.

------. (1965) 'Some aspects of urban change in Malaya, 1931-1957', *Kajian Ekonomi Malaysia* 2: 87-103.

Senftleben, W. (1978) 'Youth land settlement schemes in Malaysia', in Hill, R.D. and Bray, J.M. (eds) *Geography and the Environment in Southeast Asia*, Hong Kong: University of Hong Kong Press, pp. 225-46.

Serjan, *Datuk Haji* Mohamed Jemuri. (1986) 'The Constitutional position of Sarawak', in Trindade, F.A. and Lee, H.P. (eds) *The Constitution of Malaysia*, Singapore: Oxford University Press, pp. 114-34.

Seward, Nick. (1986) 'Balancing the redress', *Far Eastern Economic Review*, September 25, p. 77.

Shah, *Raja Tun* Azlan. (1982) 'The role of constitutional rulers: A Malaysian perspective for the laity', *Journal of Malaysian and Comparative Law* 1: 6.

Shepherd, Geoffrey. (1980) 'Policies to promote industrial development', in Young, K. *et al.* (eds) *Growth and Equity in a Multiracial Society*, New York: Oxford University Press for the World Bank, pp. 182-210.

Siddique, Sharon and Suryadinata, L. (1981-82) 'Bumiputra and Pribumi: Economic nationalism (Indiginism) in Malaysia and Indonesia', *Pacific Affairs* 54 (Winter): 662-87.

Sidhu, Manjit Singh. (1978) *Kuala Lumpur and its Population*, Kuala Lumpur: Surinder Publications.

------. (1981) 'Chinese dominance of West Malaysian towns, 1921-1970', in Sidhu, Manjit S. and Jones, Gavin W. (eds) *Population Dynamics in a Plural Society: Peninsular Malaysia*, Kuala Lumpur: University of Malaya Co-operative Bookshop Publications, pp. 87-96.

Sidhu, Manjit S. and Jones, G.W. (1979) 'Population distribution in peninsular Malaysia: Historical trends and contemporary issues', *Asian Profile* 7 (October): 459-80.

------. (eds) (1981) *Population Dynamics in a Plural Society: Peninsular Malaysia*, Kuala Lumpur: University of Malaya Co-operative Bookshop Publications.

Sin, Fong Han. (1979) 'A constitutional *coup d'état*: An analysis of the birth and victory of the Berjaya Party in Sabah, Malaysia', *Asian Survey* 19 (April): 379-89.

Singh, Mahinder Santokh, and Chi, Seck Choo. (1981) 'Spatial dynamics in the growth and development of multinational corporations in Malaysia', in Hamilton, F.E.I. and Linge, G.J.R. (eds) *Spatial Analysis, Industry and the Industrial Environment*, vol. 2, Chichester: John Wiley and Sons, pp. 481-507.

Smith, M., McLoughlin, J., Large, P., and Chapman, R. (1985) *Asia's New Industrial World*, London and New York: Methuen.

Snodgrass, Donald R. (1980) *Inequality and Economic Development in Malaysia*, Kuala Lumpur: Oxford University Press.

Specter, Michael. (1984) 'A sprawling, thirsty giant', *Far Eastern Economic Review*, March 29, pp. 23-30.

The Star, Kuala Lumpur and Penang. Published daily by Star Publications (Malaysia).

Stöhr, W.B. and Todtling, F., (1977) 'Spatial equity - some anti-theses to current regional development doctrine', *Papers, Regional Science Association* 38: 33-54.

Stöhr, Walter B. (1981) 'Development from below: The bottom-up and periphery-inward development paradigm', in Stöhr, Walter B. and Taylor, D.R. Fraser. (eds), *Development from Above or Below? The Dialectics of Regional Planning in Developing Countries*, Chichester: Wiley, pp. 39-72.

Stöhr, Walter B. and Taylor, Fraser. (eds) (1981) *Development from Above or Below? The Dialectics of Regional Planning in Developing Countries*, Chichester: Wiley.

Streeten, P.P. (1981) 'Development ideas in historical perspective', in Misra, R.P. and Honjo, M. (eds) *Changing Perceptions of Development Problems,* vol. 1, United Nations Centre for Regional Development, Singapore: Maruzen Asia, pp. 39-68.

Subramaniam, M. (1971) 'An operational measure of urban concentration', *Economic Development and Cultural Change* 20 (1) (October): 105-16.

Sullivan, Anwar and Leong, Cecilia. (eds) (1981) *Commemorative History of Sabah, 1881-(1981)* Kota Kinabalu: Sabah State Government.

Sunkel, O. (1981) 'The interaction between styles of development and the environment in Latin America', in Misra, R.P. and Honjo, M. (eds) *Changing Perception of Development Problems*, vol. 1, United Nations Centre for Regional Development, Singapore: Maruzen Asia, pp. 229-74.

Sutton, K. (1977) 'Rural land development and resettlement in Sabah, Malaysia', *Pacific Viewpoint* 18 (May): 79-92.

Suzuki, Takahiro and Cummings, William K. (1985) 'Malaysia's "Look East" policy', *Asian Profile* 13 (December): 503-9.

Sydney Morning Herald, 'Malaysia fears racial flare-up', editorial, October 1987.

Tan, Loong-Hoe. (1981) 'The State and the distribution of wealth within the Malay society in peninsular Malaysia', *Southeast Asian Affairs 1981*, Singapore: Institute of Southeast Asian Affairs, pp. 217-32.

Taylor, D.R.F. (1981) 'Role and functions of lower order centres in rural development', in Lo, Fu-chen. (ed) *Rural-Urban Relations and Regional Development*, vol. 5, United Nations Centre for Regional Development, Singapore: Maruzen Asia, pp. 265-91.

Tham, Seong Chee. (1983) *Malays and Modernization: A Sociological Interpretation* (2nd edn), Singapore: University of Singapore Press.

Thillainathan, R. (1975a) 'The public enterprise as an instrument for restructuring society: The Malaysian case', in Chee, S. and Khoo, S.M. (eds) *Malaysian Economic*

Development and Policies, Conference Proceedings Series no. 3, Kuala Lumpur: Malaysian Economic Association, pp. 77-8.

------. (1975b) 'Planning for economic equality and the role of the public sector: The West Malaysian case', in Lim, David. (ed) *Readings on Malaysian Economic Development*, Kuala Lumpur: Oxford University Press, pp. 309-20.

------. (1976) 'Malaysia', in Truong, Nguyen. (ed) *Role of Public Enterprise in National Development in Southeast Asia: Problems and Prospects*, Singapore: Regional Institute of Higher Education and Development, pp. 1-149.

Todaro, Michael. (1981) *Economic Development in the Third World* (2nd edn), London: Longman.

Tregonning, K.G. (1964) *A History of Modern Malaya*, London: Eastern Universities Press.

------. (1965) *A History of Modern Sabah (North Borneo) 1881-1963*, Singapore: University of Malaya Press.

Trindade, F.A. (1978) 'The constitutional position of the *Yang di-Pertuan Agong*', in Suffian, *Tun* Mohamed, Lee, H.P., and Trindade, F.A. (eds) *The Constitution of Malaysia -- Its Development: 1957-1977* Kuala Lumpur: Oxford University Press, pp. 101-72.

United Nations, Department of Economic and Social Affairs. (1968) 'Highlights of the Symposium on Social Policies and Planning', *International Social Development Review*, New York: United Nations.

United Nations, Committee on Development Planning. (1970) *Report on the Sixth Session, January 5-15, 1970*, New York: United Nations.

Vagale, L.R. (1981) 'Integration of socio-economic and environmental planning: An institutional framework for Nigeria', in Prantilla, E.B. (ed) *National Development and Regional Policy*, vol. 3, United Nations Centre for Regional Development, Singapore: Maruzen Asia, pp. 311-37.

Voon, Phin Keong. (1981) 'The rural development programme in Sabah, Malaysia, with reference to the 1970s', *Malaysian Journal of Tropical Geography* 3 (June): 53-67.

Voon, P.K. and Khoo, S.H. (1986) 'An overview of the impact of the petroleum industry in Kerteh, Trengganu, Malaysia', *Malaysian Journal of Tropical Geography* 13 (June): 46-59.

Vreeland, N. (1977) *Area Handbook for Malaysia* (3rd edn), Washington, D.C.: American University.

Wafa, *Syed* Hussain. (1972) 'Land development strategies in Malaysia: An empirical study', Ph.D. thesis, Stanford University.

------. (1974) *Land Development Strategies in Malaysia: An Empirical Study*, Occasional Paper no. 2, Kuala Lumpur: Pusat Pengajian Pembangunan Malaysia (Malaysian Centre for Development Studies).

Wang, Gung-wu. (ed) (1964) *Malaysia: A Survey*, Melbourne: F.W. Cheshire.

Ward, M.W. (1968) 'A review of problems and achievements in the economic development of independent Malaya', *Economic Geography* 44: 326-42.

Ward, R. Gerard and Ward, Marion W. (1980) 'The rural-urban connection - A missing link in Melanesia', *Malaysian Journal of Tropical Geography* 1 (September): 57-63.

Warr, Peter G. (1986) 'Malaysia's industrial enclaves: Benefits and costs', in McGee, T.G. *et al.* (eds) *Industrialisation and Labour Force Processes: A Case Study of peninsular Malaysia*, Research Papers on Development in East Java and West Malaysia No.1, Research School of Pacific Studies, Canberra: Australian National University, pp. 179-215.

Wheatley, P. (1966) *The Golden Khersonese: Studies in the Historical Geography of the Malay Peninsula before AD 1500*, Kuala Lumpur: Oxford University Press.

Wheelwright, E.L. (1965) *Industrialisation in Malaysia*, Melbourne: Melbourne University Press.

Wikkramatileke, R. (1965) 'State-aided rural land colonization in Malaya: An appraisal of the F.L.D.A. program', *Annals, Association of American Geographers* 55 (September): 377-403.

------. (1972) 'Federal land development in West Malaysia, 1957-1971', *Pacific Viewpoint* 13: 62-86.

Williamson, J.G. (1965) 'Regional inequality and the process of national development: A description of patterns', *Economic Development and Cultural Change* 13: 3-45.

Willmott, W.E. (1982) 'Comment: "Inequality in Malaysia"', *Pacific Viewpoint* 23 (May): 66.

Wong, J. (1979) *ASEAN Economies in Perspective: A Comparative Study of Indonesia, Malaysia, the Philippines, Singapore and Thailand*, London: Macmillan Press.

Wong, Tai Chee. (1987a) 'Resource frontier resettlement: A comparative study of Indonesian and Malaysian strategies', pre-fieldwork seminar, Department of Human Geography, Canberra: Australian National University, mimeograph.

------. (1987b) 'Regional development and resettlement strategy: A comparative study of Malaysia (FELDA) and Indonesia (Transmigration)', Seminar paper, Department of Human Geography, Canberra: Australian National University, mimeograph.

World Bank. (1955) *The Economic Development of Malaya*, Washington, D.C.: World Bank.

------. (1975) *Rural Development*, Sector Policy Paper, Washington, D.C.: World Bank.

------. (1980) *Malaysia - Selected Issues in Rural Poverty*, Washington, D.C.: World Bank.

Yeung, Yue-man. (1973) 'National development policy and urban transformation in Singapore: A study of public housing and the marketing system', *The University of Chicago Department of Geography Research Paper* no. 149, Chicago: The University of Chicago Press.

------. (1976) 'Southeast Asian cities: Patterns of growth and transformation', in Berry, B.J.L. (ed) *Urbanization and Counter-urbanization*, Beverly Hills, Calif.: Sage, pp. 285-309.

------. (1978) 'The urban environment in Southeast Asia - Challenge and opportunity', in Hill, R.D. and Bray, J.M. (eds) *Geography and the Environment in Southeast Asia*, Hong Kong: University of Hong Kong Press, pp. 17-33.

------. (1982) 'Economic inequality and social injustice: Development issues in Malaysia. A review article', *Pacific Affairs* 55: 94-101.

Young, Kevin. (1980a) 'The New Economic Policy and long-term development issues', in Young, K. *et al.* (eds) *Malaysia: Growth and Equity in a Multiracial Society*, Baltimore and London: Johns Hopkins University Press for the World Bank, pp. 60-96.

------. (1980b) 'Estimated effects of different investment levels on growth, incomes, employment and restructuring, 1975-90', in Young, K. *et al.* (eds) *Malaysia: Growth and Equity in a Multiracial Society*, Baltimore and London: Johns Hopkins University Press for the World Bank, Appendix A, pp. 289-308.

Young, Kevin, Bussink, Willem C.F., and Hasan, Parvez (eds) (1980) *Malaysia: Growth and*

Equity in a Multiracial Society, Baltimore and London: Johns Hopkins University Press for the World Bank.

Young, M.L. (1977) 'Migration and development: A case study of a rural settlement within a development scheme in peninsular Malaysia', in Salih, Kamal *et al.*, (eds) *Uneven Development in Malaysia*, Nagoya, Japan: United Nations Centre for Regional Development, pp. 18-46.

INDEX